Advance Praise for *The AI Marketing Canvas*

"Strategic marketing drives growth that can only be achieved by delivering truly customer-centric experiences. Marketers now must harness the power of AI and data to scale experiences that convert; this book gives you the foundational knowledge, framework, and inspiration to do just that."

—Christina Bottis, CMO, Coyote Logistics

"AI is something every marketer thinks they need to use, but don't really know why. *The AI Marketing Canvas* does a phenomenal job of demystifying this burgeoning capability and laying out actionable plans that allow AI to be a key differentiator that sets your brand apart. A must-read for any marketer that seeks real disruption."

—Andrea Brimmer, CMO, Ally Financial

"This is a must-read book for business leaders that want to truly understand the impact AI will continue to have on companies and brands that want to leverage customer centricity as their North Star in driving growth. It is a smart, pragmatic, toolkit-filled playbook that allows the reader to turn best-practice learning's into implementation moves, now!"

—Scott Davis, Chief Growth Officer, Prophet

"Not only do the authors make the case that AI-driven marketing is critical, but they also provide a practical and inspirational primer on how marketers can make it work for their business. This book will get any marketer both excited and prepared for the possibilities of AI marketing and eager to jump in!"

—Kelly Gillease, CMO, NerdWallet

"Whatever stage in your marketing evolution and digital customer journey, learn how to unlock the value you have already captured using AI to supercharge impact. This powerful yet digestible book gives you a step-by-step guide to take stock by asking the right questions, lay a foundation, and get started on execution. Build a road map, demonstrate success, and get the support and investment you need."

—Brett Groom, Chief Marketing Officer, ATI Physical Therapy

"Over the next ten years, AI and machine learning will transform marketing in ways far more profound than previous technology revolutions. For marketing leaders, recognizing the shift isn't enough. You have to act. This book provides a practical road map for getting started and for building sustainable advantage in the face of disruptive change."

—Matt Lawson, CMO, Juniper Square

"Through real-world, evidence-based research, Raj and Jim clearly demonstrate that successful implementation of AI and machine learning is going to result in "winner take all" scenarios. This book is a critical read to ensure that your brand ends up on the right side of that equation—the framework and practical applications that are provided will be additive whether you're at the beginning of this journey or well on your way."

—Joe Maglio, CEO, McKinney and Co.

"*The AI Marketing Canvas* offers a practical, inspiring, and grounded guide to leveraging AI as an essential tool to increase authentic connection with customers and amplify the impact of marketing today. Spanning numerous categories and useful case studies, this book is an essential read for marketers who want to win today and dominate tomorrow."

—Brooke Skinner Ricketts, CXO, Cars.com

"This book is mission-critical to marketing today, and to all business decision makers. Marketers can use this book to propel their organization forward—they can and should use this book to be a change agent within their own organization."

—Lindsay Saran, Senior Marketing Manager, Google

"Marketers have an amazing opportunity to redefine their relationship with customers through AI and machine learning. Yet, most of us are unprepared. It's time to embrace the future, and *The AI Marketing Canvas* is your guide. This book will inspire your own ideas and provide an excellent road map to bring your team and company on the journey!"

—Cassidy Shield, Vice President of Marketing, Narrative Science

"A wonderful articulation of the challenges and opportunities facing the modern CMO. Raj Venkatesan and Jim Lecinski provide a thorough and anxiety-reducing road map with tangible examples on how to integrate artificial intelligence and machine learning into a marketing organization's business strategy."

—Jim Stadler, Chief Marketing & Communications Officer, First Midwest Bancorp

"Never has it been more important for marketers to harness the power artificial intelligence (AI) and machine learning to deeply know, personalize, and engage customers. Venkatesan and Lecinski not only make the case that AI is critical to delivering customer-centric durable growth, but potentially imperative to business survival. This is an essential guide, chock-full of insights and examples, for today's modern marketer."

—Jon Suarez-Davis (jsd), Senior Vice President, Marketing Strategy & Innovation, Salesforce

"This is a book that sorts out the signal from the noise while providing actionable road maps on how AI can be understood and leveraged for business and marketing. Business leaders should read this book to gain a competitive advantage."

—Rishad Tobaccowala, author of *Restoring the Soul of Business: Staying Human in the Age of Data*, former Chief Strategist of Publicis Groupe

"Providing a great loyalty experience is about creating truly personalized, customer relationship moments throughout the entire customer experience. And loyalty is challenging to engender and difficult to maintain! Venkatesan and Lecinski give us the AI blueprint on transforming organizations into customer-centric powerhouses!"

—Chris Wayman, EVP Promotion & Loyalty, Merkle

THE AI MARKETING CANVAS

The AI Marketing Canvas

A FIVE-STAGE ROAD MAP TO
IMPLEMENTING ARTIFICIAL
INTELLIGENCE IN MARKETING

Rajkumar Venkatesan &
Jim Lecinski

STANFORD BUSINESS BOOKS
An Imprint of Stanford University Press
STANFORD, CALIFORNIA

STANFORD UNIVERSITY PRESS
Stanford, California

Special discounts for bulk quantities of Stanford Business Books
are available to corporations, professional associations, and other
organizations. For details and discount information, contact the special
sales department of Stanford University Press.
Tel: (650) 725-0820, Fax: (650) 725-3457

Printed in the United States of America on acid-free, archival-quality paper

Library of Congress Cataloging-in-Publication Data
Names: Venkatesan, Rajkumar, author. | Lecinski, Jim, author.
Title: The AI marketing canvas : a five-stage road map to implementing
    artificial intelligence in marketing / Rajkumar Venkatesan and Jim
    Lecinski.
Description: Stanford, California : Stanford Business Books, an imprint
    of Stanford University Press, 2021. | Includes index.
Identifiers: LCCN 2020041771 | ISBN 9781503613164 (cloth) |
    ISBN 9781503628045 (ebook)
Subjects: LCSH: Artificial intelligence—Marketing applications.
Classification: LCC HF5415.125 .V46 2021 | DDC 658.800285/63—dc23
LC record available at https://lccn.loc.gov/2020041771

Cover design: Kevin Barrett Kane
Text design: Kevin Barrett Kane
Diagram design: Alexandra Modie
Typeset at Stanford University Press in 10/15 Spectral

This book is dedicated to all professional marketers, and those students aspiring to become marketers, who work tirelessly every day to drive profitable incremental growth, to build long-term brand equity and to be a force for good in the world, and who are wrestling with how to achieve these goals in a rapidly changing world of marketing, customers, and technology.

The trouble is that you think you have time.
　　　　—Jack Kornfield, *Buddha's Little Instruction Book*

Contents

Notice to Readers

The information in this book, along with the forms and structures provided, is meant to serve as a helpful guide to marketing and business issues.

The author of and contributors to this book take no responsibility for compliance with the laws or regulations that govern your specific business. The responsibility for making sure everything is compliant, among other things, is 100 percent yours.

Before you implement any new information or forms, please check with your own trusted business advisers, including your own attorney, to make certain that your forms and the information you plan to implement will comply with all relevant laws, customs, and regulations.

All product names, logos, and brands mentioned in this book are the property of their respective owners and may be registered in the US Patent and Trademark Office and in other countries. All company, product, and service names used in this book are for identification purposes only. Use of these names, logos, and brands does not imply endorsement.

Figures

THE AI MARKETING CANVAS

PART 1

The Challenge and the Solution

1 The Marketer's Challenge Today

EVEN AS IT WAS STRIVING to improve the delivery of its digital products, the iconic news brand *The Washington Post* was on track to lose an estimated $40 million in 2013, when it was acquired for $250 million in cash by Amazon founder Jeff Bezos.[1]

In his open letter to its employees on April 5, 2013, Bezos wrote:

> There will, of course, be change at The Post over the coming years. That's essential and would have happened with or without new ownership. The Internet is transforming almost every element of the news business: shortening news cycles, eroding long-reliable revenue sources, and enabling new kinds of competition, some of which bear little or no news-gathering costs. There is no map, and charting a path ahead will not be easy. We will need to invent, which means we will need to experiment. Our touchstone will be readers, understanding what they care about—government, local leaders, restaurant openings, scout troops, businesses, charities, governors, sports—and working backwards from there. I'm excited and optimistic about the opportunity for invention.

Bezos understood that, like so many other businesses, the news business model had shifted from supply to demand because a few big networks (Amazon, Google, Facebook, Netflix, et al.) had reset customer expectations through increasing personalization of the customer experience.

The Washington Post is now a leading technology, software, and media company whose resources allow it to respond to changes in the customer news needs, and to shape those needs by using technology such as artificial intelligence (AI) and machine learning. AI and machine learning allows the *Post* to market better by personalizing the user's experience, supercharging it at every juncture. To wit:

- Search engine optimization serves up relevant stories based on search criteria to potential subscribers.
- Readers who come directly to the site can experience a limited number of articles for free, enabling them to experience the quality of the journalism while providing the *Post* with the opportunity to stimulate them to subscribe.
- New subscribers and casual readers alike continue to experience the quality of the product, from load speed to personalized content driven by AI and machine learning through a system called Zeus Insights, which serves up stories based on interests inferred from previously read articles. AI and machine learning technology also allows the *Post* to rapidly predict the popularity of articles, so that the newsroom can add media and links to those articles that are trending.
- Subscribers also are encouraged to add their comments to articles, in effect becoming part of the editorial process. An AI-driven comment moderation system helps the *Post* to maintain a high-quality comment section, the best of which is rolled into an adjunct publication composed of the best, most relevant comments.
- The *Post*'s AI-powered story-writing program called "Heliograf" was instrumental in its ability to produce twice the number of stories as the *New York Times* (500, versus 230 in 2017).[2]

The *Post*'s success is evident: its digital subscriber base has more than tripled in the last three years, and added well over a million new and exclusively digital subscribers in that time frame, according to a May 16, 2019, press release.[3] But that's not all. The *Post*'s main technology platform, Arc Publishing, is so successful that the *Post* has licensed it to other top publishers, broadcasters, and brands.[4] *The technology has become a new business line.*[5] All of this has returned the *Post* to profitability for at least two years running.[6]

If your brand doesn't have the resources of a giant network such as Amazon at its disposal or a technology visionary with deep pockets at the helm of your company, don't despair. There are significant gains to be had by implementing AI and machine-learning technology to supercharge your brand's customer journey by delivering the personalization that consumers now expect, no matter where you're starting.

Consider CarMax, America's largest used car retailer, where the majority of auto sales still occur in a physical store, but whose customers' buying journey increasingly begins online. CarMax.com personalizes the images shown on its website based on your search behaviors. In fact, the text and images change depending on what the site learns about you as you explore the site. CarMax.com's goal is to present you with increasingly relevant and desirable inventory, thus reducing the cognitive load and removing friction from your research process. This differentiates CarMax.com from its competitors because the site is explicitly designed to reduce the anxiety that occurs when you are researching a purchase and are overwhelmed with too many choices, particularly when it comes to high-cost items.

According to Barry Schwarz, author of a book on consumer anxiety titled *The Paradox of Choice*,[7] says that the more choices we have, the less satisfied we become. In an interview for Capitalone.com about car buying, Schwarz said, "If you buy the wrong cereal, you get to correct that mistake next week. Large decisions are not easily reversible. That's why there is extra anxiety baked into them."[8]

CarMax understands that its long-term competitive advantage hinges on its ability to collect first-party data and use it to ease the purchase process by personalizing the consumer's experience—online and everywhere. CarMax also realizes it is not competing against the best experience consumers have ever had buying a car; it is competing against the best experience consumers have ever had, period.

Let's take coffee as an example. When you launch your Starbucks app, not only can you order exactly what you want when you want it (e.g., nonfat grande iced coffee with two pumps of toffee nut syrup at 2 p.m.);[9] the app also will recommend new drinks and food based on what it knows about your purchase history and preferences. CarMax knows you expect it to deliver this same level of personalization—from the mobile marketing messages to your in-store experience. The car retailer wants to learn as much as possible about you, so that it can anticipate your needs and priorities; and it has invested heavily in technology to be able to do just that.[10] (We'll talk more about CarMax and Starbucks later in this book.)

Other brands are working through the sometimes painful process of transitioning from the old supply-driven or "analog" business model to the on-demand or "digital" business model. Many brands have yet to begin, or are in the midst of building, digital foundations that will allow them to collect the consumer data required for their marketing, and to benefit from the more advanced technology. Even brands that have substantially built their digital foundation may still be in data collection mode, and may thus be focused on learning some lessons and getting some quick wins, leading to insights that are cumulative and can be built upon.

For example, the first generation of Coca-Cola's Freestyle dispenser allowed customers to personalize their soda by mixing and matching different flavors, and this generated a ton of data about consumer preferences. The machines sent the data about combinations customers created all around the world back to corporate headquarters. This digital initiative led to the development of a successful new product in Sprite Cherry, and to an even more sophisticated dispenser that does provide one-to-one personalization: the Powerade Power Station.

On the other hand, the cost of delaying or ignoring the need to make AI and personalization a key strategic objective can be steep. For example, Kraft Heinz has signaled its intention to incorporate AI and machine learning into its operations after experiencing a sales slide and significant write-downs in the value of some of its most prominent brands in February

2019—turbulence believed by analysts to be the result of management's previously rigid philosophy of growth through cost cutting. The company appointed a new CEO, Miguel Patricio, who was formerly CMO at Anheuser Busch InBev;[11] and less than six months later it announced a new CIO in Corrado Azzarita. According to Forbes.com, Azzarita said he intends to implement "machine-learning models that crunch data such as historical sales, rivals' current promotions, and macroeconomic variables to recommend optimal promotions for Kraft Heinz brands, and other models that help it figure out the best mix of media to use to advertise products."[12]

Still, a recent study of three hundred advertisers by Advertiser Perceptions found that half of the marketers surveyed have no plans to use AI in their marketing. Said Frank Papsadore, EVP at Advertiser Perceptions, "Big-budget brands like Nike, IKEA. and Sephora are pioneering AI for marketing, but most advertisers don't have their resources, so they're focusing on more immediate marketing efforts."[13] This means if you are a marketer at a well-established firm, you may face some major internal barriers to the process of implementing AI and machine learning, some of which may require what will be rightly perceived as radical changes.[14]

The problem with this hesitation to move forward is this: Everywhere across the business landscape, the high-margin analog business model is on its way out and is being replaced by a lower-margin, digitally driven business that relies on *volume*. The significant investments required to create a successful digital business could mean that profits *will* decline before the brand emerges on the other side to new, lower unit profitability, but higher volume and lower costs, and potentially higher total profits.[15] To succeed, management must make a commitment to *investing long term and be prepared to tolerate a temporary chasm of low or no profits.* Otherwise, their brands may face bankruptcy—and they may not come out alive.

Consider all of the brands filing for Chapter 11 bankruptcy: Sears, Claire's, Toys "R" Us, to name but a few.[16] Sears, for example, has shrunk its physical footprint by 75 percent, sold critical assets, and laid off thousands of workers from its corporate offices and stores. It has emerged from bankruptcy and is opening new stores for home goods.[17] Claire's Stores, the US retailer popular with teens as a destination for ear piercing, affordable jewelry, and fashion accessories, also recently filed for bankruptcy. In doing so, it closed stores, removed $1.9 billion of debt, gained access to $575 million in new capital, and announced plans to reinvent itself as a smaller, more profitable business.[18]

Toys "R" Us shuttered its stores in 2018, with networks such as Amazon swooping in to fill the void. It was purchased in 2019 by Tru Kids Brands.[19] Tru Kids plans to revive the brand through opening smaller "experiential" stores, and is collaborating with a variety of other retailers including Target. It is also partnering with the interactive candy experience purveyor Canditopia,[20] to create *Toys R Us Adventure*, a series of interactive playrooms featuring installations that put a spotlight on Geoffrey the Giraffe, the Toys "R" Us mascot. Tru Kids Brands has partnered with the retail-as-service startup b8ta, who will be giving Tru Kids access to data and analytics to track things like foot traffic in and out of the stores to allow the company to make smarter decisions, according to Phillip Raub, b8ta cofounder and president, who says, "This year [2019]] is going to be an opportunity for us to test and learn."[21] If the brand wants to use data to promote the experience online, however, the increased enforcement of the Children's Online Privacy Protection Act (COPPA) needs to be considered to develop a responsible and ethical online strategy.

The point is, it's possible to survive bankruptcy—as well as other crises such as a pandemic or stock market bubble—and to live another day. But to survive in the longer term, we believe there's *no avoiding* this transition. Brands have to figure out how to leverage AI to serve consumers better. Why? Because the resources required to respond to this new demand economy—the demand for one-to-one personalized marketing—far outstrips human (analog) capacity.

While there's still time to catch up, there's no time to lose. Time is of the essence because, unlike the technology advances of the late 1990s, the advances experienced by brands that commit to applying AI and machine learning to their marketing now will be *exponential*. Insights obtained from customer data are cumulative, and the custom AI algorithms that are developed to leverage these insights will allow firms to provide personalized experiences—from advertising to pricing to point of sale of promotions and beyond—whose value for customers will increase exponentially over time.

In this new AI-driven business model, the *winner takes all*. Those who wait to apply AI and machine learning to their marketing will be left behind—and that could mean *the end*.

The good news is that there is still time to get in the game—if you start now. This book aims to show you how.

2 The AI Marketing Canvas

A STRATEGIC PATH FORWARD FOR MARKETERS

"We are in a rare position to create change. To reinvent what it means to be a marketer. This is your chance to be a pioneer. Don't wait for the marketing world to get smarter around you. Take the initiative now to understand, pilot and scale AI."
—Paul Roetzer, founder of the Marketing Artificial Intelligence Institute[1]

IN THIS NEW ECONOMY, one that is driven by major technological advances and disruption in the form of rapidly emerging competitors and changing marketplaces, we believe there is one way and one way only to win, and that is with AI and machine learning—deployed against a rock-solid marketing strategy. One that is grounded in proven principles for how a firm acquires, retains, and grows its customer relationships, and promotes customer Advocacy.

But that's not all. These strategies also must be driven by marketing leaders whose obsession is to find ways to use AI and machine learning to personalize the customer relationship at *every juncture*. Your mission is to use AI and machine learning to supercharge all Customer Relationship Moments, thereby providing consumers with the one-to-one personalized experience they need to find your product, buy it, buy it again, and then tell others about it.

The mission of this book is to provide a framework called the *AI Marketing Canvas* to guide you through this process. It's a road map you can use to build an effective marketing plan—one that accounts for all that is required to effectively apply AI and machine learning to your marketing—so you can win.

To validate and inform this framework, we conducted dozens of candid and thus confidential conversations with marketing leaders of big and small firms across industries, and presented portions of this material to marketing and technology groups around the world. What we learned was that very few of you are engaged to the level necessary to realize the benefits of AI and machine learning for marketing in the longer term.

Insights gleaned from these conversations were reinforced by our anecdotal surveys of hundreds of marketers we met while teaching these concepts in our executive education and training programs. More than three-quarters of those we surveyed reported that they did not feel competent when it comes to leveraging AI and machine learning for marketing.

They, and likely you, are

- hearing a lot about AI and other new technologies in the news, but struggling to determine what is hype and what is real, what's a fad or too far out to worry about, and what's here to stay;
- seeing your business change and feeling unprepared to respond;
- realizing that cost cutting alone is not a winning strategy for ensuring long-term growth in profits; and
- facing increasing competition from both niche startups and large conglomerates, and unsure how to respond.

In fact, according to a survey by McKinsey & Company published in November 2018, 43 percent of respondents ($n = 1,646$ adjusted) cited lack of a clear strategy for AI as their most significant barrier to adopting it, followed by lack of talent with appropriate skill sets for AI work (42 percent), existence of functional silos that constrain end-to-end AI Solution (30 percent), lack of leaders' ownership of and commitment to AI (27 percent), and lack of available (i.e. collected) data (24 percent), among others.[2]

And a survey by Gartner published in September 2019 cited **enterprise maturity** (staff skills, data scope or quality, and governance issues or concerns), **fear of the unknown** (*especially* of understanding AI benefits and uses), and the difficulty of **finding a starting point** (finding use cases, defining strategy, and finding funding) as the top three barriers to AI adoption. The study also calls out vendor strategy as a challenge, specifically in the areas of integration complexity and confusion over vendor capabilities.[3]

If you've been at marketing for any length of time, you likely remember the advent of digital marketing in the early 1990s, when brands struggled with whether to make their products available on this new information channel called the Internet. You probably also remember the vast sums of money that were spent reacting to management's calls to implement this newfangled technology, often with no clear view of how or what that technology was actually going to do to propel the business forward—and, later, with no ability to determine exactly how it did or did not move the needle.

If you don't remember, we do. So the mission of this book is largely to serve as an intervention, so that not one more penny is spent on shiny new technology without those decisions being based on a practical marketing strategy rooted in proven marketing principles! It's also our call to action for marketing leaders to confront and decide how they will address this critical pivot point in marketing.

THE AI MARKETING CANVAS

What you need is a "just right" solution, a guide you can use to supercharge each moment of the customer relationship journey with AI. We believe we've created that solution in our *AI Marketing Canvas*, a road map that meets you where you and your organization are right now, and shows a practical and actionable path forward.

Inspired by a traditional business model canvas, the *AI Marketing Canvas* is composed of five stages: Foundation, Experimentation, Expansion, Transformation, and Monetization. The five stages are the product of much research and many conversations with brands that are already successfully using AI to enhance their Customer Relationship Moments. In fact, we found that in brand after brand, category after category, country after country, every successful firm appears to have worked through these five stages to some degree.

To that end, we interviewed brand and marketing technology leaders at flagship brands such as Coca-Cola, Ancestry, and the *Washington Post*, among others, to isolate and identify their AI success paths in relationship to the five stages; and we won their permission to share them with you. Each stage features one detailed big brand example, along with a few shorter examples of other brands actively using AI in marketing. All are designed to provide you with as much perspective as possible on how others are using AI successfully, so that you can blaze a path forward with confidence.

You'll also notice that the AI Marketing Canvas is *customer-centric*. By placing the *customer* at the center of the discussion, the canvas and the supporting material in this book offer solutions specifically designed to help marketing managers leverage AI *to do their jobs better*—to deliver the amazing, highly personalized customer experiences that will set their brands apart and help them win.

Given the examples and cases we're providing, you might think this book is only for big brands, but nothing could be further from the truth. In fact, many of the marketing leaders we speak to are small and medium businesses (SMBs) looking for ways to use AI to compete. If this describes you, know that the principles in this book may be even more critical to securing your future because your resources are more limited. Your investment in AI has to be laser-focused and must help you do more with less. The *AI Marketing Canvas* is your road map to success, too.

THE EVOLUTION OF MARKETING

Whether or not you lived through the advent of the World Wide Web in the 1990s, it is safe to say that you are living through an onslaught of information and opinions about AI and its usefulness for marketing right now. In the past hundred years, marketing has progressed from human-curated to machine-assisted to machine-first. Human-curated recommendations have long existed as a possible buying route. Consumers seeking recommendations could rely on a personality they like and trust, someone like Martha Stewart or Shaquille O'Neal. The personality route, however, requires the consumer to

- find a personality,
- hope that personality has curated the category she is interested in (does Martha Stewart recommend hotels in Greece?),
- hope the personality has credibility in that category (Is this a real endorsement or a paid endorsement?), and
- hope their recommendation is highly current.

In the machine-assisted scenario the consumer interacts, usually online, with a product configurator that applies fixed "if-then" rules against a list of preset criteria to narrow the field of product options. The configurator route requires the consumer to find the configurator and hope that it

- covers the category she is interested in;
- has a list in the drop-down menus that matches her own personal criteria; and
- is knowledgeable, neutral, and highly current.

Clearly, both of these routes are less than ideal for buyers. There has to be a better way, and that way is to supercharge such moments in a customer relationship with AI and machine learning, so they can become personalized, or "AI Customer Relationship Moments."[4]

Though the progression of AI and machine learning technology and marketing is analogous to the evolution of the Web, the difference is that today the advancements are occurring much faster. Furthermore, rapid advances in technology, artificial intelligence, and machine learning are not just shifting the marketing landscape; they are also disrupting entire industries such as

- advertising (programmatic advertising started by Google),
- media and news (customized, bite-sized news delivery), and
- fitness and entertainment (Peloton and Amazon/Netflix).

In response, dozens of books and hundreds of articles have been published on AI and marketing, and we looked at a lot of them. Most were either too theoretical, too technical, or too hyperbolic to be useful to the marketing leader responsible for setting a course and generating results with her multimillion-dollar budget.

With so many prescriptives for how to approach AI and marketing, it can be really hard to know who to listen to—or where to start. On one hand, you have philosophers discussing how AI will save humanity, which is great but difficult to translate to how AI can help you sell more shoes or corn flakes. A little further down the continuum, you have theorists who write about sorting particular industries into categories and placing the categories in sensible relation to one another. Somewhere in the middle are the many white papers from vendors filled with technical details about what their shiny new AI and machine learning technologies can do. At the opposite end of the spectrum are the many super-short "low calorie" blog posts we see in our feeds everyday that sound important but don't really contain much substance that's helpful to an actual CMO trying to make actual progress using AI.

For a marketer, the philosophical and theoretical approaches are too high, the vendor approach is too technical, and the "twenty-eight tools" articles are too tactical. Conceptually, the material is too high or low; and mechanically, it is too basic or too specific.

Adding to the problem is the dearth of publicly available frameworks to assist CMOs and marketing leaders in taking intelligent action toward implementation. In fact, we could find only two publicly available marketing AI framework models; and as far as we could tell, neither had significant traction or widespread adoption across the marketing industry.

THE MARKETER'S DILEMMA

This AI and machine learning layer will make you, the marketing leader, more dependent on technology and finance. So it will be critical to cultivate relationships with finance and IT leaders who hold the keys to the capital expenditures and operating funds you will need to drive it all forward.

As the person who knows what's in the consumer's best interest, your job is to internally advocate for them. Your counterpart in the technology department is likely not thinking about the consumer first. Their focus is on maintenance: system upgrades, data sanitization (at least hopefully), system and data security, cost containment, and permissions management. Your finance counterpart, on the other hand, is focused on reduction: accounts receivable, manufacturing unit costs, inventory, time to delivery. IT also is focused on reduction, in terms of system total cost of ownership. Investing time, energy, and money into new technology to drive company growth or to create value through personalization is typically not high on the IT or finance agendas, for a variety of reasons.

Their interest in AI and machine learning, at least initially, will likely be in how it can improve security, effect cost savings, and improve efficiencies across an enterprise. Many AI-powered applications already exist that could do that right now. In terms of your world, AI and machine learning could certainly be used to automate repetitive, low-value marketing tasks. You could use natural language processing to write your weekly marketing status reports automatically by turning sales data into text—instead of having humans spend hours looking at dashboards and typing out documents. Great work is being done in this area, and you should investigate it to increase the efficiency of your marketing operations.

However, our focus is on using AI to drive *growth*, because that is where we believe the biggest wins will ultimately take place.

So, exactly whose job is it to focus on growth? Answer: yours, marketing leader! To win you have to grow, and the way you grow is with AI and technology, in what Phil Kotler refers to as "marketing 4.0," or what many of us call "modern marketing."[5] You will grow by using machines to add speed and personalization, and to do things at scale that wouldn't be possible if a human, or even a bunch of humans, were assigned to do them manually. Along the way you need to get your IT and finance counterparts on board, and we'll provide some tips on how to do that as we go along.

TAKE UP THE CHALLENGE NOW

We urge you to take up the challenge to drive change in your firm now, because this is your future. AI will be responsible for driving an estimated +1.2 percent GDP ($13 trillion) global economy in the next decade, according to a paper by McKinsey Global Institute.[6] That paper, "Notes from the AI Frontier: Modeling the Impact of AI on the World Economy," also says:

The impact of AI might not be linear but could build up at an accelerating pace over time. Its contribution to growth might be three or more times higher by 2030 than it is over the next five years. An S-curve pattern of adoption and absorption of AI is likely—a slow start due to the substantial costs and investment associated with learning and deploying these technologies, then an acceleration driven by the cumulative effect of competition and an improvement in complementary capabilities alongside process innovations.

It would be a misjudgment to interpret this "slow burn" pattern of impact as proof that the effect of AI will be limited—or that you have time to sit on the sidelines and wait. The size of benefits for those who move early into these technologies will build up in later years at the expense of firms with limited or no adoption.

As Jack Kornfield said in his 1994 book, *Buddha's Little Instruction Book*: "The trouble is that you think you have time."[7] So let's get started!

3 Navigating This Book

The book is divided into four parts comprising sixteen chapters, which lay out all the concepts and structures we think you'll need to be productive and successful as a marketer leading AI and machine learning initiatives in your organization.

Part 1, "The Challenge and Solution," has a twofold purpose. The first two chapters, *"Marketer's Challenge Today"* and *"AI Marketing Canvas: A Strategic Path Forward for Marketers,"* were designed to give you a thirty-thousand-foot view of the core concepts of this book. This chapter, *"Navigating this Book,"* provides a thorough overview of the concepts we'll be covering. Don't need or want this overview? Feel free to skip right to part 2. If you want to know all that we have in store for you however, read on.

Part 2, "AI and Marketing Essentials," is composed of three chapters which provide the foundational knowledge and vocabulary you need to make the best use of parts 2 and 3 of this book. *In chapter 4, "Networks and Nodes,"* we'll set the stage by talking about what we've observed are two main business models when it comes to technology, which we'll be referring to as networks and nodes. The aim of chapter 4 is to provide you with a clear picture of what each of those models are, so that you can determine which bucket you are in right now, and also determine which kind of networked business model would be appropriate for your brand. We'll also make a case for why firms that are not networks need to embrace the new world of AI and machine learning as soon as possible, because in the end it will be a winner-take-all situation—a claim we'll support with plenty of evidence throughout this book.

In chapter 5, we'll introduce you to our "Customer Relationship Moments" mental model, a universal customer decision journey model with nomenclature that can be easily adapted to a proprietary customer model if you already have one in place. We'll also walk you through the four distinct moments comprising the model: Acquisition, Retention, Growth, and Advocacy. Finally, we'll demonstrate how traditional Customer Relationship Moments differ from AI Customer Relationship Moments. We'll suggest that winning these AI Customer Relationship Moments is the objective of your AI marketing strategy. You'll be introduced to our AI Marketing Canvas as the road map you'll use to decide how best to supercharge them.

In chapter 6, "What Is AI and Machine Learning?" we'll equip you with the vocabulary and knowledge about AI and machine learning you need to communicate successfully with your data science team and technology vendors. You'll learn the categories of machine learning, as well as a bit about neural networks and deep learning. We'll conduct a brief review of data and analytics. Finally, we'll give some examples of when to use what in machine learning, so you have context for all of this information be it new to you or a review. Whatever you do, please don't skip this chapter. You will need this vocabulary to move forward and have constructive conversations with your data science contacts. Know that we worked hard to make it not just easy to read, but as interesting and relevant as possible by including many brand- and marketing-related examples.

Part 3, "The AI Marketing Canvas: Five Stages of AI and Machine Learning in Marketing," provides an overview of the canvas, and then walks you through each stage. Each chapter features brand-focused examples of what AI looks like when applied to the different Customer

Relationship Moments at that particular stage. *In chapter 7, "Elements of the AI Marketing Canvas,"* we introduce the canvas framework comprising the five stages—Foundation, Experimentation, Expansion, Transformation, and Monetization—across four Customer Relationship Moments—AI-Acquisition, AI-Retention, AI-Growth, and AI-Advocacy—and explain how best to put the canvas to use.

In chapter 8, "Stage 1: Foundation," we'll continue the conversation by zeroing in on the description and key questions specific to the Foundation stage. Foundation is about building digital infrastructure by collecting first-party data across the business—enough quality data to begin training machine learning models and supercharging Customer Relationship Moments. *Chapter 9, "Stage 2: Experimentation"* is about finding marketing activities that could be empowered with AI for some quick learning, and using AI-powered tools from third parties and vendors to get some quick outcomes in a few marketing activities. We'll also ask you to consider a new way of working: taking an Agile approach to getting AI and machine learning into your firm. (Don't panic. We'll provide an overview of what that process might look like in your culture.)

Up next is *chapter 10, "Stage 3: Expansion."* This stage is about using AI across a broader set of marketing activities and beginning the process of insourcing some development and capabilities. We'll introduce the critical role of the AI Marketing Champion, and provide some thoughts on how to develop an AI marketing team. We'll also show you the importance of quantifying the impact of the experiments you are doing in Stage 2 so that you can make a strong case for the additional budget you'll eventually be requesting. A big part of Stage 3 will be your efforts to design campaigns, run them, and then evaluate and learn from the results so you can do more of what is working and less of what isn't (along with documenting the stuff that does work for your future business case).

Chapter 11, "Stage 4: Transformation," is about using AI to automate across a complete set of marketing activities in one Customer Relationship Moment, or more deeply in one or two moments. At this point, most of your AI and machine learning capabilities should be in-house; or if you are using a partner, the development of the model should be under your (marketing's) control. At this point we'll ask you to consider whether your firm should buy a company with existing expertise, or build its own in-house. We will outline a typical process for pitching one or the other, along with a helpful form you can fill out to gauge which direction is right for you.

In *chapter 12, "Stage 5: Monetization,"* we cover how you may be able to use the proprietary models you've developed either by building in-house or by buying a company to drive new revenue streams and/or new business models, serving external customers as a platform. Caveat: Not every brand or firm will want or need to go to Stage 5, because to achieve this you must make the jump from being a node to becoming a network! (You'll understand the depth of that chasm after reading chapter 4.) Finally, *chapter 13, "Putting It All Together,"* features Starbucks, another first-class example of a brand that has traversed the five stages. In this chapter we tell that story, complete with a timeline so you can get a sense of the multitude of efforts, experiments, successes, and failures that led to the siren's massive success today.

Each of these chapters concludes with a summary and a helpful checklist to help anchor the information and make the concepts imminently actionable. We will also provide a diagnostic tool that expands on the questions raised at each stage of the canvas at the end of the book.

Part 4, "Implementation," addresses the inevitable obstacles you will face in getting AI and machine learning into your firm. It also highlights the tremendous opportunities that AI and machine learning offer in their ability to do the heavy lifting so that you can focus on increasing the quality and frequency of actual human-to-human connections with consumers.

In *chapter 14, "Managing Change,"* we'll address the reality of change through the lens of how even Google had to make this shift to AI and machine learning, first technically and then culturally. We'll show you how Google leaders followed John Kotter's change model by creating the climate for change, engaging and enabling the organization, creating short-term wins, and then reinforcing the new direction. We'll provide some guidance on how to facilitate these changes, which must happen across multiple dimensions: namely, people process, culture, and profit.

Chapter 15, "Getting Started," offers real guidance in the form of a diagnostic tool you can use to gauge where you are on the canvas, in Stages 1 through 5. You'll also learn what gaps and challenges you can expect, and how to prepare for them so that you can mitigate or overcome them. Then we'll wrap up the chapter with a sample of an AI Marketing Canvas for a fictional business, Raj's Bakery. Finally, in *chapter 16, "A Call to Action,"* we'll address how this all impacts you personally, and provide some guidance on ways to move forward wisely. We'll also point you to some next steps, including a list of things you can do right now to forward the action and enhance your career. And most important, we'll wrap with some thoughts from three marketing and business leaders on how your brand could—and, we argue, should—embrace the potential to use AI to nurture and enhance *humanity*.

These aspirations may seem noble, even lofty; but they are achievable. It all begins with your commitment to a strategic marketing approach that puts the customer at the center of everything, and the creation of a digitally driven business that maximizes the advantages that AI and machine learning have to offer. Are you up for the challenge? We thought so. Let's get started.

"A journey of a thousand miles begins with a single step."

—*Chinese proverb*

PART 2

AI and Marketing Essentials

4 Networks and Nodes

"When spiders unite, they can tie down a lion."

—Ethiopian proverb

IN 2011, the TV investing pundit Jim Cramer started referring to four technology companies—Facebook, Amazon, Netflix, and Google—as the "FANG" stocks, because they had become so big that any major move by any of them directly impacted the stock market. The way the FANGs and other technology-driven companies sell products, services, or experiences—theirs or others—has also radically impacted your world as a marketer, because it has completely upended consumer expectations around every facet of their relationship with your brand. (We realize this part is not news, but bear with us.)

These tech-driven firms are **networks**. Let's call a network a system of interconnected nodes. A **node** is an atomic element of the network. Railway systems, for example, are a network of individual train line nodes. A chamber of commerce is a network of individual local business nodes. The early telegraph systems were a network of interconnected local telegraph offices (nodes) that allowed people to communicate using Morse code. It could be argued that the Western Union Telegraph Company was among the earliest technology platforms in the United States, dating back to the nineteenth century. Note that nodes can also be freestanding and independent, often competing against powerful networks, as we will discuss below.

Networks have important advantages that force firms to pay attention to them. The primary advantage is the ability to benefit exponentially from scale, known as the "network effect." Metcalfe's Law states that a network effect exists where the cost of adding an incremental node is n and the incremental value of that node is n squared. (More current thinking has shown n squared to overestimate value, because not all incremental nodes equally add n-squared value. Some now write the network effect as $= n*(\log)n$).[1]

In the case of the Bell Telephone company, a single telephone would have been useless. But as more homes added the device, the value of the network increased because more people could talk to each other. Similarly, the more users participate in a social platform, the more valuable that network becomes to the community. In this context, Facebook, Amazon, Netflix, and Google can also be considered networks that provide value to consumers via their proprietary technology platforms—which are powered by AI.

In the 2016 book *Platform Revolution*, the authors define a platform as "a new business model that uses technology to connect people, organizations, and resources in an interactive ecosystem in which amazing amounts of value can be created and exchanged."[2] If you make and sell a tangible product, such as baked goods or tractors, through a network such as Amazon, and your *primary business model* is not driven by a technology platform that connects you directly with consumers or connects them with each other, you're most probably a "node."

EXAMPLES OF NETWORKS	EXAMPLES OF NODES
Google	Kraft Heinz
Facebook	Nike
Uber	Coca-Cola
Apple	Ford
Amazon	Levis

Netflix	Tide
Airbnb	Macy's
Zillow	Raj's Bakery

Don't get too attached to these black-and-white definitions, however, because, as you'll see, there are a few different "species" of networks. Additionally, some networks have subsections that act like nodes, while many nodes (including a few listed above) are striving to become networks! The good news is that the presence of so many nuances demonstrates that there is more than one way to reach success, as long as your business model allows you to use data efficiently to create value for the consumer.

Let's examine this idea of networks and nodes in more detail.

While networks leverage a technology platform to provide a product, service, or experience to as many consumers as possible, that is not their only agenda. A network also collects and analyzes first-party consumer data around those offerings (items searched, sales, etc.) so that it can learn more about each individual consumer and continuously fine-tune that person's experience through personalization. Networks can also opt to allow other suppliers to connect with their customers. In this case, the network lets the supplier use their platform for these transactions, and extracts a fee from one or both parties for facilitating them. Amazon, eBay, and Alibaba are examples of networks that do this.

The challenge for suppliers, many of whom are nodes (e.g., Tide, Coca-Cola), is that though they may gain access to buyers on the network's platform, they typically are not given access to any data the network collects about individuals buying their products. If the network were to share that information, the supplier might use it to establish a direct relationship with that customer and potentially take them away by nurturing them directly with personalized offerings, so that the consumer begins to buy directly from the supplier instead of from the network.

In fact, the inherent ability of the network's technology-driven platform to collect, process, and leverage massive amounts of "first-party" data and use it to provide value to users through personalization is a key component of its ability to create and sustain competitive advantage. The first-party data available to networks helps them develop product recommendations, promote the right products, develop personalized communications, and provide personalized prices. All these personalized marketing strategies are made possible by AI algorithms that are trained constantly from the first-party data collected by networks.

That said, while all network business models are powered by a technology platform, the ways those platforms are configured vary widely. In fact, it's safe to say that no two will be exactly alike.

NETWORKS

Let's examine networks first, because most nodes are scrambling to figure out how to become networks so they can have direct access to customers and their first-party data. Networks use this first-party data to develop AI algorithms that can be used to increasingly personalize your experience on their platform. Networks are like snowflakes; every one is a bit different. Some are highly pure and some are hybrids, meaning that they have many characteristics of networks but also possess characteristics more typical of nodes.

Pure Networks

Examples of "pure" networks are Facebook, Google (in particular, its subsidiary YouTube), and Amazon. We call them pure because their *primary* business model is that of a marketplace which provides a technology platform that connects buyers with sellers—or, in the case of YouTube, connects content creators with content consumers. Pure networks also have direct connections with customers, and enable them to leave and read reviews of products and services.

Airbnb, Uber, Zillow, StubHub, Houzz, Etsy, and LinkedIn also share the characteristics of "pure" networks. (For LinkedIn, a B2B network, the reviews take the form of endorsements and recommendations.) Airbnb and Uber are pure networks because they don't own anything, but just directly connect consumers to suppliers and sellers. The Zillow real estate app also is a pure network because it connects consumers directly to real estate agents. In the B2B space, LinkedIn provides a platform that ostensibly is designed primarily to connect its members with each other for networking purposes, but also with potential employers and clients. In fact, hundreds of businesses are now using technology platforms to create networks to connect consumers to suppliers of everything from photographers and dog walkers to pilots of private airplanes.[3] Apple was originally a node, but it joined the network genus (species, pure) when it created its App Store, which provides a platform for suppliers to offer their products and then enables consumers to purchase, rate, and review those products.

Some but not all pure networks also sell their own products or are in the process of bringing the ability to sell them to bear, These would include Zillow Homes, Amazon Essentials, YouTube Originals, Airbnb Experiences, LinkedIn Learning, and more. These ancillary products represent efforts to increase competitive advantage by acting more like "hybrid" networks, in order to control ever more of the consumer experience.

Hybrid Networks

A hybrid network is one in which the pure network business model of connecting consumers and suppliers through a technology platform is augmented by the firm also acting as its own supplier. Netflix is a prime example of a "hybrid" network, because its business model today is to be a creator, seller, *and* platform provider. Rather than sending you to a content creator's website (or to a channel, if you're YouTube) to consume the content, Netflix owns the entire consumer experience, from end to end. The other thing that makes Netflix unique is its focus on using data to create value for consumers. Netflix knows what each subscriber, and subscribers similar to them, are watching, and so it is able to personalize its offerings to a high degree. It is like a grocery store that automatically rearranges itself to present not just the products you buy most often, but also those it predicts you'll need or could be interested in.

You'll note there is no direct consumer connection happening at Netflix, nor does it provide a place for content creators to sell directly to consumers. If Netflix were a *pure* network, its main business would be not commissioning content, but encouraging others to post their content directly on the platform for others to watch. In other words, it would basically be YouTube!

To that end, let's dig deeper into this network definition (pure vs. hybrid) by comparing media providers.

Media Networks

A media network is a platform that delivers information or data to consumers in the form of shows, movies, and videos, which can be live or prerecorded. YouTube and Netflix are among the biggest and best known media networks. But there also are many smaller ones, such as Twitch, a live streaming platform best known for its gaming content, and TikTok, the video-sharing social networking service.

YouTube, which refers to itself as an "American video-sharing platform," has more than two billion users worldwide, equating to more than one-third of the Internet. The company claims that more than one billion hours of its video are watched daily.[4] Nearly all of its content has been made by content creators who also are users, called "YouTubers." These content creators strive to build large enough followings of subscribers to make them eligible for ads to be inserted into their video content, similar to traditional television commercials. Some of these YouTubers elect to join "multichannel networks" (MCNs) hosted on the YouTube platform.

YouTube also initiated YouTube TV, which provides access to more than seventy channels for $49.99 in 2017, and it recently introduced YouTube Music, which in December 2019 rolled out three personalized mixes: the new Discover Mix, the New Release Mix, and Your Mix—"to keep users up to date on what's just been released, and introduce them to a wider range of artists and sounds based on their personal taste."[5] Then there is YouTube Originals, a selection of commissioned content that is either free to view or ad-supported (a paid subscription allows one to view the content without ads).[6] YouTube has recently revamped and trimmed its lineup, and it has a handful of new shows slated for 2020 and in development. Rather than try to compete with Netflix and Amazon's scripted content, however, YouTube is focusing on "genres such as unscripted, educational and music artist-focused docu-follows."[7] So, even though YouTube is involved in some hybrid networklike activities, such as creation of its own content, we are defining YouTube as a *pure* network because its main business model is to provide a platform for content that directly connects outside suppliers and consumers.

Netflix is a streaming platform which began in 1997 as a video-rental firm that mailed movies to people's homes. It pioneered a subscription model where, in exchange for a flat monthly fee, customers could order multiple movies and keep them as long as they wanted. This endeared it to consumers, many of whom defected from video-rental store Blockbuster, which charged hefty late fees for movies returned after their due dates. Netflix's ability to retain customers was highly driven by customer recommendations,[8] so in January 2000 it introduced Cinematch, a recommendation system that prompted customers to rate movies using one to five stars. As customers rated more films, accuracy in predicting their preference for movies improved. By 2007, Netflix had nearly one billion movie reviews on board, and CineMatch was generating a significant portion of the firm's traffic (over 50 percent).

To make CineMatch even better at predicting how much customers would like certain movies, in 2006 it offered a $1 million prize to any group developing an engine that could beat the system's accuracy by 10 percent—a prize awarded to a firm in 2009 in exchange for the first generation of the collaborative filtering algorithm that would drive Netflix's profitability for years to come. Increases in Internet speeds and advancements in technology eventually improved Netflix's ability to successfully "stream" movies over the Internet—which increased the volume of customers and movies watched, thereby increasing algorithm prediction accuracy and thus the value of the results the recommendation engine offered to its customers.

Today Netflix operates a sophisticated technology platform which allows its paying subscribers—at this writing, 192,950,000 globally and growing—to stream video content via the Netflix app.[9] Since 2016 it has been streaming in almost every market in the world, and its goal is to ensure that users can watch the same content almost wherever they are.[10] Netflix's business model is built on the ability of its technology platform to collect first-party data about its customers so that it can apply sophisticated algorithms and predict what types of content its customers will want and when they will want it.

Note: Unlike YouTube, whose recommendations are determined by what channels viewers subscribe to and what videos they like and comment on, Netflix is doing this without direct input from its customers. In fact, Netflix discontinued the ability for customers to review, and removed all the reviews from the platform in mid-2018, citing declining use, thereby removing the means for customers to connect with and influence each other using its platform.[11] Again, because of its business model—create the product, sell it, *and* provide the platform on which the product is consumed—Netflix is an example of a "hybrid" network.

Twitch is a media network that provides a platform for "millions of people to go live every day to chat, interact, and make their own entertainment together."[12] It was acquired in 2014 by Amazon.[13] According to Twitch's website, "it's a place where creators like you can share the things you love with a community of millions and also carve out a tight-knit corner of the internet to call your own."[14] It has been described as "crowd-sourced live TV."[15] Most of the content is created within the gaming category—specifically competitive, organized video gaming, which is known as "eSports." Competitors from different leagues or teams face off in the same games that are popular with at-home gamers—League of Legends and Fortnite as examples—and viewers use Twitch to watch them play.[16] Users can view broadcasts from the website or mobile app, but those who want to broadcast and chat have to register for an account, which is free. Like YouTube, Twitch is driven by subscriptions and advertisements but also offers in-app purchases.[17]

Though eSports may be its main bread and butter, Twitch invites creators to stream about anything they're passionate about: making art, playing music, in real life (IRL) experiences, and so on. The platform offers creators three levels, which unlock additional capabilities with each "achievement," such as the ability for viewers to subscribe and eventually to advertise. As of 2019, the average viewer on Twitch watched a stream together with more than 1.274 million people watching an average of 50,800 concurrent live channels. "Every day, there's more people on this [platform] than there are on most cable networks, and during peak events, there can be over a million people in just one category," said Ben Schachter, an analyst at Macquarie Group. "This is the continued evolution of what video can be in a connected world."[18]

The platform is facing stiffening competition from other streaming platforms such as Microsoft-owned Mixer, YouTube Live, and Facebook Gaming, however. While it's still the leader over its rivals in terms of hours of content created and consumed, the number of hours watched on Twitch declined from the third to the fourth quarter of 2019 by 9.8 percent.[19] To that end, Twitch is focused on expanding its live streaming content beyond video games. Particularly interesting is its partnership with the National Football League for its Thursday Night Football games. Viewership of NFL football on the live streaming platform rose 45 percent from 2018 to 2019, according to a press release from the Canada-based gaming and esports company Torque Esports.[20] The Twitch platform is helping the league to reach fans who are watching less broadcast or cable TV in favor of over-the-top services.[21] Since Twitch provides the platform for the content creators and users, it is, like YouTube, an example of a "pure" network.

TikTok, just one of many apps owned by Bejing-based ByteDance, is another rising media network whose focus is short-form mobile videos. It is best known for its short lip-sync, comedy, and talent videos. The app provides creators with "challenges" designed to inspire engaging content. Challenges contain music tracks full of effects and filters, and AI algorithms are applied to optimize not only content creation but also content curation, recommendation, and personalization.[22] The app, which is free to download but offers in-app purchases, surpassed two billion downloads in April 2020.[23] This media network is facing some growing pains, however, as it works to grow its ad-supported platform and make things easier for advertisers. Like Twitch and YouTube, TikTok is a pure network.[24]

Marketplace Networks

Another arena in which networks operate is in the marketplace. Amazon, Alibaba.com, Facebook, and Apple's App Store can all be considered "marketplace" networks. Etsy, Poshmark, and StubHub and also are marketplace networks. Marketplace networks connect consumers and suppliers, but where possible they also encourage consumers to connect with each other by leaving product reviews. Let's look at the larger marketplace networks for comparison.

Amazon.com is a well-known large marketplace network. It operates an extremely sophisticated technology platform that allows it to offer consumers a variety of products—and, more recently, services —sourced and distributed in a variety of ways. Customers can leave product reviews on the site. It also has a professional services arm in Amazon Home Services, where one can schedule services such as plumbing, furniture assembly, and house cleaning, and the credit card kept on file is charged for the service.

Alibaba.com is China's largest international online wholesale marketplace, with buyers located in nearly two hundred countries. Its customers are typically trade agents, wholesalers, retailers, and manufacturers. In other words, it is not a consumer-facing platform. As with Amazon, B2B customers can leave product reviews on the site.[25]

Facebook is primarily a social marketplace whose main product is the content members create and share with each other. The data Facebook collects from these activities allows it to sell advertising space to brands that use the Facebook feed to sell products or services. Facebook also provides advertisers access to a "pixel" that can be installed on websites or landing pages which will deposit a cookie on the visitor's browser, so that the advertiser can then "remarket" to that visitor later.

Apple is a hybrid marketplace network that started life as a node that sold computers and other electronics. In 2008 the company debuted the first iteration of its App Store, which today boasts nearly four million apps and games (free and paid)[26] for users to download. To access the App Store you must create an AppleID, which allows Apple to collect information about what you are purchasing—though in sharing it, the company is more privacy-oriented than most.

Poshmark is a US "social commerce"–driven marketplace network with more than two million "seller stylists," and millions of shoppers. Users can buy and sell new or used clothing, shoes, and accessories; sellers can follow other sellers and gain their own followers.[27] The **Etsy** marketplace is known as a global source of unique handmade or vintage items and craft supplies.[28] Etsy provides buyers with the opportunity to rate products, whereas the Poshmark marketplace does not.

Independent Networks

Some nodes also function as "independent networks," with technology platforms that allow consumers to connect directly with them and with each other through the review process, but which do not connect them to competing brands. For example, the hoteliers **Hilton** and **Marriott** both offer rewards programs (Honors and BonVoy, respectively) that are connected to smartphone apps that allow customers to do research, book rooms, check points balances, and record their preferences—first-party information the hoteliers can use not only to better serve the customers but also to inform future business decisions about new perks and programs.

An example of a wildly successful independent network is **Starbucks**, which is built on its Starbucks rewards app, a robust customer data-collection machine first deployed in 2010. Not only does Starbucks have a rich trove of proprietary customer data, which they're leveraging to a high degree with the application of AI; they also are working with a partner to monetize this technology and offer it to other retailers. To that end, Starbucks, like the *Washington Post*, exemplifies mastery of all five stages—and we'll describe why that is in detail near the end of this book.

Walmart is also making moves to become its own network. The retailer said it's "doubling down on technology in its brick and mortar stores to better compete with Amazon" by adding pickup towers that make it easy for customers to order online and pick up merchandise quickly in a nearby store.[29] Walmart also upped its online game by purchasing the Jet.com platform, which then bought the Modcloth.com platform[30] and the Indian e-commerce site Flipkart. In May 2020 the company announced it would discontinue Jet.com, citing the strength of the Walmart.com brand. On a call with analysts, Walmart CEO Doug McMillon said he credited the acquisition for "jump-starting the progress we have made the last few years."[31]

Nodes behaving as independent networks are in the minority, but we are seeing a great deal of activity in this area, especially when it comes to bigger brands that are either doubling down on their own direct-to-consumer (DTC) product development (e.g., P&G Ventures)[32] or looking for attractive DTC brands to buy to jump the line (Unilever's acquisition of Dollar Shave Club, Edgewell Care Company's attempt to purchase of Harry's, etc.).[33]

PROVIDING CUSTOMER VALUE AT SCALE

Here's the thing: If all the big networks had done was raise customer expectations by streamlining the buying experience, nodes could probably have continued to cope with that with upgrades in technology. But streamlining the buying experience was just the beginning. Since day one, each of these networks has collected petabytes of first-party data on their customers, data they then analyze and process with powerful computer algorithms. This leads to predictions about the products or services each customer will want—sometimes before the customers are even aware they want them. In effect, networks are able to use data and AI algorithms to personalize marketing. The result is a powerful "AI machine" capable of turning massive amounts of first-party data into *predictions* that networks can use to market effectively to millions of individual segments, each containing exactly one person.

Here is why in the end, the ability to do this at scale will lead to a "winner-take-all" situation. The more people who join a network, the more information about them and their buying preferences becomes available, and thus the better predictions the AI machine can make about what they want or need at each point in their buying journey. This "flywheel" phenomenon is also called the "network effect."

THE NETWORK EFFECT

Positive network effects like those described above create a snowballing effect that provides lift. Netflix achieved a network effect early on as a DVD-only service by inviting users to review movies they watched.[34] However, it was able to achieve a more powerful network effect by shifting the responsibility for evaluating and curating films to its algorithm, which was able to deliver deeper, more accurate insights tailored to individuals. The insights gleaned from data and algorithms based on data drawn from its 192 million–plus users make this network increasingly valuable to viewers, and allow those at Netflix making decisions about content to see patterns about preferences that would be otherwise opaque. [35]

As shown in figure 1, the value of a network to its consumers increases as more consumers join the platform. For example, the value of Facebook for a person increases as more of their friends and family join the network. Also, the value of Netflix to a content provider increases as more customers

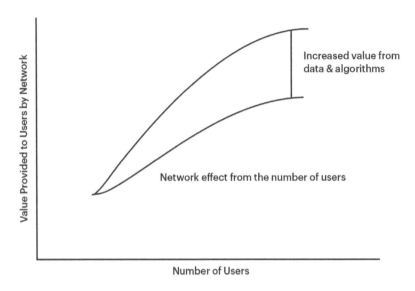

Figure 1. The network effect

join Netflix. As more *content providers* join, the value of Netflix increases for its users, attracting more new users to join the network. As more *users* join, the firm can use data about user behavior on its network to develop algorithms which provide personalized recommendations. The accuracy of these algorithms, and hence the network's value to a user, increases as more users join the network and use its services. The higher of the two S-shaped graphs in the figure represents the incremental value data, and algorithms provide consumers in addition to the value provided by just having a large number of users on the network, as shown by the lower S-shaped graph.

Now, let's look at the way network effect manifests in our other large networks.

Amazon: Amazon's powerful network effect is why large nodes such as P&G and Unilever are compelled to sell their products on its platform as well as in the local grocery store. Increasingly, Amazon is where people go to purchase consumer packaged goods, and the more people who use Amazon to reload on Swiffer or Lipton soup, the more reviews those products will receive, and the more value Amazon provides to both supplier and consumer.

Facebook: Just as the value of Bell's telephone network increased in the late nineteenth century as more people acquired the devices and connected them to Bell's wires, the value of the Facebook network has increased exponentially as the number of registered users has increased.

Apple (App Store): As more people use iPhone, messaging improves and app quality improves, making the device and store more valuable to users, Apple, and application developers alike.

Google (YouTube): Subscribers create a network effect by liking and commenting on videos, which amplifies the effectiveness of ads and improves the relevance of the videos shown to them. Signals from subscribers also impact the development of influencers on the basis of network graphs, and likely also influence the selection of YouTube originals,

The same is true with Poshmark, Etsy, StubHub, and so on. What makes those networks valuable is the number of people who both buy and sell using them. Inability to attract enough users to catalyze a network effect has led to the demise of a number of networks, some whose names you know (Google Plus) and some not so well known. For example, Sidecar pioneered the ridesharing model before Uber and Lyft, but it never became a household name because, among other things, it did not recognize the importance of building both sides of the platform: drivers and passengers.[36]

Though the road to building a network is fraught with its own issues, if you're a node with no network, you are facing some equally scary challenges that already outstrip any number of human resources you could possibly throw at them. In fact, a senior executive of one network once told us, "It's better to be the network than the node *in* the network." And that is exactly why you're seeing some nodes withdraw from their network partnerships and double down on building their own networks.

JUST LEAVE IT

For example, the apparel and footwear maker Nike recently withdrew its products from Amazon, citing the desire to "focus on elevating consumer experiences through more direct, personal relationships." The Amazon-Nike partnership began as a pilot program in 2017, which was designed to allow Amazon to act as a wholesaler of Nike products in hopes that it would stem the number of fake Nike goods available from third-party sellers. (It didn't.)[37] In that respect the pilot was unsuccessful, but a more likely explanation for Nike's abrupt departure is that the firm was looking to put more emphasis on its own online business. This makes sense considering that the company in 2019 named as its CEO John Donahoe—the former CEO at the e-commerce giant eBay!

If the desire to elevate consumer experiences is the desired result, Nike knows that to do that effectively, they need the ability to predict what consumers want; and to do that, they need direct access to the first-party consumer data—data the Amazon network is not about to share. Boding well for this direction are increasing sales attributed to Nike Direct, the arm of the company that oversees Nike.com; direct-to-consumer sales; and Nike+ digital. Nike's departure likely won't significantly impact Amazon, which already has begun recruiting Nike resellers in an effort to make sure that Nike products continue to be easily available on the Amazon marketplace.[38]

MEDIA NETWORK CHALLENGERS

Netflix, on the other hand, is experiencing new challenges as multiple competitors such as Disney+, NBC, AT&T, and HBO withdraw its content and offer it on their own media platforms. How much consumers are willing to pay for the different platforms, how many platforms they'll choose to maintain, and whether an aggregator will sweep in and create a one-stop shop of sorts remains an open question.[39]

Like Nike, Disney+ and other media challengers realize that if they want to grow, they need to act like a network by amassing first-party data and leveraging it to provide value to consumers through personalization and more. Even though Netflix is enjoying the benefit of decades of data collected on consumers, and is using algorithms to leverage insights from that data, it will have to work hard to sustain that competitive advantage as competition among media networks increases. Disney has the capability, culture, and brand trust to provide exceptional customer experiences that can only be enhanced through better first-party customer data. It is quickly building its consumer base—amassing nearly 60 million subscribers in a dozen countries in under six months—and its data and algorithms are already kicking in to personalize subscriber experience, providing the extra propulsion Netflix is now enjoying.[40]

Building a big enough customer base to get the data required and creating effective algorithms also will be the biggest obstacles facing the other challengers in streaming media. Is there room for everyone to play in this space? Time will tell. In the meantime, the consumer is the main beneficiary of the competition for their attention and their share of wallet.

After ability to attract a large enough consumer base, access to first-party consumer data will determine winners and losers regardless of whether they are networks, nodes, or something in between. A node has three options:

1. **Build your own network** (platform).
   - Walmart.com accelerated its growth by purchasing the Jet.com platform, which then bought the Modcloth.com platform,[41] and the Indian e-commerce site Flipkart, which it then absorbed it into the master brand. Recently Walmart has partnered with Shopify to enable millions of small businesses to sell on Walmart.com.[42]
   - Verizon Media Group has acquired the formerly independent nodes AOL, Yahoo, HuffPost, TechCrunch, Engadget, Rivals.com, Autoblog, and Tumblr, and rolled them up into a network now viewed by 900 million fans.[43]

2. **Collaborate with a network.**
   - Whirlpool embedded Alexa into its appliances, allowing use of mobile devices and Google Assistant or Alexa voice commands to monitor and control them remotely. Asking Alexa to preheat an oven ahead of arriving home would be one example of this.[44]
   - Target partnered with DTC brands—such as Casper, a mattress company boasting more than one million happy sleepers and 500,000 five-star reviews; Harry's, a shaving equipment and personal care company, with more than two million repeat customers;[45] and BarkBox, a curated subscription service that mails out new dog toys, treats, and other products to its 600,000 subscribers each month[46]—to gain access to those customers.

- Restaurants are partnering with online and mobile prepared food ordering and delivery marketplaces such as GrubHub, DoorDash, and Uber Eats to drive sales.[47]
- The high-end furniture company West Elm has partnered with the DTC mattress company Casper, so that shoppers can try mattresses before purchasing, and West Elm can promote its furniture to Casper customers.[48]
- Levis has partnered with Pinterest to allow the apparel maker to provide digital personalized style suggestions and visual-focused boards to millions of its users.[49]

3. **Team up with another node or research partner to gain parity**[50]
   - JP Morgan Chase is one of more than a hundred banks and credit unions that have agreed to let their customers send money with **Zelle**, a person-to-person payment network.[51]
   - A market intelligence research partner such as Numerator can create panels of consumers willing to give access to their online Amazon accounts so that their buying habits and data can be collected and crunched. This allows brands to go directly to consumers for data, and if they have a big enough consumer panels, they can approximate data knowledge.[52]

One great example of a brand that understands the importance of moving from node to network is Disney. In August of 2017, Disney chief Bob Iger announced that the company would be pulling all of its content from Netflix and making it available exclusively on its own streaming service, Disney+. Disney+ will feature content from Marvel, *Star Wars*, and Pixar, and will be the home for all of Marvel's superhero movies and *Star Wars* movies.[53] A recent report by CNBC said that JP Morgan expects Disney+ to eventually draw 160 million subscribers from around the world, more than Netflix's current 139 million—60 million of those already acquired by August 2020.[54]

Disney is not alone. AT&T CEO Randall Stephenson confirmed in May of 2019 that AT&T would pull WarnerMedia-owned content like *Friends* and *ER* from the rival streaming services Netflix and Hulu, and offer it exclusively on its upcoming streaming service.[55]

Disney had long been functioning as a node, and its business model involved licensing its content for distribution on Netflix's proprietary technology platform. The problem with this arrangement was that Disney content on Netflix improved consumer connections to Netflix, not Disney. Disney has no access to the massive amounts of data Netflix is collecting on customers who are watching Disney's content on the Netflix platform. Building its own network will enable Disney to get the data that will allow it to grow without Netflix as a middleman. The combination of first-party data and a proven ability to connect emotionally with customers is what analysts believe will give Disney+ such a good chance of success.

Disney also understands that it needs to do whatever it takes to amass as much data as quickly as possible, and so it will offer its Disney+ platform at a low cost: seven dollars a month, to Netflix's thirteen dollars. It also has partnered with Verizon to offer all Verizon Wireless unlimited customers, new Fios home internet customers, and new 5G home internet customers a year of Disney+ for free. This will ensure that Disney+ has millions of subscribers at its launch.[56] It is also already acting like a network in that it is willing to lose money for a while until it gains the subscriber base needed to catapult forward.

For Disney+ to be successful, it will have to do more than invest in content, however. It must use machine learning that leverages data to suss out the personal preferences of its audience. Consider Netflix's latest hit, *Bird Box*,[57] which follows in the successful footsteps of *Orange Is the New Black*, *Black Mirror*, *To All the Boys I've Loved Before*—all greenlighted on the basis what the data was indicating. In a December 2018 article on Slate.com titled "*Bird Box* Is a Triumph of Netflix's Data-Driven Content Machine," Aja Hoggatt says, "*Bird Box* may not be a perfect film, but it works because Netflix is delivering to an audience what their data, in defiance of conventional wisdom, has told them exists."[58]

As Netflix collects more data and deploys collaborative filtering to provide more recommendations, the value it provides to customers increases exponentially, in line with the network effect. The algorithms leverage viewing information about other customers to provide better recommendations for a customer. So the benefit to an individual customer increases as other customers join the network, and the benefit to the nodes that supply content also increases as more customers join and stay on the network. This is what makes Netflix and any other network deploying a product, service, or experience driven by data and algorithms a "winner-take-all" system, and why it will be all the more difficult for nodes that don't start now to catch up.

Networks (e.g., Alexa, Google, Siri) are also increasingly determining which *nodes* (e.g., Tide, Oreo, Pantene) are presented to the customer. The network will use its data to predict which node's product is the most personally relevant to the consumer, and that will be the one the AI-powered assistants will recommend to stock the customer's pantry, fill their makeup case, or determine what kind of automobile sits in their driveway.

This means that ultimately, the biggest threat to a node may ultimately be other *nodes* in its space that have recognized the potential of AI and are investing aggressively in the technology and data science resources to become the first choice for consumers and networks alike. Even if you are just a node competing against other nodes, to survive you're still going to need a customer-centric strategic plan for how you're going to deliver a unique buying experience to each and every customer at each moment in the customer relationship—and do it at scale. And the one and only feasible way to do that is to amass a large volume of first-party consumer data, and process it using AI and machine learning. The good news is that you don't have to radically change the essence of what you're already doing, which is driving revenue through building customer relationships and providing great brand experiences. You will, however, have to change the *way* you're doing it if you want to survive.

In the next chapter, we'll introduce our Customer Relationship Moments mental model, which is composed of four distinct Customer Relationship Moments: Acquisition, Retention, Growth, and Advocacy. We believe these four moments are key opportunities for nodes to connect directly with consumers in the one-to-one personalized experience that the networks are leading them to expect.

SUMMARY

- A network is a proprietary technology platform with the ability to connect people, organizations, and resources in an interactive ecosystem in which amazing amounts of value can be created and exchanged—and first-party data about consumers can be collected.
- A network typically provides a product or service to a consumer in exchange for a fee and/or the collection and processing of data around those offerings, so that it can learn more about each consumer in order to continuously fine-tune their experience.
- A node is an atomic element of a network.
- Freestanding nodes compete with networks built on platforms powered by AI and machine learning capable of curating the available consumer choices down to the one the machine predicts will serve them best wherever they are in the customer relationship.
- The competitive advantage of networks is the ability to use AI algorithms that are trained on the first-party data they collect about their customers to deliver personalized experiences. Doing so increases the value provided as customers engage repeatedly with the networks.
- There are several different types of networks: media networks, marketplace networks, independent networks, and hybrid networks, to name a few. What they all have in common is the platform that allows them to provide value to the consumer.
- If you're a company that makes stuff and sells it (baked goods or Caterpillar tractors), probably through or with a third-party network, you're a node.
- If you are a node, you have three options: build your own network, collaborate with a network, or team up with another node or research partner to gain parity.
- The benefit of the network to the individual customer increases as other customers join the network, and the benefit to the nodes that supply the products they buy also increases as more customers join and stay on the network.

KEY QUESTIONS

1. If you are a node currently selling through an intermediary, given your current business model, which one of the three strategies—build your own network, collaborate with another network, or team up with another node to gain parity—makes the most sense to pursue if the goal is to gain direct access to consumers?

2. What initiatives do you currently have in place to gain direct and consistent access to the first-party consumer data that will allow you to personalize the experiences of those customers at every significant moment in their relationship with your brand?

5 The Customer Relationship Moments Mental Model

"Artificial intelligence has flipped the consumer buyer's journey on its head. It creates hyper-personalized recommendations based on vast amounts of data, meaning each consumer has a journey tailored to their needs, knowledge level, and preferences."
—Nick Edouard, cofounder and chief product officer, PathFactory[1]

IF YOU'RE LIKE US, you have a favorite family-owned breakfast place in your neighborhood. You go there every Saturday, and your favorite server waves you over to their section and returns with your coffee, four creamers, and two yellow packets without even having to be asked. Then the owner stops by and asks how your spouse and kids are doing. They know their names and that one is poised to graduate from college and the other is engaged to be married.

Your server returns and asks if you want "the usual," but you tell them you've had some health issues and so need the dish to be made without certain ingredients, which they cheerfully record on their small green notepad. Your meal comes out hot and perfectly made, and the owner stops by to fill up your coffee cup. Your server drops the check along with a small to-go cup of house-made fat-free yogurt for you to try at home. Yogurt was something your doctor recommended you try. How did they know?

As a marketing leader, you are that restaurant owner. You know that anticipating the needs of your regular customers and fulfilling them flawlessly, sometimes even before they know they want something, is the key to ensuring that they never want to go anyplace else. The problem is that, instead of a hundred customers to serve on a busy Sunday morning, you have millions, and your ability to provide the one-to-one personalized level of service that is your calling card is nearly impossible. To succeed, you need a way to scale your ability to provide that one-to-one personalized experience, and that's where AI and machine learning comes in. This technology allows you to augment your ability to enhance the customer relationship at every juncture. To execute on this, however, you need a framework: something that takes into consideration the key Relationship Moments that occur between you (your brand) and your customer.

The framework we've developed is based on the Customer Relationship Moments "mental model," which is a widely known and universal model for the customer decision journey.[2] Several academic and practitioner writings indicate that customer relationships are composed of four distinct steps: Acquisition, Retention, Growth, and Advocacy. We selected this model because as a marketer, you likely are already familiar with it and probably have used it or are using it now in some way. Note: We realize that this is not the only viable customer relationship model, and that you may have your own model based on custom research and interviews with your buyers. That's OK; the goal is the same, which is to see how you can use AI to supercharge each stage of *your* proprietary customer relationship model.

Let's look at each moment in more detail:

- **Acquisition:** Customer encounters advertising or marketing that gains their attention or raises their awareness of the brand. The customer first encounters the brand when they strive to learn more about it through search and social media. This was also termed the "zero moment of truth" (ZMOT) by Google. Consider a customer signing up for a Stitch Fix subscription after watching their commercials on TV, searching for the company on Google, clicking on the organic search link, and then filling out the personalized styling questionnaire on the Stitch Fix website.

- **Retention:** Customer Retention begins at the "shelf" or point of sale, where the customer encounters the product either online or in-store and decides to buy your product. Please note that the opposite of Retention is churn; it happens when a customer decides to stop purchasing. Consider a Dollar Shave Club customer continuing their subscription. The personalized emails from Dollar Shave Club and the product experience can help establish a strong relationship with customers and strengthen Retention.
- **Growth:** As the relationship progresses, customers can grow the relationship by purchasing new products or upgrading their service levels. Consider a medical devices firm adding Microsoft Azure Analytics services to their existing Azure cloud services contract after experiencing the personalized service and usage reports provided by the Azure platform.
- **Advocacy:** Once the product or service has been procured, the customer experiences the product and then shares information with others about it. The customer, in effect, turns into an advocate for the brand. Consider a Hilton Platinum customer writing a glowing review on Tripadvisor after she has used her Hilton Honors points to stay with her family at the Conrad London St. James.

Customers interact with brands and other customers throughout this relationship, creating several *interrelated* Relationship Moments along the way. For example, the experience at the Conrad St. James hotel improves the customer's relationship with the Hilton brand, which leads to higher **Retention**, and also turns the customer into an **Advocate** for the Hilton brand. Or emails sent by Dollar Shave Club to its customers could be personalized to their preferences based on buying history. If, in addition to purchasing razors, the customer browses aftershave lotions on their website, a series of customer **Retention** emails could also be used to cross-sell aftershave lotions, leading to **Growth** by helping that customer easily learn more about other products he may prefer.

The four Customer Relationship Moments—Acquisition, Retention, Growth, and Advocacy—are represented in a continuous circle in figure 2. We use two-way arrows to show that customers can churn and be won back

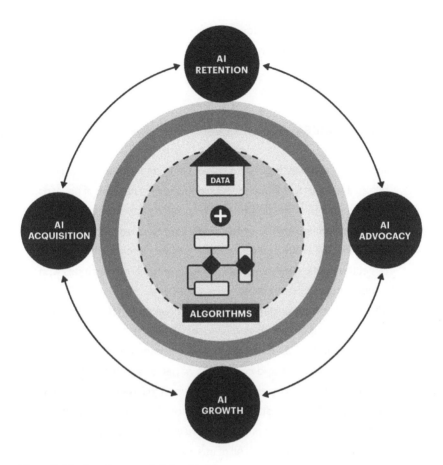

Figure 2. The four Customer Relationship Moments

through reacquisition from any Relationship Moment. When data and algorithms are at the nucleus of this model, leading to personalized interactions between the brand and the firm at each Relationship Moment, those moments become AI Relationship Moments. Note: the traditional relationship mental model would not have data and algorithms in its nucleus, and a one-size-fits-all approach would be used to develop each Relationship Moment. The theory for many years was that if you just invest the time, energy, and resources to optimize these moments in a customer relationship, you should be successful. That's not a guaranteed outcome anymore, and here's why:

There are three forces now at work that have made customer relationship management difficult if not impossible to navigate without the assistance of AI and machine learning or deep learning: advances in technology, customer connections, and information abundance.

THE THREE FORCES

1. **Technology is advancing** at light speed. For example, on a visit to a mobile ad agency in San Francisco, we were shown a network of how ads were inserted into mobile games. We found the data science that was applied to achieve this to be extremely sophisticated, and it is worth noting that the entire process of identifying the right advertisement to target the right customer was all run automatically on machines with minimal human intervention.

2. **Customers are connecting** on so many different technology platforms and in many different ways (Facebook, Pinterest, YouTube, Twitch, TikTok, Snapchat, etc.) that it has become impossible to effectively manage the volume and complexity of personalized customer engagement across channels. Further, networks that were once primarily market-based are now striving to add a social component (Amazon), and those that began as purely social networks are now entering into the marketplace (Facebook). All of this adds to ever-increasing avenues for customers to connect with each other.

3. **The information facilitated** by technology and generated by this avalanche of customer connections is creating a state of information abundance, causing consumers to experience cognitive overload, which hampers their ability to make purchase decisions.

The rather famous infographic in figure 3 was created by the social media expert Lori Lewis (lorilewismedia.com). It depicts what happened in a single 2019 Internet minute—a perfect example of all three forces at play, and visual proof of the imperative for brands to find a way to build relationships with consumers through providing hyper-relevant, one-to-one personalized experience at every juncture. If this graphic reflects just one Internet minute, consider that in one Facebook minute there are 317,000 status updates,

Figure 3. "2019: This Is What Happens in an Internet Minute." Courtesy of Lori Lewis. Reprinted with permission.

400 new users, 147,000 photos uploaded, and 54,000 links shared.[3] So just imagine how many profiles you would have to look at, how many posts you would have to read, and how many photos you would need to sift through and analyze to arrive at a reasonable prediction about how to target consumers with personalized messages. I think we can agree that it's an impossible task without the help of a powerful machine that can expedite the process.

To get a sense of how we got here and where we are going, it is useful to look at the evolution of consumer information processing over the past eight decades (1941 to present). This evolution can be divided into three distinct "waves."

THREE WAVES OF CONSUMER INFORMATION PROCESSING

The three waves of consumer information processing—mass marketing and segmented marketing, data-driven marketing, and personalized marketing (figure 4)—comprise a "long-term arc" of marketing that is reflective of the levels of data and technology available at the time. Note: These waves actually don't end; one strategy has its heyday in a certain period, and then something newer comes on the scene.

The Long-Term Arc of Marketing

Wave 1

Mass marketing (1940–60): Customer Acquisition and Retention was achieved primarily through mass advertisements and by influencer personalities who spoke directly to a primary audience. For example, Dad may have been inspired to visit a Sears store to purchase a variable speed Craftsman drill after seeing a magazine ad impelling him to "look again," and to "buy a Craftsman and be one."[4] Or Mom may have purchased a jar of Lustre Cream Shampoo based on an endorsement from actress Bette Davis, "whose beautiful hair is part of the charm that enchants millions."[5]

Segmented marketing (1960–2000): After 1960, advertisers thought much more about the concept of targeting beyond the primary audience, to secondary and tertiary audiences.

Spiegel, the company that sold apparel primarily through catalogs, is a good example of this. During the 1970s, when it began losing market share to Sears and Montgomery Ward, whose merchandise customers could return to stores, Spiegel began to target a younger, better-educated customer—primarily female, with a higher income than those of other catalog users. During this time, women were targeted according to six categories of lifestyle analytics ranging from "starting out" to "mature." This allowed Spiegel to test offers and create versions of the catalog that would best resonate with each category. It also was one of the first brands to place a plus-sized woman on a catalog cover (1991).[6]

In addition to segmenting their communications, marketers also segmented their product offerings, typically using a "good-better-best" approach. An example of segmented product marketing is Black and Decker

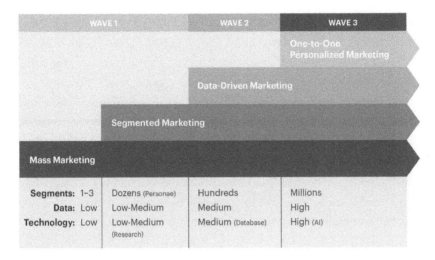

WAVE 1	WAVE 2	WAVE 3	
		One-to-One Personalized Marketing	
	Data-Driven Marketing		
	Segmented Marketing		
Mass Marketing			

Segments: 1–3	Dozens (Personae)	Hundreds	Millions
Data: Low	Low-Medium	Medium	High
Technology: Low	Low-Medium (Research)	Medium (Database)	High (AI)

Figure 4. The long-term arc of marketing

creating Dewalt, a separate higher-end tool brand, for contractors, because it had learned that contractors and expert tradespeople didn't want to be seen using the same brand of tools as the casual weekend do-it-yourself homeowner. The higher-end professional tool line was a huge success that actually ended up outshining its household sibling.[7]

Wave 2

Data-driven marketing (post-2000): The advent of the World Wide Web and digital marketing ushered in the ability for marketers to use even more data and move from a few segments to hundreds. Early on in this wave, you may have been intrigued enough by Travel Channel cable TV network host Samantha Brown's tour of Paris to contact your travel agent and book a trip because of your perception of her as a trusted advisor. You also may have seen her show on the Travel Channel and used a new search engine called Google to find out about flights and hotels. To try to get the cost of the trip down, you may have gone to a site called Priceline.com to use its configurator to search for hotels in Paris, sorted by price and neighborhood, and then spend a bit of time parsing through the results.

Fast forward to 2020. A search request for "Paris" on Google returns a staggering 4.1 billion results; a search for "Paris travel," 1 million results.

A search for "Paris hotels" on Priceline returns 2,698 results, though using its configurator to narrow to "Eiffel Tower" gets those results down to 135. Which is a doable number, if you are sure you want a hotel near the Eiffel Tower, and want to spend the time required to evaluate all 135 results.

By the way, many in the financial services industry were early adopters of data-driven marketing, because the collection of consumer data to make decisions about credit worthiness and other things was baked into their business model. To understand how they are using that data to target customers today, you need only to take stock of the vast number of credit card applications and solicitations to open new bank and investment accounts that fill your mailbox each day.

Wave 3

One-to-one personalized marketing (now and future): Getting back to that trip to Paris you're planning, chances are you've watched several videos about Paris on YouTube to get the "inside track." You're also a HotelTonight. com subscriber who has invested time in filling out a profile. When you search for "Paris, Eiffel Tower," the system serves up ten to fifteen results precisely curated to your preferences—curation that gets better and better as you "train" it by telling it whether you liked your stay or not. The key here is that the HotelTonight system is not giving you one million or even 135 options. It applies algorithms to the information you've provided, and serves up the five or six options that best match your criteria. All the options and bits of information that HotelTonight.com presents are curated and personalized for you specifically, through its application of machine learning to your profile.

And that letter you received from JPMorgan Chase? It probably wasn't written by a copywriter. Rather it likely was generated by a machine that is looking at what it knows about you and has made a prediction about what you want and need from your financial institution. (We'll talk about how JPMorgan Chase does this in chapter 9.)

AI and machine learning provide the algorithms that marketers of nodes (brands) can use to curate the information customers receive, transforming information abundance into information perfection and allowing you to harness all three forces to achieve a level of *personalization that fosters intimacy and loyalty.*

How you respond to the *current* wave of consumer information processing—millions of segments and a high level of data and technology (AI)—*and* manage the three forces—advancing technology, connected consumers, and information abundance—will determine how successful you are in supercharging your Customer Relationship Moments—Acquisition, Retention, Growth, and Advocacy—and transforming them into the AI Customer Relationship Moments that will allow you to *win it all.* As Karl Wirth, CEO of Evergage (a Salesforce company) said in his 2019 article for Entrepreneur.com, "A good personalized experience occurs when a company, in each moment, understands you as a person, decides what the best experience for you would be, and responds with relevance."[8]

So what exactly are the differences between traditional Customer Relationship Moments and AI Moments? Let's walk through the customer experience of each, comparing an imaginary health club called "Peach" with a potential series of experiences with the exercise equipment and media company Peloton.

TRADITIONAL CUSTOMER RELATIONSHIP MOMENTS VS. AI MOMENTS

Let's say your New Year's resolution is to lose weight (stimulus). You're super-serious this time, so you're especially interested in personal training. You see an ad on TV for a local gym: Peach Athletic Club (PAC). You go online to search for reviews about PAC, and discover that it has several membership levels: blue, silver, and gold. Intrigued, you drive to the local Peach gym, about ten minutes away. You wait fifteen minutes until a salesperson becomes available. The salesperson gives you a tour, telling you about all the features and benefits and the membership special that's ending shortly. To sweeten the deal, the salesperson offers you a few free sessions with one of the club's personal trainers. Those are the magic words and so you sign up (Acquisition). After a few visits (Retention), you decide you love this gym (or not), and, hoping to save others some time, you go online and write a review (Advocacy). You decide to continue with personal training, even though it's expensive, and you expand the gym membership to a family plan to include your spouse and kids (Growth). You get a new job in a new city, and so you look on the website for a way to cancel your membership. Not finding anything there, you call the gym—only to be told that not only do you need to give thirty days notice, but you also must come to the gym to sign paperwork in order to effect the cancellation.

These are moments in a traditional customer relationship that live solidly in the second wave of marketing. Now let's see what those moments might look like as AI Moments.

It's January 1 and you're determined to lose weight this year (stimulus). You've seen a few ads on TV about your local gym and have seen the Peloton outdoor ads, so you're *aware* that both options exist, but neither brand comes immediately to mind as a solution. You go online and search for "fitness routines for 43-year old men." The search engine, using an algorithm, serves up a Peloton ad. This ad is personalized to your preferences (running or cycling) through predictions made by a machine, which recognizes pictures you have posted in and browsed on in your Facebook profile and in other online social media profiles such as Pinterest.

You click on the ad, which takes you to a landing page that has been dynamically generated to align with what the machine knows about you. It contains, among other things, all the routines that can be customized to your lifestyle, along with detailed feedback and customized calendars. The content the machine has generated for you hits its mark, because now you're intrigued and excited about the possibilities. Depending on where you live, you could walk to the local Peloton studio, purchase a Peloton bike, or download the Peloton app to try the routines and personalized data about your workout regiments and health—complete with music that is customized for you based on your initial choices (Acquisition).

Upon exploring the app, you discover that it not only allows you to connect with others, but also connects you with a specific trainer (live or avatar), who advises you about your personalized routines based on your strengths and interests. This data is cycled back into the machine to help not just you but also other customers like you (Retention). If you are happy (or maybe not), you write an online review about Peloton and its studio, connect with others who train with you (Advocacy), get feedback for improvements from an algorithm based on data collected during Acquisition, decide to purchase a Peloton bike, or subscribe to another routine that works for you and is recommended by the AI algorithms (Growth).

This is a made-up story, based on experience and research about Peloton, to show the potential for AI to impact the entire customer journey. Now, here's a real-life example of how Peloton is using AI to grow its business.

Peloton has been running Facebook ads for years, and was using both broad targeting and lookalikes to achieve its goals; but it wanted to grow faster, so it tapped the ad technology firm Lightning AI to help accelerate the process.[9] Lightning AI's algorithms identified user groups that were highly likely to purchase Peloton bikes (Acquisition). Within two weeks, more than five hundred different interests and behavioral targeting groups were tested on Facebook. Within two months, more than a thousand combinations were tested. In addition, Lightning AI led Facebook prospecting campaigns for new Peloton bike sales, which drove 26 percent of total purchases from prospecting (Growth). Lightning AI's algorithms created scale, and the new audiences it found performed better than the broad audiences and lookalikes Facebook had offered.

The company also has added AI to its sound design with Super Hi-Fi. Peloton says, "With this partnership, Peloton becomes the first and only fitness service to leverage AI for intelligent audio experiences. Peloton Members will experience powerful enhancements architected from the ground up for their service powered by technology that understands the nuances of music with a depth similar to a human DJ."[10] Side note: Peloton is one of many fitness brands that collect data. Consider wearable Fitbit (a node), which was recently acquired by Google (a network). All such brands collect a lot of data, and a logical next step would be to focus on Wave 3: one-to-one personalized marketing.

So where do all these Peloton AI Moments lead? For one thing, as a customer you're happy to get a service that would otherwise cost a ton to get from a fitness trainer. Second, the feedback, the personalized music, and the connection with other riders make you use the product more (Retention, Growth, Advocacy). These two things, especially in the fitness world, are signals to Peloton that you are getting better and feeling better, and are more likely to go back and use the product again. This increases the value of the product to you over time (Retention), and makes you more likely to tell others about it (Advocacy). In the meantime, Peloton is also learning about you and others like you, and is using that information to develop and pitch the right products to you at the right time.

These new AI Moments are the new personalized way in which customers will experience all the moments in their customer relationship (Acquisition, Retention, Growth, Advocacy) as a result of advances in artificial intelligence and machine learning. The long-term implications of the three forces and the current (third) wave cannot be overstated. If you're a "Peach Athletic Club" still using second-wave strategies to market to consumers, with no road map for moving to a third-wave personalized approach—think chatbot technology to automatically schedule tours, and AI-powered email marketing—you will not be able to compete in the long term with the richness of the AI- and data-powered experience of a Peloton, or with anyone else.

Another way to think about how AI and machine learning can supercharge your Customer Relationship Moments is through the lens of "buying pathways." Figure 5 depicts three customers, their buying pathways, and their choices, along with the personalized interactions driven by consumer insights that brands can have with their customers. Let's unpack each path using a fictional brand and retailer. (If consumer electronics is your category, however, our hope is that you'll be inspired by the possibilities.)

John's Buying Pathway

While watching a Saturday college football game on ESPN, John sees a television ad for "Fab" LED TVs that promotes great prices for the holiday season (Stimulus/Acquisition). John uses his iPad to go to the Fab website to learn more about the product. The website uses his location information to highlight the closest Primo Purchase store, where John can check out the great prices it has on Fab TVs (Location/Acquisition).

John responds to this personalized information on the website by making a trip to the Primo Purchase store to check out the picture quality of

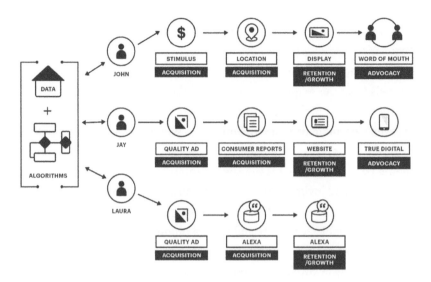

Figure 5. Buying pathways

FabTVs. He likes the product and is close to purchasing, but does not want to wait in line to complete the purchase, and then have to figure out how he's going to fit the big box into his small car. He takes a picture of the Fab TV on his phone, and the Google Lens feature automatically provides a link to a display ad from Fab TV that highlights free shipping for online purchases and 10 percent off all sound system purchases made directly from Fab Company. He clicks on this display ad and purchases the TV and the sound system from the brand's landing page, which is customized for the display that John has clicked. He has now moved from Acquisition to the Retention/Growth phase.

After a month has passed, John really loves the TV and sound system, and decides to write a review for the product on Fab's website. As he does this, he proceeds to the Advocacy phase of the customer relationship.

Jay's Buying Pathway

While on his way to the subway, Jay notices an advertisement on a digital display board for a new Swell laptop. While on the train, he logs onto the Consumer Reports website, whose reviews he trusts. He looks up its Swell brand report, and is impressed with the features and performance ratings (Acquisition). He goes to the Swell website, reads the consumer reviews, and purchases the top-of-the-line model to be delivered the next day. Thus, Jay proceeds from the Acquisition moment to the Retention moment.

Upon delivery of the laptop, Jay also discovers the 10-percent-off coupon for Swell's portable printer—the quality of which he validates by looking at Consumer Reports. Impressed by the review, he fills out the form on the landing page, and purchases the Swell printer. The page asks for additional information, and invites him to download an app from the Apple store that offers detailed videos for setup, an easily searchable manual, and a link to a curated catalog of accessories and related products Jay can purchase. This demonstrates the Growth moment.

Blown away by Swell's end-to-end intuitive support and customer care, which is powered by a chatbot (Retention), Jay posts a picture of his new laptop and printer on Instagram, recommending the brand to his followers, and includes the hashtags #SwellLaptop and #SwellPrinter, which reside at the center of the Advocacy customer moment.

Laura's Buying Pathway

While at her kitchen table drinking coffee, Laura leafs through the latest issue of *Parents* magazine and notices a print ad for her preferred baby shampoo from a brand she loves: Baybee. This is a stimulus that lives in the Acquisition moment. Remembering that she's almost out of shampoo, she says, "Alexa, order one bottle of Baybee shampoo." Alexa replies that it has found two sizes, and asks which one she would prefer. Laura chooses the smaller bottle even though it's more expensive, because it's easier for her to handle when she has her hands full bathing her young daughter. Alexa places the order, using Laura's credit card on file with Amazon. Alexa then asks Laura if she is ready to reorder baby lotion and baby wipes, and Laura says yes—a Growth moment. Alexa also asks if Laura would like to subscribe to receive shampoo, lotion, and baby wipes automatically, and then guides her through the process of doing so, which is Retention.

To be clear, AI Moments don't *replace* Customer Relationship Moments. Rather, they affect the customer's experience of each moment in a specific way. To marketers this is really important, because it means that if the competition is fully leveraging AI to supercharge *its* Customer Relationship Moments, one will be left behind.

Before we begin our journey through the five stages, let's take a break and synch up on what we mean by "AI" and "machine learning," so that we can provide you with some basic computer science concepts that you really need to know. Relax, breathe, and have no fear—we promise it won't be too technical. Onward!

SUMMARY

- The customer relationship mental model we are using has four steps: Acquisition, Retention, Growth, and Advocacy. However, you can swap these out for whatever model you are using, and it will still work.
- There are three forces at work which have made the customer relationship difficult if not impossible to navigate without the assistance of AI and machine learning: advances in technology, customer connections, and information abundance.
- AI and machine learning provide the algorithms that marketers of nodes (brands) can use to curate the information customers receive, transforming information abundance into information perfection and allowing you to harness all three forces to achieve a level of personalization that fosters intimacy and loyalty.
- Consumer information processing has experienced three distinct waves which reflect the levels of technology in play. They are Wave 1, mass marketing and precision marketing; Wave 2, data-driven marketing; and Wave 3, personalized marketing.
- How marketers respond to the current wave of consumer information processing and manage these three forces will determine whether they can create the AI Moments required to win it all.
- **The AI Moments are the new personalized way customers will experience all the moments in the customer relationship (Acquisition, Retention, Growth, and Advocacy) as a result of advances in artificial intelligence and machine learning.**

KEY QUESTIONS

1. Which Relationship Moments (Acquisition, Retention, Growth, Advocacy) are you able to identify and track for your customers?
2. When do your customers experience information abundance, and how can AI help you improve your customer experience through curation of the offers?

6 What Are Artificial Intelligence and Machine Learning?

"I want you to be smart consumers of analytics."
—Raj Venkatesan's advice to his students

ARTIFICIAL INTELLIGENCE (AI) is the capability of a machine to accomplish tasks in a "smart" manner, where the machine is a high-powered computer system equipped with the ability to process massive amounts of data quickly and accurately. AI is a broad term that has several different dimensions: rules-based expert systems, robotics, natural language processing, vision, speech, and machine learning, to name a few. And while these dimensions of AI are distinct, today many of them are working in concert to achieve a specific outcome. Think of IBM Watson's ability to beat out top champions at *Jeopardy!*—an example we'll describe in more detail later.

As the title of this chapter suggests, we will be looking at AI primarily through the lens of *machine learning*. That's because most of the marketing opportunities that will be available to you likely will be led by the machine learning dimension of AI.

If you're reading this book, we're betting you've read more than a few of the myriad articles on AI. You've likely also noticed that not everyone talks about AI in exactly the same way. In this chapter we aim to clarify those key technical concepts and provide you with the vocabulary critical to your ability to understand the capabilities and potential of AI and machine learning. Don't worry—we won't try to turn you into a computer scientist. We just want to give you the tools you need to communicate effectively with your data science team and be a smart consumer of technology, so that you can press AI and machine learning into service to supercharge each and every moment of your customer journey.

If you walk away with nothing else from this chapter, make it this: When it comes to marketing, AI equals prediction. This means predictions that allow you to more confidently answer questions such as "Who is the best target?" "What should the message to them be?" and "Where should we place that message for best results?" You're already doing all this manually. The goal is to use AI and machine learning to do it all better and faster, so that you can improve outcomes and create a competitive advantage!

Caveat: We have made some strategic choices about what information to include and omit, and about how deep to go based on practical relevance and our experiences working with thousands of marketing managers. However, all the information presented here is consistent with the more complex scientific and academic principles.

The overall goal of this chapter is twofold:

- to provide you with a foundation of knowledge that allows you to better understand subsequent information you may want or need to consume on this topic, and
- to equip you with core concepts you need to understand concerning what is possible and how to communicate effectively to direct your data science team and/or your third-party vendors.

We'll begin by providing you with a very brief historical context for how we arrived at the current state of AI beginning in 1950, when the English mathematician Alan Turing published a paper asking the question, "Can machines think?" Next, we'll define exactly what machine learning is, and illustrate its different "categories" using the example of Airbnb. We'll also define neural networks and deep learning, and then show you how machine learning assisted by neural networks and deep learning allowed IBM Watson to beat two champions at the TV question-and-answer game *Jeopardy!* and enabled Google's DeepMind product Alpha Go to beat the world champion in the abstract strategy board game called go. (By the way, the latest is for DeepMind, that chess and go were child's play; it now beats humans at multiplayer games as well.)[1]

Speaking of questions, here's one: Is machine learning different from statistics? We'll clear that up for you. Finally, we'll outline the key machine learning *techniques* and how they are organized using their analytical objective; and then, through some examples, we'll convey what they mean to you as a marketer tasked with making decisions about your brand. Our goal is to make this a critical nuts-and-bolts chapter you'll actually enjoy reading. Let us know how we've done by connecting with us on LinkedIn (we'll accept) and leaving us a message.

JIM LECINSKI: www.linkedin.com/in/jimlecinski
RAJ VENKATESAN: www.linkedin.com/in/education-marketing-consultant/

Ready? Here we go.

ARTIFICIAL INTELLIGENCE: A BRIEF HISTORY

In 1950 the English mathematician Alan Turing published one of the earliest papers on AI, titled "Computing Machinery and Intelligence." The paper began by posing the simple question "Can machines think?" Turing proposed a method for evaluating whether machines can think, in the form of an imitation game. This game challenged a human interrogator to distinguish which response to the same question was given by a human and which was given by a machine, solely on the basis the content of the responses, and without physical clues. This method became known as the Turing test. Though imperfect, computer scientists continue to use the Turing test and various versions of it to explore questions the field of AI seeks to answer.[2]

Another key moment occurred in 1956 when John McCarthy, a professor at MIT and Stanford University who is now widely recognized as the "Father of AI," defined artificial intelligence as "systems that perform actions that if performed by humans would be considered intelligent." Then, in

1958, McCarthy created Lisp, which became the standard AI programming language. Lisp is still used in robotics and other scientific applications, as well as in Internet-based services such as credit-card fraud detection and airline scheduling. Lisp also paved the way for voice recognition technology, including Apple's personal assistant application, Siri.[3] Excitement around the new field of AI and the potential for sentient machines attracted large amounts of funding initially, and science fiction further drove up expectations. By the 1970s, however, lack of specific goals for funding and failure to demonstrate commercial value of AI led financiers to pull out, resulting in what became known as the "AI winter."[4]

In 1981, the Digital Equipment Corporation (DEC)—incidentally, the main hardware vendor for the AI community in the 1970s—started using R1, an "expert" system (also known as a *rules-based* system) primarily to assist in the manufacture of its VAX-11/780 systems. R1's *input* was a customer's order, and its *output* was a set of diagrams displaying the spatial relationships among the components on the order. These diagrams were used by the technician who physically assembled the system. A major part of R1's task was to notice which components were missing and add them to the order, eliminating delays due to missing parts.[5]

An expert (rules-based) system is a form of AI because it uses knowledge acquired from human experts in the field to solve a specific problem. Although the results of expert systems were not as grand as financiers initially had hoped, these systems were successful commercially and brought funding back to the field. For example, by 1986 it was estimated that R1 had saved DEC an estimated $40 million annually.[6]

AI research has advanced quite a bit since then, most notably in producing systems that have evolved from using sets of rules to guide outputs to being data-driven. Today, in fact, most dimensions of AI including machine learning are data-driven. The exponential increase in computing power (e.g., TPUs) and the decrease in computing costs (i.e., Moore's law) are key factors in the emergence of data-driven AI at scale.[7]

One important advancement in data-driven AI occurred in 2006 when the AI researcher Fei Fei Li, then a professor at the University of Illinois at Urbana-Champaign, began work on a "computer vision" project that would become known as ImageNet. (Dr. Li is now a professor at Stanford and co-director of the Stanford Institute for Human-Centered AI.) ImageNet's goal was to create one huge real-world data set by mapping the entire world of *objects*. This was achieved by leveraging Amazon's Mechanical Turk service to label millions of individual images.[8] This is important because before ImageNet, most computer scientists did not realize that a large real-world data set was the missing link to being able to train machines to accurately identify unlabeled objects. ImageNet also allowed neural networks to enter the mainstream for image recognition. (A neural network is a machine learning technique in which a computer learns to perform a task by analyzing training examples. We'll talk more about neural networks later in this chapter.)

ImageNet today is an image database of over fifteen million labeled high-resolution images belonging to roughly twenty-two thousand categories.[9] As a result of ImageNet, dozens of new AI research datasets have been introduced over the past ten years. For example, Google introduced its Open Images database in 2016. Open Images offers an image data set so granularly labeled it can be used to train a multilayered neural network from scratch. ImageNet, Google Open Images, and other image datasets facilitate machine learning by providing a source of training data that enables machines to recognize similar, unlabeled objects.

At this point you may be thinking you need a massive dataset compilation in your firm to use AI. Fear not! The datasets built by Google, ImageNet, and others are available to everyone. You also can use neural networks that Google and others have built as a starting point, without having to invest the time and resources needed to build one from scratch yourself.

In summary:

- AI is composed of a number of dimensions of which machine learning is just one.
- The Turing test is still the gold standard when it comes to deciding whether machines can think.
- The definition of artificial intelligence, according to John McCarthy. is "systems that perform actions that if performed by humans would be considered intelligent."

- For all the excitement about AI in the 1950s, financiers pulled out by the 1970s because no one could figure out how to commercialize AI; and this led to the "AI winter."
- In 1981, DEC developed a rules-based "expert" system that saved them money, and so paved the way for other firms to begin monetizing AI.
- The ImageNet project initiated in 2006 allowed machines to become data-driven by providing access for the first time to a massive amount of "training data."
- ImageNet led to Google and others developing even more sophisticated datasets, which in turn led to the development of neural networks.

So now that you have a sense of the key moments in the development of artificial intelligence and a sense of the key concepts, we can dive deeper into the dimension of AI we are most interested in as marketers, and that is machine learning.

WHAT IS MACHINE LEARNING?

Machine learning occurs when a data set is loaded into a machine which then processes it by applying one or more computer *algorithms* to arrive at a series of *predictions*.[10] A computer algorithm is a well-defined procedure that allows a computer to solve a problem.[11] An algorithm is typically preceded by a qualifier, as in *search* algorithm, or *classification* algorithm.[12] Only rarely in machine learning is a single algorithm used; typically several algorithms are deployed in a certain sequence and at lightning speed. To keep this simple, we'll talk about them as one unit.

One example of an algorithm in action is Google search. When you type your search request into the box on Google's home page, Google's machine applies a proprietary and ever-changing *search algorithm* to your request to decide what information to retrieve for you from its mass of available data. The more relevant data the machine receives, the more accurate its predictions become, because the algorithm can use this influx of information to continuously refine its predictions—that is, to *learn*. As the algorithm "gains experience," it also becomes increasingly applicable to other future contexts.

You've experienced machine learning if you've let Google complete your sentences while writing an email in Gmail. Google's machine notices what you've written instead of its suggestion, and uses its *content* algorithm to make a better prediction in the next email. The best-known use of machine learning, however, is in image recognition. For example, a robust image-based data set combined with algorithms can allow a machine to accurately *predict* whether an image is a furry dog or a mop, based on the characteristics it has "observed" in other similar images that have been labeled one or the other.

In 2015, Tensor Flow, an open-source code library that helps developers develop and train machine learning models and build neural networks, accelerated mainstream businesses' ability to build and train their own image recognition systems for use in a commercial setting.[13]

A few examples of image recognition systems in action include:

- a bakery in Japan that employs a point of sale that can scan and identify more than a hundred different types of pastries, tally them up, and allow the customer to pay with minimal human intervention;[14]
- a Nature Conservancy initiative which uses image recognition and its own data sets to detect and classify species of the catch from fishing boats to control illegal, unreported, and unregulated fishing practices that affect the balance of marine ecosystem;[15] and
- carmaker KIA's interactive campaign, which profiled participants' image content online, assigned them to lifestyle groups based on those images, and matched them to the cars that best fit their style among the thirty-six different car styles offered.[16]

In summary:

- An algorithm is a well-defined procedure that allows a computer to solve a problem.
- In machine learning typically, several algorithms are deployed in a certain sequence and at lightning speed.
- You've experienced machine learning if you've let Google complete

your sentences while writing an email in Gmail, because it predicts and then learns from your corrections.

- Image recognition is currently the best known use of machine-learning-based AI.
- The open-source code library Tensor Flow accelerated mainstream businesses' ability to build and train their own image recognition systems for use in a commercial setting.

CATEGORIES OF MACHINE LEARNING

Machine learning operates in four main categories: regression, dimensionality reduction, classification, and clustering. Dimensionality reduction and clustering fall under the commonly used term of unsupervised learning, and classification and regression belong to the category of supervised learning techniques. These methods originate in statistics, the field of data collection, organization, analysis, interpretation, and presentation. Machine learning, in the form of deep learning (part of reinforcement learning), also operates in areas that do not come from statistics, most notably artificial neural networks. We'll discuss neural networks and deep learning in detail a little later.

Let's start by looking at the four main categories in action through the example of Airbnb, beginning with regression and dimensionality reduction.[17]

Founded in 2008 and based in San Francisco, Airbnb is an online platform that connects owners of homes, condominiums, apartments, villas, and even castles to prospective renters. Its goal is not only to keep all of its properties rented at all times, but to maximize the profit from each property. To determine how best to maximize profit, Airbnb needs a way to analyze and make predictions about its key revenue drivers.

In this example, Airbnb wants to increase revenue by optimizing pricing. One way to achieve this is to examine the relationship between user sentiments and variables such as property cleanliness, cleaning fees, and price using a *regression* model. (Regression is a statistical method that allows you to examine the relationship between two or more variables. The good news is that the machine handles all the computational and statistical heavy lifting!)

Let's say an Airbnb marketer's data source is the reviews of properties. The problem is that the Airbnb raw data at this point is "unstructured," thus not usable in the regression model. To overcome this, an algorithm must be applied to turn those written words (or groups of words) into numeric values—that is, "structured" data that represents quantifiable consumer preferences. Note: The reduction of text into numbers also falls into the machine learning category of *dimensionality reduction*, the process of reducing a large number of random variables under consideration to a smaller set of principal variables.

Airbnb then chooses to perform a high-level analysis of this review text (or data) by creating a "polarity metric" to represent the sentiment of the customer reviews for a property. To do this, it imports the raw text review data into a sentiment analysis tool (qdap library in the statistical package R), which produces a numeric score that captures the sentiment of the reviews.

With variables assigned, the qdap "polarity algorithm" is then applied. Natural language processing algorithms such as qdap, which take raw text data and convert it into numeric sentiment scores, use a prespecified dictionary of positive and negative words, as well as context shifters (words around the positive and negative words), and assigns a numeric value to each review, positive and negative. The polarity algorithm in qdap computes the weighted average of positive and negative words in a sentence, and the weights are dependent on the combination of the words and the context shifters.

Once a numerical value is assigned to the sentiment present in each review, Airbnb's marketing managers can use *it* as a variable in a regression analysis designed to optimize revenues, just as it would any other variable. In that scenario, Airbnb's regression analysis might use price, review sentiment, and property attributes such as fees and number of bedrooms to predict the number of reviews, a measure of property demand. The predictive model built with regression will allow Airbnb to predict property demand at different price levels, and then choose the price that maximizes property demand.

In summary:

- Machine learning operates in four main categories—regression, dimensionality reduction, classification, and clustering—which originate in the field of statistics.

- Regression is a statistical method that allows you to examine the relationship between two or more variables.
- Raw text data isn't usable in a regression model because it is considered "unstructured data."
- To overcome this, an algorithm must be applied to turn the text into numeric values, or "structured" data.
- Machine learning allows one to apply sophisticated tools such as the sentiment analysis tool qdap, which produces deeper insights far faster than any human or group of humans could achieve.
- The reduction of text into numbers is a form of *dimensionality reduction*—the process of reducing a large number of random variables under consideration to a smaller set of principal variables.

The other two categories of machine learning are classification and clustering. It's appropriate to talk about them together, because classification and clustering are also at the foundation of neural networks, which we'll talk about next.

Classification is the process of predicting the label or category of an item based on a group of data points. Those data points are assigned to characteristics. Characteristics are values that usefully describe the distinctive nature of the things you wish to classify. Simple example: If you're classifying moths, some characteristics would be wingspan, mass, and antennae length.

Staying with Airbnb, suppose the firm wants to identify guests most receptive to buying additional services such as Airbnb Experiences. In this case, Airbnb's marketers would use guest characteristics such as age, family composition, prior locations visited, the number of experiences available at a location, and other relevant factors to *classify* customers into different tiers based on their frequency of experience purchases in the past. The classification algorithm would sift through the past data on customers to help Airbnb identify rules that can be used to predict purchase of experiences. An example could be customers who are twenty to thirty years old and single, have visited beach locations that have more than twenty experience options, have purchased an experience during every other visit, and so on. These rules would let Airbnb score customers who are now looking to rent a property also suggest some experiences through emails, if they score high on their chance of purchasing experiences.

Clustering is a machine learning technique that involves the grouping of customers or data points.[18] Clustering analysis allows you to gain valuable insights from your data by seeing which groups the data points fall into when the *clustering* algorithm is applied. Clustering is used in targeted marketing, customer segmentation, and recommender systems. A cluster analysis could be used by Airbnb to segment customers based on the characteristics of the properties they have rented, such as ratings on accuracy, communication, cleanliness, location, check-in process, and value. The output from the cluster analyses would provide segments based on their property preferences.

For example, Airbnb could use one segment's preference for cleanliness, and another's preference for easy and relevant communication with the host, to create personalized advertisements to target customers on Facebook. To target customers, the segments would need to be profiled based on their demographics and other variables that Facebook provides. These profile variables would be used to identify new prospects for Airbnb, and also target these prospects with the right message.

In summary:

- Classification is the process of predicting the label or category of an item based on a group of data points, which are assigned to characteristics. For example, some characteristics of a moth would be wingspan, mass, and antennae length.
- Machine learning's classification algorithm can sift through past data on customers to identify rules that can be used to predict purchase of Airbnb's experiences product.
- Clustering is a machine learning technique that involves the *grouping* of customers (or data points).
- A cluster analysis could be used by Airbnb to segment customers based on the characteristics of the properties they have rented.
- When it comes to regression and clustering, the machine learning and traditional versions are essentially the same. Clustering is almost

exactly the same, and in regression the machine enables automation of variable selection to include a wider variety of data, and to process more predictors.

Another aspect of machine learning, specifically deep learning, operates in the area of artificial neural networks. Let's define neural networks first.

NEURAL NETWORKS

An artificial neural network is a set of algorithms, modeled after the human brain, that are designed to recognize patterns. Conceptually, a neural network is composed of inputs, hidden layers composed of nodes or "neurons" that do the work, and outputs.[19]

Neural networks help us cluster and classify data. They help to group or *cluster* data according to similarities among the example inputs, and they can help *classify* unlabeled data when they have a labeled data set to train on (think ImageNet)—thus helping the computer improve its "perception" and "learn."[20] An object recognition system powered by a neural net, for instance, might be fed thousands of labeled images of cars, houses, coffee cups, and so on, before it could find visual patterns in new, unlabeled images that consistently correlate with particular labels. The aforementioned Japanese POS system that can identify more than a hundred different pastry types likely was fed hundreds if not thousands of labeled images of maple melon pan before the system achieved the level of perception required to be useful.

For Airbnb, photos can make or break a user's decision to rent. So in 2018 the firm undertook a project to categorize its massive database of listing photos into different room types using computer vision and deep learning. This categorization project served two purposes. It would allow Airbnb to group photos of the same room type together to provide a simple home tour. It also would make it much easier for Airbnb to validate the information about the rooms provided by the host.[21]

Airbnb used image classification similar to ImageNet with the goal of presenting the photos that guests would be most interested in first, to be able to validate the information provided by hosts, and to help hosts learn how to make their images more appealing in a scalable way. To achieve this, it chose an off-the-shelf neural net model called ResNet50, and customized it to its needs. Airbnb's data scientists then sought a reliable way to label the data, and experimented with some training options. The result was that Airbnb can now ascertain with 95 percent certainty that, for example, an image the machine identifies as outdoor is in fact an outdoor image, and that an image classified as indoors is also an indoor image. This shows the value of a company taking advantage of its direct-to-consumer data and custom-built algorithms to outperform even the industry state-of-the-art models.[22]

One could see Airbnb extending this capability to allow guests to search within its website for houses with the characteristic "lake view" in a certain location—say, Geneva, Switzerland. Airbnb's system would then serve up some houses with lake views based on the images posted by the hosts.

In summary:

- An artificial neural network is a set of algorithms modeled after the human brain, which are designed to recognize patterns.
- Neural networks help us cluster and classify data, with the goal of helping the computer to improve its "perception" and "learn."
- Image classification has enabled Airbnb to present the photos guests would be most interested in first, and validate the information provided by hosts.
- Airbnb's use of its own direct-to-consumer data and custom-built algorithms led it to outperform industry state-of-the-art models.

DEEP LEARNING

So if you've ever asked Siri or Alexa to make a phone call for you, or used Google's language translation application, you've experienced deep learning in action. Deep learning (DL) is the application of machine learning's neural networks to complex problems, allowing the machine to learn from its mistakes and to assess its own probability of reaching a correct result or, in other words, develop its own "intuition."[23]

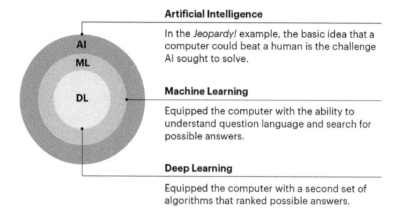

Artificial Intelligence

In the *Jeopardy!* example, the basic idea that a computer could beat a human is the challenge AI sought to solve.

Machine Learning

Equipped the computer with the ability to understand question language and search for possible answers.

Deep Learning

Equipped the computer with a second set of algorithms that ranked possible answers.

Figure 6. AI, machine learning, and deep learning

For our purposes, when we talk about machine learning we will assume that it also may include some aspects of deep learning. Though they are different terms, today AI, ML, and DL, and neural networks typically work in concert, as shown in figure 6. A great example of this was IBM Watson's performance in 2011 as a contestant on the classic TV game show *Jeopardy!*

WATSON AND *JEOPARDY!*

Watson began as one of IBM's "Grand Challenges," a multiyear initiative involving its hardware, software, services, and research divisions, which starts with a clear goal that is currently considered "impossible."[24] IBM conducts these Challenges because it knows that even if the goal turns out not to be possible, the results will be valuable and the company's collective knowledge will be advanced. IBM Watson, Deep Blue (the machine that beat grandmaster Garry Kasparov at chess),[25] and the Blue Gene supercomputer[26] were outcomes of IBM Grand Challenges.

For the Grand Challenge posed in the mid-2000s, Paul Horn, then director of IBM Research, was in favor of developing a machine that could win the Turing test by fooling a human into thinking they were having a conversation with another person. Horn thought a machine beating a person in *Jeopardy!* would be a step in that direction. He approached the EVP of IBM's software group, Charles Lickel, with the project, but Lickel was not onboard until, at dinner one night in a restaurant, he watched the patrons clear out into the bar to see whether *Jeopardy!* champion Ken Jennings would continue his winning streak. (He did.) Lickel then managed to convince his very skeptical team to take on the *Jeopardy!* Challenge.

Jeopardy! is a classic quiz game in which the answers are given first, and the contestants supply the questions. If a player's response is correct, they get an amount of money they have wagered; if incorrect, they lose that amount. It is an incredibly complex game, in that it requires not only encyclopedic knowledge but also the ability to recall that knowledge quickly, as well as the ability to interpret convoluted and often opaque statements, the ability to buzz in quickly and strategically . . . and a smidgen of luck.[27]

To meet this Challenge, the IBM team needed to develop a "question-answering" machine. The result was DeepQA, a software architecture that examined natural language content not just in the clues set by *Jeopardy!* but also in some *two hundred million* pages of stored data. This system was named Watson after IBM's founder, Thomas J. Watson, and was the first system with the ability to answer the questions posed in natural language—language that has evolved naturally in humans through use and repetition.[28] Watson's ability to analyze and understand what the clue was *asking* is an example of machine learning in that the system used algorithms to analyze the various ways in which the question could be interpreted, and then searched vast amounts of internal data for plausible answers.

Additionally, considering the penalty a player faced for an incorrect answer, Watson also had to be confident in its response before buzzing in. This is where deep learning came in. Watson used a second set of algorithms (DL) to find evidence to support or refute possible answers and rank them, while limiting its offering of an answer to the instances where it was confident in its response.

In February of 2011, Watson was represented on the *Jeopardy!* podium by a vertical computer monitor with IBM's Smarter Planet logo, which turned green when the system answered correctly and orange when its answer was wrong. Though Watson received the clues via text instead of from host Alex

Trebek, it played the game in just the same manner as its human counterparts did. Over three consecutive episodes, Watson successfully competed against two of the show's greatest champions, and won the first-place prize of one million dollars.

IBM continued to further develop and commercialize its "cognitive computing" abilities, and its technology is deployed in a wide swath of industries such as food, medicine, and travel. And even though IBM sold its marketing and commerce solutions, including Watson, to a private-equity company in 2019, it plans to continue its collaboration with the new owner.

In summary:

- Deep learning (DL) is the application of machine learning's neural networks to complex problems, allowing the machine to learn from its mistakes and assess its own probability of reaching a correct result—or, in other words, develop its own "intuition."
- Today AI, ML, and DL, and neural networks typically work in concert, as in IBM Watson's performance on *Jeopardy!*
- IBM Watson, Deep Blue (the machine that beat grandmaster Garry Kasparov at chess), and the Blue Gene supercomputer were all outcomes of IBM Grand Challenges.

DATA AND ANALYTICS

We can't talk about AI and machine learning or deep learning without talking about data, because to be able to learn and adapt, machines require *massive* amounts of data. There are basically two ways to talk about data. One is through the lens of *machine learning*, which originates from the newer field of computer science; and AI and the other is through *statistical modeling*, an older field which is derived from pure mathematics. Aatash Shah, CEO of Edvancer Eduventures, defines the two this way:

- Machine learning is an algorithm that can learn from data *without* relying on rules-based programming.
- Statistical modeling is a formalization of relationships between variables in the data in the form of mathematical equations.[29]

Machine Learning	Statistics
Learning	Estimation Fitting
Hypothesis Testing	Confirmatory Data Analysis
Example/Instance	Data Point
Network/Graph	Model
Weights	Parameters
Supervised Learning	Regression/Classification
Unsupervised Learning	Clustering
Feature	Covariate
Label	Response

Figure 7. Machine learning vs. statistics

However, Carnegie Mellon professor and statistician Larry Wasserman asserts that the two fields address the exact same concepts, but just use different terms (figure 7).[30]

So what is the difference between machine learning and statistical modeling? The short answer, says Wasserman, is there is none. Both fields are concerned with answering the same question: How can we learn from data? Pressed to further distinguish the two fields, Wasserman offers that "statistics emphasizes formal statistical inference (confidence intervals, hypothesis tests, optimal estimators) in low dimensional problems. Machine learning emphasizes high dimensional prediction problems." He then quickly adds that this is an oversimplification because as both disciplines advance, the lines between the two blur more and more. In fact, the collaboration and overlap between these two data-driven disciplines results overall in better predictability and decision making.

WHEN TO USE WHAT IN MACHINE LEARNING

Machine learning is a powerful tool, but to use it effectively you first need to clarify what it is you want to achieve. Are you interested in summarizing historical information? Do you want to know what would happen if you took action a, b, or c, or a combination thereof? Or do you want to figure

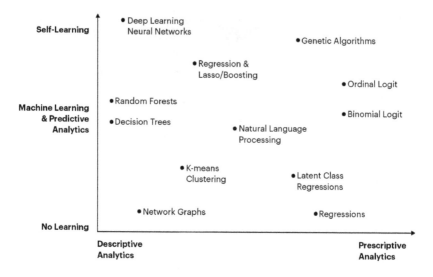

Figure 8. An analytics framework

out why a problem is happening and the best action to take to correct it? Understanding what you want to achieve will help you determine which machine learning technique can best assist you.

Machine learning techniques span a continuum in both analytics type and machine learning type, as reflected in figure 8.[31]

Organizing a Framework for Different Analytics Techniques

Descriptive Analytics

Descriptive analytics explores data to summarize historic information. Typical questions answered by descriptive analytics include "What happened?" "When, where, and how often did something happen?" "Why did something happen?" or "Is a certain event abnormal?"

For example, Hilton Hotels may be interested in knowing the percentage of rooms booked in a property during the holiday season, the percentage of bookings that have come through Tripadvisor, the number of Facebook posts made by customers about their stay, the value of friends on the customers' network on Facebook, and whether the drop in bookings in a certain property in March is consistent with historic trends and with trends in other properties in that region.

Network graphs are a descriptive technique Hilton could use to map customers' social relationships and learn about better customer targets for seeding viral marketing campaigns. Pivot tables, correlations, histograms, and data visualizations are other good examples of descriptive analytics.

Predictive Analytics

The term "predictive analytics" refers to methods that allow you to forecast outcomes or answer, "What will happen at different levels of input?" Machine learning techniques have primarily focused on predictive analytics models that are capable of harnessing several variables to forecast a particular event. For example, the Hilton hotel chain may want to predict the level of occupancy of a property based on historic occupancy rates, the chain's characteristics such as star ratings (five stars, four stars, etc.), Tripadvisor reviews, local events, or property features.

Managers could use decision trees, or an ensemble of decision trees called random forests, for this purpose. Lasso regressions allow managers to automatically select a smaller set of effective predictors from a large set of candidate variables with the specific goal of improving predictions across several possible samples of the data. For example, managers at Hilton can use Lasso regressions to predict occupancy rates, similar to decision trees. Hilton would also be interested in knowing whether a customer is likely to continue booking in their properties, or is more likely to switch to other hotel chains such as Marriott or Airbnb.

Neural networks and deep learning extensions of neural networks allow managers to predict customer retention by incorporating *all* the information about the customer's interactions with the brand: type of booking, type of trip (business or leisure), visit day of week, customer loyalty status, trends in customer bookings, customer demographics such as age or income, property manager ratings, hotel customer food preferences, and more.

Image classifiers and translation algorithms made popular by Google also use deep learning algorithms. These algorithms are also called "self learning," because they are capable of updating the model specifications themselves on the basis of new data, without human intervention.

Prescriptive Analytics

Prescriptive analytics are useful when managers are interested in the answers to questions such as "Why is something happening?" and "What is the best course of action to maximize the key performance metric?" In addition to predicting customer churn, a Hilton manager may also want to know whether certain special offers available to platinum-level members, such as lounge access, are effective in building customer Retention. While predictive models can predict an event, they are weak in determining whether a certain promotion is causally linked to an outcome such as customer retention. This prevents management from designing better offers to maximize retention.

This is where prescriptive analytics such as multiple linear regression and logistic regression (binomial or ordinal) can be useful. Prescriptive analytic techniques are less of a black box and can deduce the marginal effect of each individual treatment or marketing campaign on outcomes such as customer Retention. The drawback is that they don't handle a large number of independent variables very well, and their predictive power is typically lower than that of predictive analytics techniques.

One interesting technique is genetic algorithms. These are algorithms inspired by Darwin's theory of natural selection to solve *optimization problems.* They are a good solution, especially with incomplete or imperfect information, or even limited computational capacity. They use a process of evolution that begins with one set of variables and then intentionally and rapidly creates a series of subsequent "generations," complete with mutations, to arrive at an optimal solution to a stated optimization problem.[32] Here's what genetic algorithms look like in action.

Optimizely is a customer experience optimization software that uses genetic algorithms to, among other things, figure out what website features customers like, so that it can provide an increasingly personalized site experience. For example, the blender manufacturer Vitamix was seeing an 80 percent abandonment rate of its website shopping carts. To engage return visitors and encourage them to convert to checkout, Vitamix used Optimizely X Web Personalization. The new experience added a "minicart" functionality to Vitamix's site, which showed a personalized list of items for purchase and a brightly colored call to action. By delivering this personalized experience to return visitors, the team was able to improve order conversions for this audience by 13.7 percent.[33]

In summary:

- Two ways to talk about data are through the lens of *machine learning*, and through *statistical modeling*.
- The two fields address the same concepts but use different terms. Both fields are concerned with answering the same question: How can we learn from data?
- Machine learning is a powerful tool, but to use it effectively you first must clarify what it is you want to achieve.
- Network graphs, regression, K-means clustering, natural language processing, and ordinal and binomial logits (see figure 8) are examples of machine learning *techniques*.
- Machine learning techniques can use descriptive, predictive, and prescriptive analytics or a combination thereof (*x* axis). The process ranges from no learning to predictive to self learning (*y* axis).
- Descriptive analytics explores data to summarize historic information.
- Predictive analytics allows you to forecast outcomes or answer the question "What will happen at different levels of input?"
- Prescriptive analytics are useful when managers are interested in the answers to questions such as "Why is something happening?" and "What is the best course of action to maximize the key performance metric?"
- Genetic algorithms can solve optimization problems by using a process inspired by Darwin's theory of natural selection.

Data-driven AI is already at work improving customer experiences through personalization—sometimes even without the customer noticing it. And the machine learning dimension of AI is rapidly approaching a level at which it makes better predictions on its own, constantly, while you are sleeping (as opposed to advanced analytics by itself, which only gets better when you have a meeting every Friday to discuss a spreadsheet, agree to a change or improvement, and then go to implement it the following week).

Though making improvements through meetings and manual intervention may be what we're all used to, future success lies in the strategic implementation of AI-powered systems that can deliver automated improvements to the customer experience at every significant marketing moment. It's about giving machines examples that allow them to make highly accurate predictions so that you can use them to do marketing that will transform those Customer Relationship Moments into AI Moments.

Now that you have the basics of AI and machine learning under your belt, let's move onto the real reason you're here—to learn how the AI Marketing Canvas can help you create a solid strategy for supercharging Customer Relationship Moments at every opportunity.

PART 3

The AI Marketing Canvas

FIVE STAGES OF AI AND MACHINE LEARNING IN MARKETING

7 Elements of the AI Marketing Canvas

With machines that can experiment with tactical marketing execution far more speedily, systematically and consistently than any human, the marketers that want to make best use of these machines will require frameworks (and mindsets) that support and encourage iterative learning and experimentation.
—Konrad Feldman, founder and CEO of Quantcast[1]

WHAT IS YOUR PLAN FOR AI IN MARKETING?

Let's say your CEO stops you in the hallway and says she has read an article about AI and marketing in the *Wall Street Journal*, and asks what your strategy is for applying AI to marketing. Many marketers (not you) would answer her with something tactical and executional like, "We are testing YouTube's new machine-learning-powered ad placement tools to automatically serve the most efficient combination of ad formats at the individual user level."[2] The problem with that response is (a) it's about tactics, and thus does not answer her question, which is about your strategy; and (b) it's not going to do anything to position you for asking for more resources to expand your initiatives later.

Strategy at its foundation is about making choices.[3] It's making a bet. In other words, saying, "If I choose X series of actions (which includes tactics and execution), Y outcomes should happen." It's not about trying every new shiny object and activity in marketing. It's about making some assumptions and then creating a thoughtful, comprehensive plan filled with activities that you believe will result in three things:

1. incremental profitable growth;
2. brand equity built over time; and
3. good outcomes for your team, company, and community.

For your CEO, for your team, and for *yourself*, you need a strategic plan for how to use AI in marketing! You need a strategy to get your marketing from being 100 percent hand-developed and hand-determined today, to being machine-assisted, if not machine-determined, tomorrow.

Between our executive education classes and consulting projects, we encounter a wide swath of senior marketers, and we've been asking them what their plan is for applying AI to marketing. The consensus is that this is a very difficult question to answer. It's hard for a few reasons. Few marketers have a good grasp on AI and machine learning technology, and on how to apply it to those four Customer Relationship Moments. Also, there is no real AI- and marketing-specific strategic road map or planning tool template they can use to confidently chart a path forward. This much is clear: without some guidance, brands will either remain paralyzed and do nothing, or aim too high and do too much involving tactics only, which can lead to catastrophic failure.

Note: Failure can be useful. When done incrementally, it allows you to learn safely. More about that will be discussed in chapter 10. The failure we're referring to here may be something like the launch of an expensive initiative that took a million dollars and a year to develop but doesn't deliver any consumer value. It's an important distinction. To fill this strategic void, we've created a strategic planning template for how to implement AI into your marketing toolkit. We call it the *AI Marketing Canvas*.

WHAT IS THE AI MARKETING CANVAS?

You already know what marketing is, but it's useful in this case to define the other terms, "AI" and "canvas."

Artificial Intelligence, or AI, is the capability of a machine to accomplish tasks in a "smart" manner, where the machine is a high-powered computer system equipped with the ability to process massive amounts of data quickly and accurately. (We covered all the elements of AI you need to know in chapter

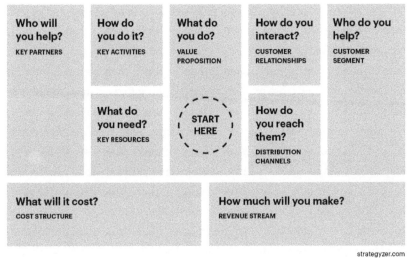

strategyzer.com

Figure 9. A business model canvas. Source: Strategyzer.com. Design inspired by DIYtoolkit. org. CC-BY-SA 3.0.

6.) The word "canvas," of course, is widely used to convey a meaning in business strategy. You may be familiar with the popular "business model canvas," first proposed by Alexander Osterwalder in a 2004 dissertation, as a managerial tool that would allow a firm to easily express its business logic.[4] It's one way to distill all the critical strategic components of a business with nine building blocks all in a one-page visual, as seen in figure 9. The format of this traditional business model canvas is the inspiration for the AI Marketing Canvas.[5] Presenting all the key elements of the business on one page allows you to see the "big picture" and make better decisions about what you might need and want to do to achieve your objectives. The typical business model canvas is composed of a firm or product's key strategic "building blocks": value proposition, infrastructure, customers, finances, and so on.

We are big fans of the business model canvas and teach it in our MBA classes, and so we naturally thought a one-page strategy format would lend itself to the framework we wanted to create. After numerous iterations inspired by helpful feedback from many great marketers, and some help from our talented graphic designer, we arrived at the AI Marketing Canvas.

The AI Marketing Canvas is a framework you can use to plan and execute informed strategic action on AI and machine learning for marketing at whatever stages (there are five) you're energizing right now—whether you're still building your digital foundation, or you already have a solid digital/data analytics foundation in place and are looking to the canvas to help you navigate from one stage to the next. You can use the AI Marketing Canvas to explain to your marketing peers and management the different levels of AI and what you want to do with them as a node. It also serves as a road map for what is required if your firm aspires to operate more like a network.

Let's look first at a condensed version of the AI Marketing Canvas in figure 10, so that you can get your bearings. There are five stages that every successful brand addresses. They are, in order, Foundation, Experimentation, Expansion, Transformation, and Monetization. The way the AI Marketing Canvas works is that you start at the bottom and work your way up through the stages. As you ascend, more and more AI and machine learning is at work, personalizing more and more relationship moments in the consumer's experience. Each stage has specific objectives, and as you ascend through the stages the objectives from the previous stages will continue to be in play. For example, if you are leveraging AI-informed programmatic advertising in Stage 2, you likely would continue that as you pushed your AI and machine learning capabilities further in Stages 3 and higher.

Think of the AI Marketing Canvas as a game board. The more squares you can cover, the more AI will be applied to each Customer Relationship Moment, and the better able you'll be to create the personalized customer experience that will allow you to "win" those moments, now and in the future.

Going back to the scenario that opened this chapter, if you've used the AI Marketing Canvas to to create an AI strategy—instead of telling your CEO, "We're testing YouTube's new machine learning powered ad placement tools," your better and more strategic short statement could be this: "We have developed a strategic road map called the AI Marketing Canvas that lays out a path for our organization to advance in five specific stages or levels of competence over time, deliberately and systematically moving us 'from zero to hero' with AI, in accordance with best practices of leading brands. I'd love to share it with you." This level of response also functions

THE AI MARKETING CANVAS

	AI ACQUISITION	AI RETENTION	AI GROWTH	AI ADVOCACY
STAGE 5 MONETIZATION	AI to drive significant new revenue streams and/or new business models. Serve external customers as a platform.			
STAGE 4 TRANSFORMATION	AI to automate complete set of marketing activities across full customer journey. Strong in-house competency. "Build or Buy."			
STAGE 3 EXPANSION	AI across a broader set of marketing activities. AI Marketing Champion named. Efforts coordinated, and in-house capabilities begin to develop.			
STAGE 2 EXPERIMENTATION	AI-powered tools from third parties and vendors to get some quick learnings/wins at individual moment(s) in the customer journey. "A thousand flowers..."			
STAGE 1 FOUNDATION	Prerequisite to doing any AI or machine learning.			

Figure 10. Overview of the AI Marketing Canvas

as a first step to getting C-suite support for funding of all the other options you'll be presenting later on.

THE COMPLETE AI MARKETING CANVAS

Now let's take a look at the full canvas (figure 11). You'll notice that each level has specific objectives, and key questions for each stage and each Customer Relationship Moment. Don't worry about exactly what to put in there just yet; we'll go into detail about that in part 4 of this book. Your job here is to familiarize yourself with the canvas and its guideposts.

Remember, you start at the *bottom* with Stage 1 (Foundation), and work your way up the canvas to Stage 2 (Experimentation), Stage 3 (Expansion), Stage 4 (Transformation), and finally, if appropriate, Stage 5 (Monetization). Eventually you will recreate this canvas and begin to populate it with the AI and machine-learning approaches required to supercharge the Customer Relationship Moment or moments at the stage on which you're currently focused. We'll show you a completed example later.

We also encourage you to use this canvas in your long-range strategic marketing planning to communicate to stakeholders the people, processes, and culture shifts that likely will be required for successful—and profit—in the long term. Hopefully, you are already through building your digital foundation; but even if you're not, keep reading. In chapter 8 we'll provide some work-arounds that will allow you to get the AI and machine-learning show on the road so that you can use the results to build a case to management for getting that done.

Now that you've seen the AI Marketing Canvas and know how it works, it's time to begin our journey through the five stages, beginning with Stage 1 (Foundation).

SUMMARY
- The AI Marketing Canvas is a one-page strategic road map or template you can use to add AI and machine learning to your marketing tool kit.
- The canvas was inspired by a business model canvas that originated with a 2004 dissertation by Alexander Osterwalder.
- The AI Marketing Canvas reflects five main stages that all brands we've

THE AI MARKETING CANVAS

	AI-ACQUISITION	AI-RETENTION	AI-GROWTH	AI-ADVOCACY
STAGE 5: MONETIZATION Uses AI to drive significant new revenue streams and/or new business models. Serve external customers as a platform.				
Key Questions: • What is the business model? • How could AI generate a new revenue stream?				
STAGE 4: TRANSFORMATION Uses AI to automate across complete set of marketing activities across one Customer Relationship Moments or deeply in one or two Customer Relationship Moments. Most capabilities in-house or with partner whose advanced development product is under marketing's control.				
Key Questions: • Should I build in-house or buy a company with the capabilities? • Where will I find the talent required? • What AI practices set our marketing practices apart?				
STAGE 3: EXPANSION Uses AI across a broader set of marketing activities; beginning to in-source development and capabilities.				
Key Questions: • Do I go deeper into this Customer Relationship Moment or branch over to the next one? • Who is my internal core competency team across functions?				
STAGE 2: EXPERIMENTATION Uses AI-powered tools from third parties and vendors to get some quick learnings/ wins and outcomes in a few marketing activities.				
Key Questions: • What are the personalization value pockets? • Where's the data? • Which Customer Relationship Moments will I focus on first? • Which vendor has the appropriate AI-powered tools?				

STAGE 1: FOUNDATION (Prerequisite) – Begin building digital infrastructure by collecting first party data across the business. Seek adequate amounts of quality data to begin training machine learning models and supercharge customer relationship moments.

Key Questions:
• Do we have first party, second party, and/or third party data on customers and prospects?
• Are the processes for collecting data automated?
• Can we store and access structured and unstructured data about customers/prospects in a consistent and reliable manner?
• Can we connect all the information to obtain a single, comprehensive view of customers/prospects?
• Does the data cover a large number of customers/prospects over a sufficiently long period for AI/ML algorithms to be effective?

Figure 11. Full AI Marketing Canvas

studied have gone through to successfully use AI to supercharge their Customer Relationship Moments.

- Those stages are Foundation, Experimentation, Expansion, Transformation, and Monetization.

- Each stage involves several key questions you should be able to answer before energizing initiatives in that stage.

- When your CEO or your team asks, "What's the plan for AI and marketing?" you can now say you are following the five stages of the canvas to increasingly implement AI deeper across your marketing tool kit.

- A diagnostic at the end of this book will help you revisit and integrate all this material and figure out where your firm is on the continuum, so that you can decide what to do first, second, and third.

8 Stage 1: Foundation

Tall buildings need stronger foundations. The edifice of the modern corporations will be built on the foundation of data they use to constantly learn from.
　　　　　　—Sunder Madakshira, head of marketing, Adobe India[1]

THE FIRST STAGE of the AI Marketing Canvas, Foundation (figure 12), speaks to the digital infrastructure required to consistently collect "first-party" consumer-focused data across the business—quality data you can use to begin to train the machine learning models.

The key questions for implementing the Foundation are:

- Do we have first-party, second-party, and/or third-party data on customers and prospects?
- Are the processes for collecting data automated?
- Can we store and access structured and unstructured data about customers and prospects in a consistent and reliable manner?
- Can we connect all the information to obtain a single, comprehensive view of customers and prospects?
- Does the data cover a large number of customers and prospects over a period sufficiently long for AI/ML algorithms to be effective?

| STAGE 5 |
| STAGE 4 |
| STAGE 3 |
| STAGE 2 |
| **STAGE 1** |

THE AI MARKETING CANVAS

FOUNDATION (Prerequisite) – Begin building digital infrastructure by collecting first-party data across the business. Seek adequate amounts of quality data to begin training machine learning models and supercharge customer relationship moments.

Key Questions

- Do we have first-party, second-party, and/or third-party data on customers and prospects?
- Are the processes for collecting data automated?
- Can we store and access structured and unstructured data about customers/prospects in a consistent and reliable manner?
- Can we connect all the information to obtain a single, comprehensive view of customers/prospects?
- Does the data cover a large number of customers/prospects over a sufficiently long period for AI/ML algorithms to be effective?

Figure 12. AI Marketing Canvas, Stage 1

Starbucks, for example, has amassed a database of 17.6 million active Starbucks Rewards members, as part of a program it deployed more than a decade ago. These members provide Starbucks with a mind-boggling amount of valuable personal data. Such data is useless, however, unless there exists an efficient and accurate way to process it and extract insights from it. The only way to achieve that is to engage technology to help, and that is exactly what Starbucks has done with its Deep Brew initiative.[2] In the company's Q4 and fiscal year 2019 annual report, Starbucks president and CEO Kevin Johnson wrote, "We are leveraging AI technology in many ways as part of an initiative called Deep Brew. . . . Deep Brew is . . . already being applied to personalize customer offers and recommendations on our mobile app to improve the customer experience.[3]

If, like Starbucks, you aim to personalize the consumer experience, you need to know firsthand what consumers are doing at every relationship moment. To achieve this, you first need a reliable way to acquire clean data. You must build a digital infrastructure that will produce outputs you can feed to AI and machine-learning systems. These systems will then learn from that data, and use those insights to make predictions about what your consumers actually want.

Without a robust digital infrastructure in place, you won't be able to amass the volume of clean data the machine systems (algorithms) need to produce meaningful outputs (predictions). To amass those millions of loyal users who are the main source of data for the Deep Brew initiative, Starbucks has made continuous refinements to the technology in and around its Rewards app over a period of *ten years*. If you weren't fortunate enough to have started building it ten years ago as Starbucks did, the next best time to begin is *today*.

We'll revisit Starbucks in chapter 13 as a prime example of a brand that has successfully energized all five stages of the AI Marketing Canvas.

BECOMING DATA-CENTRIC

If your firm's ultimate goal in developing your Foundation is to hone your ability to track consumer behavior and preferences, you'll want to focus on getting the following things into place.[4]

- **Automation of basic processes** involving substantial amounts of data—especially in areas where intelligence from analytics or speed would be an advantage. An example of this is an insurance firm that automates its processes for collecting benchmark pricing data so that it can update its quotes every fifteen minutes.
- **Structured analytics** and **centralized data processes,** with reporting that provides a big-picture view across channels. For example, a retail category manager should have access to a complete picture of historic

customer data. so that they can see things like which products have been popular with which customers, what has sold in which channel, and and between which products have customers switched.

- **Connected databases** and the ability to collect and store first-party customer data whenever possible (as in the case of Starbucks Rewards).
- **Data quality processes** which ensure that the way data is collected (input) and delivered (output) is uniform and complete (i.e., "clean"). For example, the product reviews are all recorded accurately, and are attributed to the right customer who wrote the review and the right product.

Again, the goal here is to gain access to tons of *clean* data collected directly from consumers, which can then be fed to a machine that runs algorithms on that data so it can learn and predict things about those consumers. If you're a larger firm, you probably alreayd have some systems in place that will allow data to be transferred directly from your database to the machine doing the work. However, the more divisions and channels you have, or the more you've grown through acquisition, the more challenging it will be to connect and standardize that data. Once everything is finally in order, however, the benefits will accrue faster, because you will be starting with more data. On the other hand, if you're a small firm with one product and a direct-to-consumer relationship, transferring the data to a machine may be as simple as exporting the data to a .csv file for upload to the machine. The point is that if you want to personalize your marketing, you have to be focused on capturing as much consumer-focused data as possible.

Describing exactly how to proceed with building your digital foundation is outside of the scope of this book; and besides, many great books have already been written on the topic. *The Digital Transformation Playbook* by David L. Rogers (Columbia Business School Publishing, 2016), is one of the best, and *Data Advantage* by Martínez Aguilar and José Antonio (Amazon Digital Services, 2018) is another one we like. In *Data Advantage*,[5] the authors say this: Data and information are the fundamental tools for decision making and for finding opportunities. The more and better data that you can activate will improve your company, and will in fact create more data. Of course, having this data is a condition of achieving further success, but you need to make use of it wisely in order to reap those benefits. If your firm is already there, great! Take your customer-focused data and proceed to Stage 2, with our blessing.

Caveat: Even if your firm is already in motion, realize that it can take a while—sometimes a few years—for your firm and its technology team to build its digital foundation—that is, to shift from solely using a traditional data schema to using a customer-focused data schema.

In truth, when it comes to your firm's digital foundation, there is no "final" destination. Once you get enough infrastructure in place to apply AI in a meaningful way, you will continue to refine your foundation, as different sources of data and different ways of storing and gleaning insights from it arise. The important thing is to work as hard as you can to get your digital foundation in place, so that you can begin an effective journey through the stages outlined in your AI Marketing Canvas.

In the next section we'll examine the difference between "traditional" data schemas and the customer-focused schema that you'll be creating.

THE TRADITIONAL DATA SCHEMA VS. THE CUSTOMER-FOCUSED DATA SCHEMA

The Traditional Data Schema

The "traditional" data schema in most firms is focused on reporting by entity (lawn and garden, sporting goods, fashion), basic customer information (name, shipping address, email), and sales. It is focused on tracking the performance of a *function*, as shown in figure 13. In this figure, which could reflect the traditional data schema of a CPG company, data is collected and stored separately by functions such as manufacturing, retailers, and the firm's finance and sales organizations. If you're the marketing leader for Raj's Super Soap brand, looking for data, and your firm is limited to the traditional data schema, here is the type of data that will be available to you (maybe).

The factory can provide you with data about how many of each SKU were produced, and which stores they were shipped to.

The retailers can provide data on things like how many Raj's Super Soap SKUs they have sold in what category, and on which days they have sold the most.

Function-First Approach

Data is organized by functional variables.

Figure 13. The function-first approach

Your finance department can tell you how much Raj's Super Soap you've sold this month, whether you're on track to meet your goals, and which products are performing. The sales organization can tell you information about your customers (big box stores, department stores, etc.); but in a traditional data schema, it will have no direct insights into the consumers who are buying those products.

The Customer-Focused Data Schema

A customer-focused data schema calls for tracking *consumer* behaviors and preferences. As part of its digital foundation, your firm should be connecting all its data, so that you can use it to make predictions about consumers and can personalize their experience. Data is organized per customer, and AI supercharges the data to generate custom creative messaging for each customer in real time, to create a flow that looks more like the one in figure 14.

In a customer-focused data schema, the consumer experiences many forms of stimulus as part of the Acquisition process. They may see your TV or print ad, visit your optimized website, see an optimized display ad while they're searching Google, or hear about your brand on social media. Let's say as a result of that stimulus, the consumer takes action.

- She calls the 1-800 number offered by your TV commercial; and the agent answers and collects her name, street address, and email; or
- she visits the website listed on your magazine print ad and trades her email for a free ebook full of laundry tips, and acquires a cookie on her browser that allows you to remarket to her later; or
- she clicks on the display ad, which again offers her an opportunity to trade her contact information for more valuable content; or
- she sees your ad on social media offering a coupon for one dollar off her next purchase of XYZ soap. She clicks the link and trades her name, address, email, and other personal information in exchange for it; or

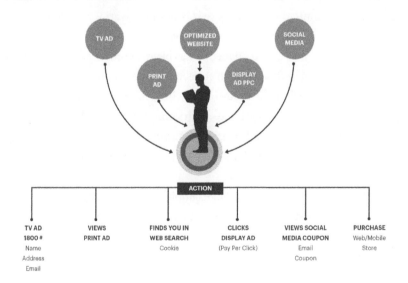

Figure 14. The customer-first approach

- she goes to your website using her mobile device, puts in her information, and subscribes, so that a predetermined amount of XYZ soap is delivered to her home every month.

To achieve the one-to-one personalization you're after, your mission must be to find as many ways as possible to track and collect customer-focused data at every Customer Relationship Moment.

If you have no customer-focused data, does that mean you have to wait to play? No! You likely *do* have access to some data; you just have to know where to look. And the further behind the curve you are right now, the more important it is that you do start to play. You need to begin to amass a series of positive data-driven outcomes—in other words, evidence of what the firm has to gain, but also of what it's losing out on by not getting the rest of its digital house in order post haste.

THE NEED FOR "CLEAN" DATA

To get started, all you need is a concentration of *clean* customer-centric data around at least one moment in the customer relationship. If your firm is still fine-tuning its digital foundation, you may find that there is a lot of data, but it's all locked up in disparate systems. And even if you had access to that data, it would be of limited value because it is not necessarily customer-centric. That's OK. Here are a couple of work-arounds.

Your best bet is to go after data that has been automatically captured with technology, meaning that it's been collected without human intervention. If a human is responsible for inputting the information, we can pretty much guarantee that there will be issues with consistency; and that's a problem, because for the machine to learn, the data you give it has to be *clean*.

Here are some places to look for machine-generated data:

- programmatic advertising (for example, doubleclick data);
- Google analytics, which automatically records who is doing what on your site;
- cookies (all-digital access across platforms);
- web analytics data from Google analytics;
- your website (product subscription information and direct sales);

- RFM tables from your direct marketing / direct mail / catalog team (here, tracking stimulus data is easiest, and you know whether they bought or not, to create the need and the urgency for the rest);
- Adobe or Hubspot, which will tell you when customers have visited, how many visits they have made, what transactions have occurred, how much money you have spent on digital and display ads, search, and so on;
- customer relationship management (CRM) systems such as Zapier;
- enterprise sales management systems such as Salesforce.com; and
- data from paid advertising campaigns on Facebook and YouTube.

Once you have the clean data, the next step is to see where else you can identify and capture inputs and outputs that advance your knowledge of who your customers are and what you know about them over time. Here you'll be looking to extract consumer data from existing systems in your firm—including unstructured data such as product reviews that reside on your website or in customer service databases. (Use techniques such as dimensionality reduction to turn unstructured data into structured data, as described in chapter 6.)

If you are selling a product or service directly to the customer, the information should be there. However, if you are a big brand that sells to a distributor such as Walmart or Amazon, the amount and value of the consumer data you will receive from them will be limited. That's why you need to put into place a way to identify and connect with consumers directly. You need a way to track their behaviors—whether they have visited your store or website, whether they click on your ads, and so on—that the machine can use to predict and provide output.

You may already be

- trading coupons for customers' email addresses (and more);
- trading whitepapers for information (B2B);
- providing a store locator with functionality through a mobile app;
- participating in loyalty programs in which the provider gives you access to the data;
- asking for callback numbers on customer service calls, which can be matched with data from third-party vendors; or

- collecting email addresses and zip codes at the sales counter, which you can use to find out more about customers from third-party vendors.

Note: Certain businesses, such as insurance, financial services, hotels, and airlines, already have this information, because it's part of their business. These firms already know who their consumers are and have been collecting information about them for a long time. Thus, they have a head start in that respect.

Getting your data house in order is about locating and organizing sources of clean first-, second-, and third-party data so it can be fed into a machine that will apply algorithms to process it at light speed and find patterns that will lead to predictions about what the consumers want and need. In the simplistic example in figure 15 you'll note that the machine is taking in not only first-party DTC data collected from web browser cookies, but is also processing second-party data perhaps obtained from a noncompeting brand in the same category, plus data from an aggregator, which has been gleaned from publisher databases.

Let's take a closer look at the different data types.

- **First-party data,** also known as DTC or "direct-to-consumer" data, is information you, the "first" party, have collected about your current audience. The most valuable data type, it is typically collected through website cookies and is a key component of site retargeting and CRM retargeting. Another very effective method of collecting first-party data is through a loyalty program. Once you amass enough first-party data, the machine will be able to begin making predictions about what the consumers' wants and needs will be in the future.[6]

- **Second-party data** is another company's first-party data, typically acquired by making an arrangement to swap data with trusted partners who serve the same customers. This can be useful for beginning to expand your consumer network. For example, if your firm sells baby clothing, you might arrange to swap data with a retailer who sells baby soap, because you both will have relevant first-party data about the customers who are buying in the same category.

- **Third-party data** is the product of data aggregators, who typically purchase it on a large scale from publishers. The benefit of this data set is that it is extremely large; the downside is that it is available to everyone, and thus is not unique.

Third-party analytics can provide granular consumer data such as browsing behavior and customer preferences, and can aid segmentation of your customers by product and insights into what they like. It's also useful for audience targeting and audience extension. For example, you could use third-party analytics to determine if a consumer who is reading about Samsung monitors is also looking at Dell products. Third-party data also can be collected by vendors on web properties they don't own. For example, a vendor may strike a deal with a sports website to cookie users who reach that site, and then sell that data to a consumer goods brand for its own use.[7]

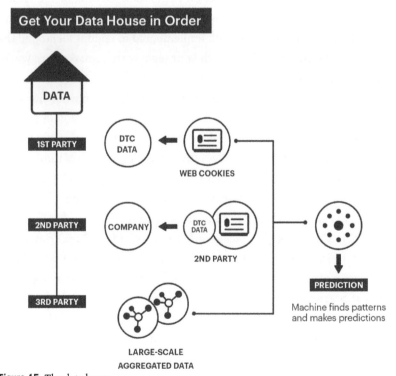

Figure 15. The data house

Once you have enough *clean* first-party consumer data, you can begin to augment your AI and machine-learning marketing efforts with second- and third-party data, each of which provides you with different opportunities to learn more about those consumers. Wherever you are right now, the overarching goal of building your digital foundation has to be to find a way to connect with customers *directly* so you can track them through the Customer Relationship Moments over time.[8] Maybe that's an app (e.g., Starbucks, Regal) or a direct to consumer (DTC) offering (e.g., Dollar Shave Club, Casper) that allows you to sell directly to customers.

IMPORTANT NOTE ABOUT DATA COLLECTION AND PRIVACY

It's critical that you carefully consider what you are doing and how you're doing it when it comes to data collection. Be aware there are rules you must follow, depending on what data you're collecting and where: for example, the California privacy law, the Children's Online Privacy Protection Act (COPPA), the General Data Protection Regulation (GDPR), or the Health Insurance Portability and Accountability Act (HIPAA), to name just a few. More rules are being discussed and implemented in regions all around the world. It's vital that you check with your legal team to make sure you're fully compliant![9]

To that end, beyond laws and regulations which govern what one "can" do, there are a host of other opportunities in the "should we" column, which are guided by ethics, morality, and cultural norms. University of Chicago economist Richard Thaler describes it this way: "A good rule of thumb is we shouldn't impose a set of rules that will create moral outrage, even if that moral outrage seems stupid to an economist.... If you treat people in a way they think is unfair, then it will come back and bite you."[10]

In their 2019 book *The Intelligent Marketers Guide to Data Privacy: The Impact of Big Data on Customer Trust*, Robert W. Palmatier and Kelly D. Martin offer a series of tenets to keep in mind for effective privacy when marketing.[11] The best practices for responsibly managing customer data, according to these authors, relies on establishing a trusting relationship with customers and emphasizing data security. A relationship based on trust requires equitable transactions between customers and your organization (not just the brand). It involves only collecting data that is absolutely necessary for providing value to consumers, and providing them with tools they can use to monitor how your firm is using their data, along with the ability or right to tell you not to use any of it!

Customers also appreciate firms that compensate them for the data they provide—for example, rewards or product discounts as well as free access to services such as credit monitoring that they can use to ensure the well-being of their data across firms. To achieve this, data privacy must become a top management priority, with a strong data security process in place, which includes tracking and reporting on metrics around customer data security and privacy. These activities also must be proactive, and not a knee-jerk reaction to the need for regulatory compliance.

The bottom line is this. In today's environment, data privacy is a *strength* in your marketing strategy, and thus needs be addressed as such. Your customer has the data you need to be successful in your marketing efforts. Your success in collecting that consumer data hinges on their confidence that you will respect that information, protect it, and use it responsibly. It is in your organization's best interest to attend to their concerns.

NOW, NEXT, AND LONG

While there are ways to move forward *before* your digital foundation is complete, there is a limit to what you can and should do if that is your "now." It may be tempting to jump into "next" and "long" before you're ready—beginning to bring in sophisticated AI solutions or other technologies before your processes are fully automated and your structured analytics and data processing capabilities are in place.[12] The problem is that without adequate clean data, you're not going to get the results you want. You'll likely create a lot of unnecessary complexity and chaos trying to manage disparate systems and partnerships, and you could spend *millions* in the process.

How important is clean data to success? Even Google Images needed clean data, in the form of ImageNet's hand-labeled images, to train its machines to determine what its images were. ("Is this a dog or a mop?")

In researching this book, we talked to marketing leaders of some really big brands who said AI for marketing is not even on their radar for a variety of reasons, including lack of good customer-focused data. If that's you, don't despair. Respect your firm's overall "digital status" and work within the constraints of the clean customer-focused data you have. Find a source of clean customer data and *get started*. You're still ahead of the game—but the gap is closing.

In the next section, we'll take a look at Stage 1 in practice by examining Unilever, one of many brands that has successfully built a foundation that allows it to leverage clean consumer data and AI to advance its business worldwide.

STAGE 1 IN PRACTICE: UNILEVER

With annual sales of over 50 billion euros, Unilever is one of the world's top consumer products companies, selling 400 brands—Dove, Axe, Knorr, Lipton, Rexona, Magnum, Dollar Shave Club, Seventh Generation, and scores of others—in 190 countries. Its digital foundation employs a platform approach (Microsoft Azure), which is underpinned by a "data lake" approach.[13] A data lake is designed to hold, process, and analyze structured, unstructured, and streaming data. Data is stored in its native format and processed only when needed, which is more efficient and allows them to scale operations more quickly. Data lakes are typically used in conjunction with traditional data warehouses. Unilever is now using AI across its business in at least three main areas: business planning, manufacturing, retailer and distributor sales, and marketing.[14]

- **Business planning:** Sales and operations forecasting has evolved from regression and spreadsheet-based forecasting—and the need for business users to harvest data from disparate systems—to AI-driven forecasting with data drawn from one central repository: the data lake. Said Jane Moran, Unilever's global CIO,[15] "With some of these tools we are building out data catalogues; that helps our business community really trust the data. And trust is an important thing, to get your employees to really use the analytics you're providing."[16]

- **Manufacturing:** Using data streaming from sensor-equipped machines, Unilever is creating digital models of its plants. This "digital twin" strategy uses machine learning and artificial intelligence to analyze massive amounts of data from connected devices so that plant engineers can make adjustments leading to more efficient and flexible production—for example, to predict the correct order of processes to get the most efficient batch time for shampoo or detergent.[17]

- **Retailer and distributor sales:** Sales recommendations to its millions of customers—retailers and distributors—are now fully digitized, using AI to predict the right assortment at the right time and the right price.

- **Marketing:** Unilever is using AI, machine learning, and voice-related technologies to deliver personalized and immersive experiences to Unilever's consumer platforms such as All Things Hair (allthingshair. com). The company is also building its own database using online customer registrations, third-party sites that consumers visit, and data from store loyalty cards.[18] Unilever also is looking to the capabilities of its twenty-eight "people data centers," which offer in-house programmatic capabilities, real-time insights, and in-house content production to advance toward its goal of one-to-one marketing at scale.[19] One example is a proprietary real-time media mix model.

As if that's not enough, Unilever is also using AI in its recruiting process, which it has said has cut some seventy thousand hours from interviewing and analyzing candidates.[20] Here's our take on how Unilever could leverage the principles of Stage 1 (Foundation) in its marketing (figure 16). Before it could apply AI in these advanced ways, however, it first had to establish a data foundation. To learn more about Unilever's approach, we reached out to Peter ter Kulve, chief digital and growth officer, and president of its Home Care business unit.

Peter says Unilever recognized that marketing decisions such as promotional spending and discounts to retailers could be made better with data-driven predictions. To achieve this, Unilever used the "first party + second party + third party" method. It tagged all it media and related it all back to a single device ID. The attitudinal data, where possible, was matched with behavioral transaction data. Adobe has been Unilever's key partner in making all this happen.

THE AI MARKETING CANVAS: Unilever	
STAGE 1: FOUNDATION (PREREQUISITE)	
Begin building digital infrastructure by collecting first-party data across the business. Seek adequate amounts of quality data to begin training machine learning models and supercharge customer relationship moments. (Note: The individual moments are not in play at this stage.)	
Key Questions	
Do we have first-party, second-party, and/or third-party data on customers and prospects?	Data about customer preferences on digital platforms, and tagged media communications.
Are the processes for collecting data automated?	Yes, after obtaining customer consent, Adobe helps us record digital marketing communications and customer response automatically. Data on promotional spending allocations to all retailers is recorded automatically.
Can we store and access structured and unstructured data about customers/prospects in a consistent and reliable manner?	Yes, we have developed databases with an Adobe interface. Data is centrally stored on the Microsoft Azure platform, which acts as a unified "data lake."
Can we connect all the information to obtain a single, comprehensive view of customers/ prospects?	We can obtain a single view of customer's activity on digital platforms, and in responses to digital marketing communications, but transaction databases are with retail partners.
Does the data cover a large number of customers/prospects over a sufficiently long period for AI/ ML algorithms to be effective?	Yes, in places like Thailand, we have access to data from about 70 million people over multiple years.

Figure 16. AI Marketing Canvas: Unilever

One example of this involves Thailand, a country of around seventy million people, where Unilever has been offering stickers on Line, the popular social network. In one campaign for Dove, a sticker set amassed more than six million downloads. This added customer information to Unilever's database, which now reflects almost a *third* of the Thai population.[21] This foundation of user data now allows Unilever to move to data-driven marketing, and to begin applying AI and machine-learning techniques necessary for one-to-one personalized marketing at each moment in the customer relationship—especially while launching new brands or product components. It also reinforces Unilever's approach to AI, which Peter ter Kulve describes as looking for "value pockets"—areas of the business where better decision-making can lead to better outcomes.

Regardless of where your firm is in the construction of its digital foundation, finding a way to move forward must become a priority; so locate a source of clean data and go! Beginning the process of working with AI will allow you to demonstrate the potential of AI and machine learning to management, and may help to bump it and your firm's overall digital transformation to the front of the line.

In the next chapter, we'll start to unpack how you can empower existing marketing activities for some quick learning with AI-powered tools from third parties, and cover the advantages of taking an Agile approach to getting AI and machine learning into your firm.

CHECKLIST

- Have customer-focused database or access to source of clean data.
- Be able to track a customer over time in at least one Customer Relationship Moment.
- Be able to use data given regulations.
- Have data rich enough in volume and variety to enable use of AI.
- Focus on "now," rather than on "next" or "long."

SUMMARY

- Stage 1: Foundation (prerequisite)—Begin building digital infrastructure by collecting first-party data across the business. Seek an adequate amount of quality data to begin training machine learning models and supercharge Customer Relationship Moments.
- Foundation is about developing the ability to see what consumers are doing at every moment of truth over time, and organizing that data so that a machine can use it to learn and make predictions about what consumers want.
- It is composed of automated basic processes, structured analytics, centralized data processes, solid digital infrastructure with connected databases, and data-quality processes.

- Begin tracking consumer behavior and preferences in addition to departmental data (traditional data schema vs. customer-focused data schema).
- Find a source of clean data. Your best bet is machine-generated data by programs such as Google Analytics, Website subscription and direct sales info, RFM tables, and CRM systems.
- Find ways to connect with the consumer directly by trading a coupon or white paper for their email address, participating in a loyalty program, or asking for callback numbers on customer service calls.
- Seek to match first-party data with second- and third-party data to complete the profile of individual consumers.
- Practice good data-privacy hygiene!

Foundation is very much about "now," and getting the data house in order. Proceed to "next" and "long" with caution.

9 Stage 2: Experimentation

You no longer need to be completely integrated to be successful.
What you need to be is fast.

—Peter ter Kulve, president of home care at Unilever[1]

FIRST-PARTY DATA IN HAND, you're ready to jump in and begin learning how experimenting with AI and machine-learning applications can help you with your marketing initiatives in Stage 2 (figure 17).

MISSION OVERVIEW
In Stage 2, your goal is to take your data and apply AI-powered tools from third parties and vendors to get some quick learning and some and wins in a few marketing activities. Figure 18 provides a road map that reflects the process and a general sequence of events.

ORGANIZING A BUDGET
Your first task here is to shuffle your existing budget to divert dollars from human-led marketing to AI-led marketing for a series of small AI "skunk-works." You also may already have some budget set aside for these kinds of initiatives. This is your opportunity to use it to experiment and collect some evidence around the impact that AI and machine learning can have on your marketing—without the need to sell a big internal initiative.

STAGE 5
STAGE 4
STAGE 3
STAGE 2
STAGE 1

THE AI MARKETING CANVAS

	AI ACQUISITION	AI RETENTION	AI GROWTH	AI ADVOCACY
STAGE 2: EXPERIMENTATION Uses AI-powered tools from third parties and vendors to get some quick learnings/wins and outcomes in a few marketing activities.				
Key Questions: • What are the personalization value pockets? • Where's the data? • Which Customer Relationship Moments will I focus on first? • Which vendor has the appropriate AI-powered tools?				

Figure 17. AI Marketing Canvas, Stage 2

With your budget identified, the next step is to identify the following three internal processes that will guide your AI and machine learning experiments:

1. Find source(s) of clean consumer data.
2. Identify value pockets.
3. Select vendor(s).

Finding Source(s) of Clean Consumer Data

If your company has a solid digital foundation and plenty of clean *accessible* consumer data, you can skip to the next section. If not, here are some potential to-dos:

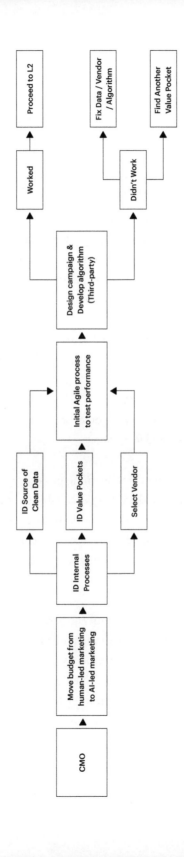

Figure 18. Mission overview

- Reach out to your salesperson in charge of programmatic advertising, and ask for a .csv file of the contact information collected by the system.
- Schedule a meeting with the person who has access to Google Analytics for your brand website to see what data is being collected.
- Reach out to your database administrators for your website, and find out what and how much product subscription information, cookies, and direct sales data there are.
- Reach out to your direct marketing / direct mail /catalog team and get them to track and send you reports on stimulus data.
- Connect with your Adobe or Hubspot account executive and ask them to provide you with an orientation of all the data they have been collecting.
- Meet with the sales department to see what if any consumer data is being collected by their CRM system or in their enterprise sales management system.
- Meet with the person running paid advertising campaigns on Facebook, Instagram, YouTube, or other social media, and see what data is being collected and from whom.

What type of AI and machine-learning project you start with will depend on the type and volume of data that is available to you. If you are fortunate enough to have access to a lot of clean first-party consumer data, that's great. However, if you've got a limited amount of clean consumer data to work with, start by using AI and machine learning where the data quality is sufficient.

Identifying Value Pockets

In any case, your first step is to identify an area for improvement. It could be just one Customer Relationship Moment on one product on one campaign. Select one issue, opportunity, or process, in one Customer Relationship Moment (or stimulus) where data-driven predictions and personalization would add value for consumers. Peter ter Kulve, president of home care at Unilever, refers to these opportunities as "value pockets":

Look for value pockets—problems data and machine learning can solve—and then identify a vendor who has the capability to help you do this. Work with that vendor (new or existing) to develop some short-term programs to get some quick learnings. When we say quick, we mean one quarter—six months, max.

For example, when Budweiser was looking to reach users on the Chinese messaging, social media, and mobile payment app WeChat, it tapped RikaiLabs to create a branded AI chatbot using a WeChat miniprogram called MiniBots. A miniprogram is an app within the WeChat app for brands. A MiniBot combines the functionality of a chatbot and an app to create a rich user experience.[2] When it comes to value pockets, it's useful to vet each opportunity by asking the following questions.

- Do I have data about customer preferences in this Customer Relationship Moment?
- Would personalization of the Relationship Moment to consumer preferences be viewed as valuable by the customer?
- How does the application contribute to that?
- What *new* insights can the application provide about consumers?
- How does the application solve their pain points?

Remember, you're not looking to implement a comprehensive application across all the Customer Relationship Moments or marketing mix just yet. That will come later. You just want some quick learning for stimulus or individual moments, so that you can start building a case for how AI and machine learning can work in your firm.

Selecting Vendors

The final step is to meet with your existing marketing vendors and your agency, and take an inventory. What AI is already running? And what else is available but not turned on? What consumer data already lies within your walls, and within the walls of those applications? Then, on the basis of specific pain points, value to the customer, and/or disruption opportunities, look for new vendor partners whose technology can advance your efforts in those areas. Use the form below as a checklist to organize your vendor conversations: first with your top existing vendors, and then with potential new vendors you've identified either by referral or by searching online.

Top Existing Vendors	Consumer data collected (Type/ amount)	Do they have an AI solution?	How tech can help: -Pain point +customer value +disrupt disruption	Testing (Y/N) and details	Outcome?	Plan to scale/ expand?
Ex. ABC Co.						
Potential New Vendors	Consumer data collected (Type/ amount)	What is their AI solution?	How tech can help: -Pain point +customer value +disrupt disruption	Testing (Y/N) and details	Outcome?	Plan to scale/ expand?
Ex. XYZ Co.						

Figure 19. Vendor checklist

Vendor Checklist

Note: It's in your vendor's best interest to get more people using more features, because more people using more new features means more results they can talk about with others. If they are simply turning on additional features, you could make a strong case that there should be no additional costs—unless you add onto or change the scope of an existing project, which is another option. The reason why we recommend starting this way is that we want you to get your hands in the dirt, as soon as possible. So upload that data, turn on that feature, try that new app, and *take note of what happens.* That said, remember, the machines will need time to learn; so don't expect your next batch of emails or adwords to magically deliver better results than your manual (human) approach.

In fact, when using Google's "Smart Bidding" feature, for example, it is not uncommon to see a *worse* outcome for a short period, while the machine learns. Stay the course! Let the machine learn. If you apply an expectation of "instant improvement" to this experiment, you'll cut it off too soon. Ask your vendor partner how long before you can expect to see better results from their AI-driven technology.

A NEW WAY OF WORKING (AGILE)

This transition may be challenging. You were likely trained in a system that said it's about home runs, big ideas, and control: one winning Super Bowl commercial, one perfect proprietary software system. You have also learned from numerous sources—maybe even from direct experience—that failure, even the *appearance* of failure, should be avoided at all costs. The good news is that digital marketing created a pocket where the new "test-and-learn" approach was acceptable. When it comes to AI and machine learning, however, a test-and-learn *culture* is now *essential.* In fact, perfectionism is a recipe for failure in the new world of modern marketing. To win, not only do you have to take some calculated risks; you also have to move *fast.*

Enter the "Agile" organization. The Agile Method originated in software development, but the philosophy is increasingly being applied across disciplines to increase the velocity of improvements to marketing, product development, and more. In an Agile firm, the focus is on making small improvements relentlessly, in "sprints" that last weeks rather than months, the sum of which add up to massive growth. It's about working in small teams and using the principles of continuous design improvement and testing based on rapid feedback to achieve the best outcome for the consumer. In fact, one of the biggest differences between the traditional "waterfall" and the Agile approach is that the consumer's role is not just important to the initiative's success—it is *essential*.[3]

Here are two books you can read on the Agile Method applied beyond software development that should give you a good jumpstart. One is *Agile for Everybody* by Matt LeMay (O'Reilly Media, 2018). The other is an older book titled *The Goal*, by Eli Goldratt (North River Press, 2014). There's also a more recent graphic novel version of *The Goal*, published in 2017. What's nice about *The Goal* is that it is anecdotal, which makes new concepts somewhat easier to wrap your head around.[4]

DESIGNING CAMPAIGNS AND DEVELOPING THIRD-PARTY ALGORITHMS

Your vendor partners and suppliers are specialists that can help you and your team determine how their technology can move the needle with those consumers and better understand the potential for how AI and machine learning can supercharge your Customer Relationship Moments. Challenge your internal staff to work with these specialists to apply their algorithms to your clean data, thus experimenting with AI and machine learning for one Customer Relationship Moment (Acquisition, Retention, Growth, Advocacy) across as many channels as possible—emails, landing pages, banner ad copy—anywhere you're making a prediction. Then track your results against the human-led way.

Remember that at this point you haven't yet asked for any additional budget or additional head count; you're just taking your existing budget and using it to run AI and machine-learning experiments with outcomes that allow you to compare the old and new ways. Look for bright spots. Where did you get lift? What has improved? Then ask, "Why was this successful? How can we scale it?"

Caveat: Whether things have worked is not a straightforward determination. When you conduct experiments, you need to decide whether you're measuring target ROI, customer lifetime value (CLV), brand equity, and so on. The measurable is what will determine your inference about whether an experiment has worked.

At a very basic level, the first thing you need to understand is whether your vendor can in fact provide personalization! You'll want to see proof that their AI capabilities can indeed deliver individualized messages and product offerings to consumers for whom you have data. Once personalization has been achieved, then look to see whether it has had an effect on customer engagement. For example, you could consider the rate at which cross-sell offers have been successful from a personalized email campaign that has populated products to cross-sell from a recommendation algorithm.

Once you achieve success with a campaign, repeat it and see if you can achieve consistent gains. Be sure to measure the delta between what you have been doing versus the AI and machine-led results. Think of this as an A/B test, or a "challenger-versus-champion" approach. Track the performance of these campaigns closely because you'll be using these outcomes to make a case to management for the capital and operating budget you'll start to need to energize the next layer of activities in Stage 3.

Following are some quick examples of brands using Stage 2 approaches.

STAGE 2 EXAMPLES: CHASE, KIA, CHECKLI, ALASKA AIRLINES, RED HAT

- **JPMorgan Chase** is boosting the effectiveness of customer *Acquisition* by using AI and machine learning to optimize the messaging for its digital advertising and direct mail. (Persado).[5]
- **Allstar Kia** is supercharging customer *Acquisition* with an AI-driven chatbot which enables prospective customers to chat directly with its conversational assistant (Ad-Lingo).[6]
- **Checkli,** an SAS provider of checklists, is empowering *Retention* by using AI-powered email optimization to increase its mobile app engagement and decrease spam reports (Optimail, since acquired by Strong.io).[7]
- **Alaska Airlines** is supercharging *Retention* by using a third-party AI

application to customize the mobile experience for its customers (Optimizely).[8]

- **Red Hat** is a provider of enterprise open-source solutions that uses third-party AI search to supercharge *Retention* by continuously optimizing the support content on its website, so that its customers can find the most relevant answers to their questions quickly and thus be more likely to renew their subscriptions (Lucidworks).[9]

- **Bonobos** is an online menswear company that has established a long-term partnership with a third-party AI-driven audience behavior platform for real-time advertising targeting of consumers who exhibit the desired online browsing behavior. This partner's algorithms dynamically adjust the levels of prospecting and retargeting to reach the best matches and drive them to purchase (*Acquisition, Retention, and Growth*) (Quantcast).[10]

Remember, the canvas isn't a report card. It's a *game board* on which the object is to light up as many squares as possible—so you can *win*.

Now, let's revisit one of the aforementioned brands, JPMorgan Chase, so that you can get a better sense of Stage 2 in practice.

STAGE 2 IN PRACTICE: JPMORGAN CHASE

Not so long ago, a consumer's main experience with the JPMorgan Chase financial services brand was a one-to-one transaction with a bank teller through a drive-through window or at the counter inside the bank—often after a few minutes waiting in line. Based on the consumer and the kind of account they maintained, they might be referred to a bank executive to talk about additional products. The point is that the quality of the brand experience hinged primarily on the skillfulness of those individual human touchpoints.

Today most people conduct their banking online, and so the Chase brand experience now occurs largely through the ads that consumers see. Chase spends a huge amount of money on advertising—$5 billion annually[11]—certainly a big factor in their success. To see whether AI could improve engagement with its ads, in 2016 Chase began a pilot program with the AI marketing technology company Persado (persado.com), beginning with its cards and mortgage businesses. Use of the technology has since expanded across platforms.[12]

"Machine learning is the path to more humanity in marketing," said Kristin Lemkau, CMO of JPMorgan Chase, in a press release.[13] She also said that the technology "rewrote copy and headlines that a marketer, using subjective judgment and their experience, likely wouldn't have. And they worked." Chase has stated that ads created by Persado's machine learning performed better than ads written by humans, with a higher percent of consumers clicking on them—more than twice as many, in some cases. The difference can be as simple as what word choice resonates with consumers. Persado technology generates creative content using data science and AI to render copy proven to be the most compelling message to individual customers and segments of customers.[14] The tech world is mesmerized with media and media placement: Where does this ad appear? That is important; but if the messaging isn't optimal, the ad will not be as effective, and money and opportunities to endear consumers to the brand will be wasted.

Persado's "message machine" offered Chase an advanced marketing language knowledge base of more than one million tagged and scored words and phrases.[15] The machine generates display ads, and over time it learns what is most effective—what type of language and what sentiment works in what situation. That information can then be shared with internal and agency creative teams, and added to creative briefs. Chase has used the Persado message machine to redraft marketing messages for its card and mortgage businesses. It has extended the application of Persado's technology to generate copy for direct-response marketing campaigns across its personal banking, home lending, and wealth management segments, and for ideation of digital advertising such as display ads and Facebook ads.[16] It also hopes to use the technology in its internal communications, and in customer-service prompts.[17]

Van Diamandakis, former Persado CMO in residence and CMO advisor for technology consultancy Firebrick, put it this way: "A great way for brands to successfully apply artificial intelligence and machine learning to their business is to get started with one use case and work with a specialized AI technology vendor with proven success."[18] In this case, Chase started with a well-defined trial in 2016 and expanded the Persado relationship enterprise-wide, powered by the consistent delivery of business results. Here's our take on how JPMorgan Chase Financial Services could leverage the principles of Stage 2, Experimentation, in its marketing.

THE AI MARKETING CANVAS: JP Morgan Chase Financial Services				
	AI-ACQUISITION	AI-RETENTION	AI-GROWTH	AI-ADVOCACY
STAGE 2: EXPERIMENTATION What marketing activities could be empowered with AI for some quick learnings? Uses AI-powered tools from third parties and vendors to get some quick learnings and outcomes in a few marketing activities.	Machine-generated personalized copy for digital advertisements and direct mail.			
Key Questions				
What are the personalization value pockets?	Consumer search data, consumer browsing history, consumer prior search and display click-through			
Which customer relationship moment will I focus on first?	Focus first on customer acquisition			
Where is the data?	Consumer search data, consumer browsing history, consumer prior search and display click-through			

Figure 20. AI Marketing Canvas, JPMorgan Chase

THE JPMORGAN CHASE FINANCIAL SERVICES AI MARKETING CANVAS

Your job in Stage 2 is to take your clean consumer data and engage specialists to come in and apply their AI and machine-learning technology to that data for one or two targeted value pockets in at least one Relationship Moment. Using this third-party AI and machine-learning technology to gain broader insights about consumers and their preferences will increase your ability to personalize your offerings and communicate effectively with them at every moment.

Now that you have some "old way" vs. "new way" results that show how AI and machine learning can not only create more value for your consumer in at least one Customer Relationship Moment, but also lift for your brand, you are ready to move to the next stage.

In the next chapter, we'll be looking at ways you can take your Stage 2 wins and expand them to additional customer moments, or go deeper on the one you're already working on with Stage 3.

CHECKLIST

- Select a limited number of Customer Relationship Moments that you want to try to improve—perhaps just one moment on one product in one campaign.
- Identify a partner or vendor who has already built AI-based systems to do this. It could be a current vendor, or a new one you select.
- Shift some budget from "doing things the way we've always been doing them, human-led," and funnel it into testing this new machine-led approach
- Be patient and run a few cycles or "tries" at whatever you chose to do, to determine if you can get lift.
- Create a way to track performance so that you can communicate the value of AI and machine learning for marketing to management.

SUMMARY

- Stage 2: Experimentation—What marketing activities could be empowered with AI for some quick learning? Use AI powered tools from third parties and vendors to get some quick learning and outcomes in a few marketing activities.
- Start small and focus on quick learning.
- Look for bright spots, and then try to replicate them.
- This is a new way of working that requires different skills, so be prepared to manage that change.
- The stages are not a report card; they are part of a game board "canvas" intended to help you make the most of the resources you have.

10 Stage 3: Expansion

With AI and machine learning, it's all about continuously find-
ing the edge that exists between humans—marketers and
consumers—and machines. That edge is constantly moving as AI
ecosystems automate more and more capabilities that were once
considered uniquely human.

Once you have proof of concept that AI-powered marketing
can really have a significant positive impact on your business, the
next step is to make a big bet to fully transform your marketing.

—Ed Breault, CMO, Aprimo[1]

IN STAGE 3, you'll lean on your experience using AI and machine learning to create value for consumers and insights for your team in at least one
Customer Relationship Moment, as you begin to scale up your activities
(figure 21). Your primary mission in Stage 3 is to expand the application of
the machine learning you piloted and proved in Stage 2, going either more
deeply into the same Customer Relationship Moment or extending it to an
adjacent moment, where data-driven predictions and personalization would
add value for consumers.

A few helpful questions to ask:

- What other marketing processes can you start to automate?
- Can you expand it across products, divisions, regions, campaigns,
  and so on?

Exactly how you approach Stage 3 will depend on the size and structure of your firm and your role's span of control. In case you're wondering, yes, you can be in Stage 3 in one moment and in Stage 1 or Stage 2 in another. There's also no need to go all the way up one channel (i.e., through Stages 1 to 5 in the Acquisition moment) before you move on to applying AI and machine learning to the other customer moments.

Remember, it's a "game board" on which the objective is to advance each Customer Relationship Moment as far and as quickly as time and resources permit. By Stage 3, not only do you have a bunch of AI and machine learning plates spinning; you also are in the process of cultivating key relationships inside and outside the organization. Figure 22 provides a flow chart that gives you a thirty-thousand-foot view of all that needs to happen. Let's unpack it.

| STAGE 5 |
| STAGE 4 |
| **STAGE 3** |
| STAGE 2 |
| STAGE 1 |

THE AI MARKETING CANVAS				
	AI ACQUISITION	**AI RETENTION**	**AI GROWTH**	**AI ADVOCACY**
STAGE 3: EXPANSION Uses AI across a broader set of marketing activities; beginning to in-source development and capabilities.				
Key Questions: • Do I go deeper into this Customer Relationship Moment or branch over to the next one? • Who is my internal core competency team across functions?				

Figure 21. AI Marketing Canvas, Stage 3

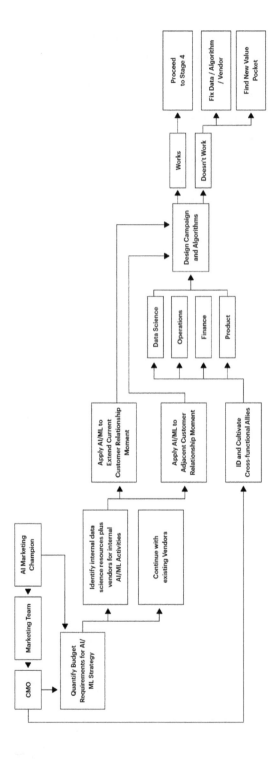

Figure 22. AI implementation workflow

APPOINT AN AI MARKETING CHAMPION

The AI Marketing Champion will oversee all of your AI and machine-learning marketing initiatives, and function as a translator between marketing and data science. This "marketing technologist" will not just understand data and marketing and be excited about the possibilities that AI and machine learning can create; they'll also have some technology in their background, including some Agile-based software project management experience. In this role, the person will act as an advocate for all of your AI and machine learning marketing efforts, and will work with internal staff to reinforce how important these initiatives are to you and the firm. Additionally, they will identify resources, cultivate vendor relationships, and look for value pockets. They also will help you create a business case that will allow you to promote your activities across silos and eventually go to management to secure additional resources (CapEx and OpEx). On the technology side, the AI Marketing Champion will manage the Agile process and the implementation of algorithms. And when the time comes, they will be the one to help you explore the pros and cons of leveraging internal resources to create models you can use to make in-house investments as opposed to engaging an outside strategic partner.

While the Champion leads, coordinates, and drives things forward, it's everyone's responsibility to get onboard, and yours to lead the charge by developing a strong AI marketing team.

DEVELOPING AN AI MARKETING TEAM

You've been encouraging staff to conceive of and participate in running one-off experiments on one Customer Relationship Moment with the help of third-party vendors, and that's great. To become an AI-first marketing team, however, you'll need to expand those one-off experiments into team initiatives in which one-off experiments become multiple experiments where the "new-way-versus-old-way" outcomes are tracked, and results are recorded, on a dashboard that everyone can see.

Through this process, you will begin to move your AI and machine-learning marketing efforts from the periphery of your marketing strategy to the center. What's happening with everyone's experiments will become a standing item on your monthly meeting agenda. Additionally, processes for onboarding new vendors will now be standardized, and workflows will be established. The goal is to embed the use of AI in marketing into the fabric of your department while you work on getting buy-in from key stakeholders across the firm.

All this change—new, more collaborative ways of working, new skill sets, and yes, new leadership approaches—means that you likely will find yourself immersed in the management of a pretty significant culture shift that will require people in your department to

- acquire the willingness and ability to tolerate failure and learn to fail fast;
- collaborate and share best practices and learning, so that everyone gets smarter together; and
- accept that they now live in a world of continuous learning, which you will support by sending them to AI conferences (which you pay for), encouraging them to buy and read AI Marketing books (which you pay for), and bringing in external speaker and experts to share their experiences with AI marketing (with lunch and learns that you pay for).

A detailed description of exactly how to manage the necessary organizational changes is beyond the scope of this book; but in chapter 14 we will provide some guidance for how to think about it, and what to look out for when you start the process. For now, just know that a significant internal corporate culture component will needs to be addressed, and that this will affect your ability to move up through the AI Marketing Canvas effectively.

QUANTIFY IMPACT AND BUDGET REQUIREMENTS

Everyone's efforts at this stage need to be focused on quantifying the marketing ROI of the new way versus the old way. These tangible, repeatable outcomes are the evidence you'll need to build a rock-solid business case for funding additional AI and machine-learning-driven marketing initiatives. You need to assiduously create this body of proof, because at the end of the day you are asking them to make a big bet about an approach they likely won't automatically understand. You'll also be starting the process of identifying places where it might make strategic sense to lessen your dependence on vendors and their models. To do this, you'll want to identify internal data science resources and engage them to design some machine-learning models and run some experiments in-house.

For areas where it makes sense to continue with a partner, you'll want to identify the best of the best and let them do what they do best, so that you can focus on making sure the customer is experiencing maximum value from your experiments. Consider recent DTC newcomers Dollar Shave Club (recently acquired by Unilever) and Harry's (nearly acquired by Edgewell Personal Care). The founders had the brand and the vision; but all of the logistics, from manufacturing to storefront to product delivery, are executed by vendor specialists that are coordinated by the brand.[2]

It's critically important to have actual results that show improvement via AI and machine learning over what you were doing before, so that you can show that what you've been doing is not only already ROI-positive but also a potentially large strategic opportunity worth additional investment. The metric we recommend is marketing ROI (MROI), defined as "the financial value attributable to a specific set of marketing initiatives (net of marketing spending), divided by the marketing 'invested' or risked for that set of initiatives."[3]

MROI = (Incremental financial value generated by marketing - Cost of marketing) / Cost of marketing

Use MROI to show the incremental financial value generated from your AI and machine-learning initiatives, and compare that to the MROI of your current best approach. The difference between the two will be the "net lift" or incremental impact of a machine-first way of doing things.

INTERNAL AI AND MACHINE-LEARNING ACTIVITIES

As your AI efforts expand and become increasingly customized, you may not want to be tethered forever to third-party vendors. In Stage 3, you are looking for ways to do some things in-house by tapping into existing data science capabilities within the firm. The goal here is to expand your internal abilities to use and gain insights from data beyond the "black box" functionality your current vendors provide.

A good place to start building your in-house competency is by taking advantage of the emerging trend of "data science as a service," sometimes abbreviated as DsaS. Instead of relying solely on third-party vendors or hiring your own data scientists to build your own models from scratch, there are a number of available solutions that allow you to plug in your existing data and apply an "off-the-shelf," ready-to-use AI model instantly. Two examples of DsaS machine-learning solutions for marketing applications are Intersect Labs (intersectlabs.io) and Aible (aible.com). Both offer integration with popular data tools like Tableau and SalesForce, allowing marketers to make predictions and run "what-if" scenarios in-house quickly and easily. All it takes to get started with these solutions is your data and a little time from your marketing analyst. If, however, you have internal access to data scientists, you can go one step further and have them assemble your own models and applications using machine-learning libraries.

For example, Google has a number of "off-the-shelf" AI-driven solutions in the form of machine-learning libraries. They're akin to website code libraries or plugins. For example, if you needed a countdown timer for your website, you wouldn't build it from scratch; you would download a plugin to your website theme, customize it, and switch it on. This is the same idea. Machine-learning libraries can be customized to assist with things like visual classification, search (Tensor Flow), and product recommendations (Amazon Personalize).[4] Similarly, you can get word sourcing from IBM Watson, because Watson ingests all of every page on the Web, as well as all of Wikipedia, and thus has that corpus inside of it to learn. This means you can just select the piece you need and then adapt it or augment it for your needs. "You" means some developers and data scientists who know how to pull in and configure these solutions.

As part of this process, you want to be looking for ways to use AI and machine learning to further supercharge an existing Relationship Moment and/or begin to apply it to an adjacent moment. Here are a couple of examples of what each of these ways looks like.

SUPERCHARGE EXISTING MOMENTS: WARBY PARKER

Warby Parker began life as a website offering a more cost-effective alternative to traditional eyewear retailers, initially shipping to customers five pairs of frames to try on in the comfort of their own homes. It likely is using machine learning to encourage engagement and send personalized messages to customers who browse the site but leave without purchasing.[5] Warby Parker also has gone deeper into its Acquisition moments with its new Virtual Try On app. Those who have the iPhone X now have the option to try on virtual frames using Warby Parker's new augmented reality app. This app overlays a computer-generated image of the frame onto an image of your face. Apple's Face ID creates a map of your face, allows the tool to recommend frames it thinks will look best, and provides you with a 3-D preview (Acquisition).

In terms of Retention, Warby Parker is also using machine learning to crunch customer data to determine where best to locate new retail stores.[6] And, according to its 2018 sustainability report, "a state of the art machine learning system automatically figures out the topic of incoming support emails, and routes them to the appropriate Customer Experience specialist," allowing the company to answer customer support emails 60 percent faster than the previous manual system (Retention).[7]

EXTENDING AI AND MACHINE LEARNING
TO ADJACENT MOMENTS: WALMART

When a customer opens the Walmart app, it displays a page that is personalized with items they have previously purchased (Retention). Once the customer has placed an order, Walmart predicts when they will arrive at the store (Retention). If your goal is to achieve quick learning, you'll want to go with whichever approach—deeper into an existing moment or extending to adjacent moments—is easier to implement.

IDENTIFYING AND DEVELOPING AN AI
MOMENTS CROSS-FUNCTIONAL TEAM

Next, you'll want to begin developing a cross-functional team composed of C-Level roles from finance, product development, and operations. This is especially important when you are moving to an adjacent moment, because often the locus of control of other moments is shared. A good book on this topic is *Reorganize for Resilience: Putting Customers at the Center of Your Business* by Ranjay Gulati.[8]

The first step is to figure out who your C-level allies are. If you're going to be able to expand beyond your internal team, cross-functional leadership has to buy in. Do your homework and be specific. For example, identify in-house capabilities: "Who do I have in the building who can do advanced data work?" Or, "I need 1.5 analysts to help my department do *x*, and here's why."

DESIGNING CAMPAIGNS AND ALGORITHMS
(TESTING AND LEARNING)

This is a four-step process that involves working closely with your data science contact.

1. Identify a value pocket around which to design an experimental campaign.
2. Figure out what you are trying to predict, and work with your data science folks to come up with some algorithms.
3. Create and run an AI and machine-learning experiment to explore the value pocket.
4. Evaluate the results.

If it works, great! The next step is to use what you've learned to expand the applications. In other words, proceed to Stage 4! If it doesn't work, try to isolate the problem, so that it can be fixed. Since you have already done the work to ensure that the consumer data you are using is clean (at least we hope so), you may have to tinker with the model. If you're doing this process with a vendor and they are not delivering the results you're after, you may need to find another resource. If the experiment fails, remember that it's OK. Failure is part of the process. Don't dwell on it. Simply find another value pocket, devise a new experiment, and rerun the process.

Another possible scenario is that your experiment will answer one question and pose another, and that's a good thing. Why? Because a big part of this process is knowing the right questions to ask. We'll see how that happens in the story of Compare.com, a brand that has successfully used this four-step design, test, and learn process.

DESIGN, TEST, AND LEARN IN ACTION: COMPARE.COM

Compare.com (Compare) is an aggregator of automotive insurance that allows customers to generate real-time quotes from affiliated insurance providers. It is owned by the Admiral Group (Admiral), one of Britain's largest insurance companies, established in 1993.[9] In addition to its low-cost online auto and home insurance offerings in Europe, Admiral also owns several auto insurance price-comparison sites, such as Confused.com in the United Kingdom and its equivalents in Spain. The company entered the US market in 2009, with Richmond, Virginia–based Elephant Insurance, which followed Admiral's successful direct-to-consumer business model by serving customers via the phone and Internet. After much analysis, Admiral decided that the US market was ready for its own insurance price-comparison website (modeled after the already successful UK-based site Confused.com), and launched Compare.com (then called comparenow.com) in 2013.

Admiral's goal, through Compare, was to make finding the best car insurance price "a much easier, much quicker process" for US drivers, at a time when doing so was inefficient and messy, despite the legal mandate for nearly all US drivers to have insurance, depending on their state's policy. Initially, Compare faced a "chicken-or-egg" situation when it came to getting insurance carriers to join the site; but the company pressed on with its marketing and advertising strategies, and turned the corner in 2015 with a partnership allowing Google access to Compare's forty-one different insurance partners for its own comparison platform, Google Compare.

Compare's value proposition is in providing real quotes from insurance providers; so the more carriers it has on its platform, the more value it can provide to its customers. Conversely, the more customers Compare can say have used its platform to purchase insurance products, the more easily it can bring additional carriers onboard. In this way, Compare (a node) is functioning as a network, insofar as it is not the one providing the product. Rather, it is providing a technology platform consumers can use to purchase products from an insurance carrier, and is presumably collecting a fee from the carrier for facilitating the transaction.

Compare worked with three main channels to acquire customers: TV advertising, Google AdWords (PPC), and advertising on broker websites, where some basic information was collected from the consumer before they were passed onto Compare.com. Though the leads received from the broker channel were the most cost-effective, they also presented the lowest completion percentage. Consumers had just answered basic personal information through the broker sites, and they likely didn't want to fill out another substantially longer questionnaire through Compare.com—even though the effort would lead to a list of actual bindable quotes tailored to their situation, which they could click to buy immediately from the insurer's site.

Compare's marketing team also performed before-and-after and A/B testing to optimize the language, cadence, and subject lines of its marketing emails, in order to draw people to the site. In A/B testing, a control case was compared to one or more test cases to determine which version was preferred by consumers. The control case in these tests was usually referred to as the test condition, and for Compare's marketing group it was the marketing email methodology that had been used prior to testing.

Like its parent company, Admiral, Compare enjoys a very transparent company culture in which failure is acceptable. It is also known for its test-and-learn culture, which is deeply rooted in the Agile development process, and in which it conducts regular test sprints as it tweaks its site. Regardless of how the consumer arrived at the site, Compare's challenge was to figure out the best way to engage them, compel them to fill in the entire form, and complete a purchase. The problem was that most visitors weren't doing those things. In fact, by early 2016, Compare had seen completion rates decrease from a high of 18 percent in January to just 12 percent in March—a 33 percent decline in three months. This was a critical firm-level strategic challenge, because Compare.com is only paid when customers accept a quote provided by the insurance partners on the platform, and the questionnaire is the vehicle by which the required information is collected from the prospective customer.[10] So in this example, the designated value pocket was to increase the number of website visitors who completed the online questionnaire required to generate a bindable quote—in other words, step 1.

To address this, Compare began looking for answers to two main questions: Does showing predicted rates earlier increase completion rates, as compared to the standard questionnaire process that withholds quotes until the end of the process? And if the answer is yes, which customer groups responded best to those estimates, and where should estimates occur in the questionnaire process? Compare.com engaged an intern who developed a basic algorithm that would predict potential customer savings from auto insurance, and would provide estimates earlier in the questionnaire completion process.

Considerations:

- How and where should an estimate option be presented, and to whom (i.e., who would be in the test vs. control groups?).
- What information should be provided to those test customers?
- How many questions are sufficient to provide a reliable estimate, and what is the minimum amount of information needed to provide an early estimate?
- Should the accuracy of the predicted quote change as more questions are filled out, or is a single estimate sufficient?
- What text or copy will draw customers to the predicted quote?

In other words, Compare figured out what they were trying to predict, and worked with a data science intern to come up with some algorithms: step 2.

The next step for Compare (step 3 in our process) was to create and run an AI and machine learning experiment to explore the value pocket. The first test around quote estimates (step 3) helped Compare.com conclude that quote estimates using a state's lowest monthly rates had the biggest impact on completion rates (step 4). This led Compare back to step 3 for a second experiment, which examined a new problem: How would customers react to a pick-your-path option? In this alternative, consumers had the option to defect from the full questionnaire and fill out a shorter questionnaire (seven questions) that would give them a customized quick quote. Analysis of this experiment revealed that the quick-quote option further improved completion rates for the site.[11]

Note the feedback loop between steps 3 and 4. The first experiment revealed a second important opportunity to exploit Compare's selected value pocket.

Following are examples of three additional brands using Stage 3 level approaches in their marketing campaigns.

STAGE 3 EXAMPLES: UNILEVER, THREAD, INTELLIGENTX

- **Unilever** uses Google Cloud's Cloud Vision API to extend the reach of its marketing campaigns. In one example, a three-day Valentine's Day campaign for Close-Up toothpaste in Asia, Unilever used Google Cloud Vision to analyze user-generated content around its campaign hashtags and Valentine's Day. Those insights led to the creation of six-second bumper ads which were deployed daily on Instagram, Facebook, and YouTube. To monitor online comments about the campaign and ads, Natural Language API was used, allowing Unilever to fine-tune the message and delivery of the ads that resonated most with its audience across social channels (Acquisition).[12]

- **Thread** uses AI to personalize wardrobes for people. Each personalized shopping specialist (a single human) serves up to fifty thousand customers. You tell the shopper you need an olive green jacket that will look good on you. Thread has developed an algorithm that collects information from all the different websites and partnerships the company has built, and distills that data down to two or three options, which the shopper passes on to the customer. With AI, Thread can scale a very few shopping specialists to be able to serve tens of thousands of people, and still deliver one-to-one personalized service (Retention and Growth).[13]

- **IntelligentX,** a UK-based beer company, creates four different foundational varieties of beer—Black AI, Golden AI, Pale AI, and Amber AI—which are offered via a subscription service. An early approach directed customers to visit a URL on the label that asked a series of ten questions about the beer they tried. Customers who participated (80 percent) have provided the company with 100,000 data points. This data is processed by an AI algorithm, and then the brewer decides whether or not to heed the algorithm's advice. Founders Hew Leith and Rob McInerney believe that, rather than replacing a brewmaster, AI gives insights to help a brewmaster be better equipped to make decisions on the basis of customer feedback.[14] Today, customers can use an app to connect directly with the algorithm to provide feedback which leads to a new set of beers that are further dialed into their taste (Growth).[15]

To better understand all that can be accomplished in Stage 3, let's look at one facet of an iconic brand for which artificial intelligence is truly at the foundation of everything it does: Coca-Cola.

STAGE 3 IN PRACTICE: COCA-COLA

One of Coca-Cola's first steps toward using AI across a broader set of marketing activities was a big investment in a drink dispenser, Coke Freestyle, which allows consumers to mix their own drinks (Retention). Through descriptive analytics harvested from the machine, Coke was able to identify the mix of Sprite and cherry flavoring as one of the most popular combinations. This data led to the development of Sprite Cherry—a quick win in product development (Growth). Coke also uses this data to allow its customers (e.g., Five Guys, Wendy's) to right-size its inventory in different places. Since the drink dispensers give them real-time data on usage, they can use machine learning to ensure that stock-out is minimized.

The first generation of Freestyles collected first-party data that revolved around the *product*; and that is still true, according to Thomas Stubbs, vice president of engineering at Coca-Cola Freestyle. He says, "The company has billions of rows of data from our dispensers, which allow us to identify consumer trends and interests, and how tastes are developed, regionally, in supermarkets and other outlets. We gain enormous insights from the dispensers, and use that mass of data in a variety of ways. Everything about the machine, whether data on the pour that just happened, or ongoing operations, or the ability of the consumer to build custom mixes or drinks, is controllable via API. This gives us an enormous runway for innovation and personalization based on consumer preferences and tastes."

Coca-Cola sells through other channels, such as retail stores and online, but what Freestyle makes them really good at is *listening*. "Freestyle is a huge source of real-time data directly from a consumer touchpoint, which allows for 'mass personalization'—in this case a new product, Sprite Cherry," says Stubbs. "The data revealed the trends, and we could then make business decisions based on that information."

To increase its ability to connect directly with the consumer mixing the drink, Coca-Cola also integrated the Freestyle experience into mobile apps, which connect via Bluetooth to an even more sophisticated dispenser: the Coca-Cola Freestyle 9100. The mobile app collects limited consumer information and allows consumers to earn rewards, scan codes from bottle tops and other merchandise, and engage in location-specific experiences. In terms of the new Freestyle 9100 dispenser, the app also allows you to tee up not only *your* custom drink mix, but also a mix for a friend—before you get near the machine. Once at the venue, you can connect to the fountain and the drink will be dispensed. Now, app users provide Coke not only with mix preferences, but also with information it can use to further personalize the Coke experience for them.[16]

Note: Many brands featured in this book are pursuing AI on multiple stages via different initiatives. So, while this example of how Coke is using AI fits into Stage 3, as you'll see shortly, it has extended its learning from Freestyle to allow sports team trainers at Louisiana State University (LSU) to create one-to-one personalized drinks for athletes via its Powerade Command Center (Growth), an initiative residing at Stage 5, Monetization (more about that in chapter 12).

COCA-COLA AI MARKETING CANVAS

At some point you will emerge from this experimental, tactical, "trial" period of AI and machine learning. You will have become adept at using the existing technology to personalize the consumer's experience and create value for them, and you'll deeply understand the impact that AI and machine learning have on your Customer Relationship Moments.

You may also have maxed out the existing capabilities of some of your third-party AI providers. Your needs will have become so specific that your vendor will have to start writing custom code to meet them. When you reach this milestone, it will likely make sense to begin to bring those capabilities

THE AI MARKETING CANVAS: Coca-Cola				
	AI ACQUISITION	AI RETENTION	AI GROWTH	AI ADVOCACY
STAGE 3: EXPANSION Uses AI across a broader set of marketing activities; beginning to in-source development and capabilities.		Smart Drink Dispenser "bot"	Mobile App: Sprite® Cherry (new product)	
Key Questions				
Do I go deeper into the Customer Relationship Moment or branch over to the next one?		Continue to deploy dormant features on the Freestyle 9100 to delight and surprise consumers. (Deeper)	Develop a mobile app, and new products that can expand the customer relationship to more consumption and variety of products. (Branch Over)	
Who is my internal core competency team across functions?		We would need to collaborate with product development, and operations teams.	We would need to collaborate with app development, product development, and operations teams.	

Figure 23. AI Marketing Canvas, Coca-Cola

in-house, engage with a strategic partner, or acquire a company that can do it for you, because the proprietary models you build in the future will create strategic advantage.

CHECKLIST

- Decide whether to go deeper on one Customer Relationship Moment or on an adjacent moment, on the basis of the richness of the value pocket and what consumers would find valuable.
- Compile a summary of the results and financial impact of your results to this point, in preparation for Stage 4 activities.
- Identify and appoint an AI Marketing Champion, and develop an AI marketing team.
- Draft a strategy, and quantify impact and budget requirements.
- Begin building internal competency in AI and machine learning by investing in training.

- Start developing a cross-functional team composed of C-level roles from finance, product development, and operations.
- Test, learn, and adjust your models and approach on the basis of what the data is telling you.

SUMMARY

- Stage 3: Expansion—Use AI across a broader set of marketing activities, beginning with in-source development and capabilities.
- Lean on your experience using AI and machine learning to create value for consumers, and insights for your team, for at least one Relationship Moment as you begin to scale up your activities.
- The primary mission in Stage 3 is to expand the application of the machine learning you piloted and proved in Stage 2, either more deeply into the same Relationship Moment (or stimulus) or to an adjacent moment where data-driven predictions and personalization will add value for consumers.
- How you approach Stage 3 will depend on the size and structure of your firm and your role's span of control.
- Identify and appoint an AI Marketing Champion and an AI marketing team; quantify impact and budget requirements; continue internal AI and machine-learning activities; identify and develop an AI/ML cross-functional team; and design, test, and learn from campaigns and algorithms.
- When you start maxing out the existing capabilities of third-party AI providers, it's time to create a plan to bring it in-house, with or without a strategic partner, or buy a company to help.

With Stage 3 competencies securely under your control and working, it's time to scale things up. In the next chapter we'll take you through the key strategic decisions the firm must make and the actions you must take to chart the next phase of your efforts to further supercharge Customer Relationship Moments with AI and machine learning in your marketing.

11 Stage 4: Transformation

People tend to think more tactically than strategically. AI is a strategic function; you have to think one year ahead. I don't think it's possible now to do great marketing without AI.

—Azadeh Moghtaderi, VP data science
and analytics, Ancestry[1]

IF STAGE 3 is about seed planting, Stage 4 is about scale and execution. Stage 4 is about using AI to automate across a complete set of marketing activities, and beginning the process of identifying strategic capabilities and moving them in-house in a way that makes the most sense for your firm (figure 24).

Your objective at this stage is to become the best in class when it comes to using AI to automate *all the moments in a customer relationship,* and so you will continue your efforts to expand in those areas as appropriate (figure 25). That means you are deploying AI consistently, and that both you and the machines (algorithms) are learning from the outcomes. You're using all of this to increase the returns curve, so as to produce more and more irrefutable evidence that AI and machine learning add value to the customer experience and provide lift for your brand. Most importantly, you are now playing the AI and machine-learning-for-marketing game for keeps, using every available resource because in the end you know it will be "winner take all."

STAGE 5
STAGE 4
STAGE 3
STAGE 2
STAGE 1

THE AI MARKETING CANVAS

	AI ACQUISITION	AI RETENTION	AI GROWTH	AI ADVOCACY
STAGE 4: TRANSFORMATION Uses AI to automate across complete set of marketing activities across one Customer Relationship Moment or deeply in one or two moments. Most capabilities in-house or with partner whose advanced development product is under marketing's control.				
Key Questions: • Should I build in-house or buy a company with the capabilities? • Where will I find the talent required? • What AI practices set our marketing practices apart?				

Figure 24. AI Marketing Canvas, Stage 4

Whether you're ready to progress to Stage 4 depends on the following:

- Do you have an adequate amount of reliable, clean data across all Customer Relationship Moments? We can't overstate how critical this is. There's an old data processing adage that applies here, which is, "Garbage in, garbage out."
- Does your marketing strategy call for AI and machine-learning algorithms that require customization beyond vendors' off-the-shelf products?

- Are there proprietary AI capabilities that, if developed, would set your marketing practice and your business apart or eventually become a new source of revenue?

Why consider bringing AI and machine learning capabilities under your control—meaning bringing them away from a third party in-the-box solution provider? Because your large trove of data about the customer relationship now represents your strategic advantage. That means you need to own the processes and the resulting feedback loops around that data, 100 percent. You now should have some learning and wins you can share and use to make a business case for the need to customize algorithms beyond what existing

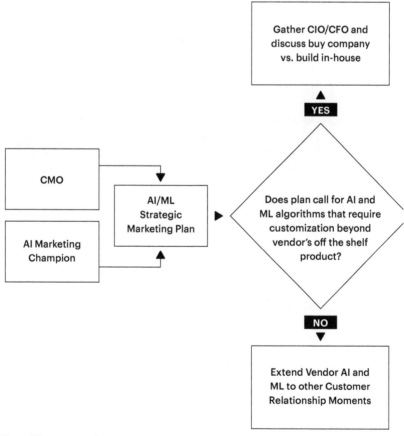

Figure 25. Strategic planning

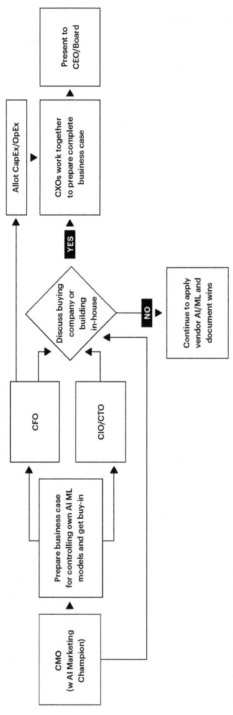

Figure 26. Getting team buy-in

models can provide. If the answer is yes, the question becomes, "Do you build that model in-house, engage a strategic partner, or purchase a company (and its expertise) to do it?" Whichever way you decide to go, the goal is the same: Create excellence across the firm for AI and machine learning for marketing, with the objective of developing a competitive advantage. Figure 26 outlines a typical process for pitching a "buy-versus-build" initiative.

In your quest to determine whether to buy or build expertise, you'll want to look at how much customization of algorithms is already happening, and ask the following questions:

1. As we expand to other moments, are our existing off-the-shelf algorithms up to the job?
2. If customization is required, is it something that creates strategic advantage for the firm?
3. If it does create strategic advantage, do we build those models in-house, purchase a company to build them for us, or do a combination thereof? (This is a strategic decision that needs to be addressed by the strategy committee and the board.)

EVALUATING BUY/BUILD OPTIONS

Determining which way to go is a matter of examining combinations of cost, timing, and degree of difficulty. In the imaginary example depicted in figure 27, option 1 is to go in-house, which would take two years and cost $1.5 million with a 60 percent likelihood of success. According to your research, it looks as though option 2, purchasing a company to do the same thing, would cost twice as much, but would be easier, faster, and provide a higher likelihood of success. Option 3 is much more expensive and much harder. You get the idea.

In addition to the variables of cost, degree of difficulty, timing, and success ratio, there is also the matter of which tack will best align with the culture of your firm. For instance, if your firm has an "Acquisition" culture, management's decisions will likely lean that way. The question then becomes, "What companies are available that have the expertise you need at a price your firm is willing to pay?" Additionally, the history of successfully

EVALUATING BUY/BUILD OPTIONS				
Approach	Cost	Degree of difficulty	Time / advantage	Likelihood of success
Option 1: Build in-house and add staff	$1.5MM	10/10	24 mos	6/10
Option 2: Purchase company	$3MM	6/10	3 mos	8/10
Option 3: Purchase company and support with in-house data science	$4.5MM	9/10	4 mos	9/10

Figure 27. AI and machine learning: Build vs. Buy

integrating incoming companies needs to be considered, which is another board-level question.

If data science skills and talent are already in-house, it may be possible to draw from those internal resources to create a cohort who can build the models you need. And if you can't find a company that is doing what you are looking to do, you may *have* to build your own cohort.

To give you a clearer picture of what Buy-vs.-Build might look like, we've profiled four companies: two that have built models in-house, and two that have purchased companies with existing models and expertise.

STAGE 4 EXAMPLES: DISNEY, CARMAX, MCDONALD'S, ULTA BEAUTY

Building Models In-House

Disney has developed scientific and technological innovations in its own in-house research lab, Disney Research.[2] There are actually three sites with research areas including machine learning and data analytics, visual computing, robotics, and human-computer interaction. One current example of the application of Disney's machine-learning capabilities is the development of MagicBand: a theme park–wide pass that tracks customers' movements, analyzes purchasing habits, and reports the real-time data to Disney. The purpose of this innovation was to streamline the customer experience by helping Disney staff (known as "cast members") anticipate customer behavior and make quick decisions around adding staff or incentivizing guests to head to another ride or attraction (Retention/Growth). As a result of this investment, the efficiency and capacity of the parks have improved, operating margins have increased, and traffic trends continue to be strong.[3] Customer Relationship Moments impacted are Retention and Growth, in that they are leveraging data to incentivize guests.

CarMax starts the majority of its relationships online (Acquisition); however, almost all of its sales occur in the physical store (Retention). When visiting CarMax.com, you're shown some initial results; and then the text *and* images change on the basis of what the site learns about you from your search activity.[4] This capability, a form of collaborative filtering, is particularly interesting because it involves filtering of images, not just text. In fact, Carmax invested in a photo lab to take high-quality photos of cars, which enabled it to better train its image recognition algorithm to present personalized photos of cars to customers.[5] CarMax compiles a vast amount of data every year through the different areas of its operations;[6] it sells more than 700,000 cars per year as a company.[7]

Proprietary algorithms drive CarMax's inventory management and pricing decisions, which allow it to adjust inventory to customer demands in real time, in stores across the nation. According to a presentation at the 2019 Spark+ AI conference by Todd Dube, senior solution architect at CarMax responsible for data science and machine learning platforms, "a key initiative for CarMax is enabling their data scientists and analysts to leverage machine learning and their massive volumes of sales, clickstream and other data to drive an omni-channel experience with a goal of creating a personalized customer experience online and anywhere."[8] Customer Relationship Moments impacted are Acquisition (data-driven online sales and marketing) and Retention (sales in physical store).

Buying a Company

McDonalds purchased the Tel Aviv– based personalization and decision logic tech startup Dynamic Yield in March 2019, and has integrated its technology into the drive-through experience at seven hundred McDonald's restaurants in North America so far. The technology personalizes menu displays and digital signage based on real-time signals, such as trending food items, time of day, restaurant traffic, and a customer's own choices (Retention/Growth). This technology also will allow McDonald's to add more personalization features into the McDonald's app (Advocacy). Former McDonalds CEO Steve Easterbrook noted in a 2019 earnings call that the recommendation algorithms built into the drive-through menu boards already have generated larger orders (Growth).[9]

At some drive-throughs, McDonald's also has tested technology that can recognize license-plate numbers. This allows the company to create a list of suggested purchases on the basis of a customer's previous orders, if the person agrees to give McDonalds access to that data (Growth).[10]

Ulta Beauty in 2018 acquired technology start-ups QM Scientific and GlamST. GlamST offers mobile, Web, and in-store virtual makeover tools that use augmented reality to provide virtual try-on for hair color, makeup, and eyebrow shaping (Retention). QM Scientific offers an AI-powered shopping assistant that learns each individual customer's preferences and habits over time, thus enabling devices, apps, or bots to respond with relevant and timely answers and suggestions (Retention). Today, an AI-based skincare virtual beauty advisor is also available on Ulta.com. The virtual advisor enables guests to browse Ulta's skin care assortment by concern or by product. It also asks a series of dynamically generated questions and presents a set of personalized recommendations of products that can be further reviewed and purchased (Growth).[11]

"Both GlamST and QM Scientific bring technology leadership, guest experience, focused capabilities, and the right cultural fit," said Prama Bhatt, chief digital officer at Ulta Beauty. "We now own the technology assets to support our digital experience roadmap."[12] In an interview with us, Prama also shared her thoughts on the collection of customer data and the future of third-party technology vendors. She said they are choiceful around customer data and are able to deliver more consistent and connected customer experiences by owning that data, as opposed to being solely dependent on a third-party vendor who executes on their behalf. (Note: You will recall our discussion of customer-focused data needs in chapter 8; Ulta is doing exactly that to lay the foundation for their AI activities.)

"As retailers, the ultimate goal has to be to create a single view of our guests' interaction with Ulta Beauty and the signals they send us, so we can better understand our guests and build strong customer relationships," says Prama. "To do that, we'll need access to the collective data." She also said she anticipates that third-party vendors will increasingly enter into strategic relationships in which they provide brands with access to customer-focused data, and in the process become part of a brand's marketing ecosystem.[13]

Now that you have seen some examples of AI and machine learning "buy-vs.-build" strategies, let's take a look at a company that is a great example of Stage 4 in practice: Ancestry.

STAGE 4 IN PRACTICE: ANCESTRY

If you have ever researched your family's history, you may be one of three million paying subscribers who have tapped Ancestry's extensive collection of more than 10 billion digitized historical records. Since 1996, users have created 100 million family trees containing more than 13 billion ancestral profiles, and have uploaded more than 330 million photographs, scanned documents, and stories to their individual trees.[14]

Founded as a publishing company in 1983, Ancestry is now the largest genealogy company in the world, operating a network of genealogical, historical record, and genetic genealogy websites such as Ancestry.com, AncestryDNA.com, Newspapers.com, and FindAGrave.com, to name just a few. Its mission is to "harness the information found in family trees, historical records, and DNA to help people gain a new level of understanding about their lives." In 2017 the company reported $1 billion in revenue.[15] Today, Ancestry is a prime example of a firm that employs AI and machine learning across all the moments in a customer relationship, and in multiple stages up to Stage 4 of the AI Marketing Canvas (figure 28).

ANCESTRY'S AI MARKETING CANVAS

To learn more about Ancestry's use of machine learning in marketing across Customer Relationship Moments, we spoke with Todd Pollak, senior vice president for global customer success and product commercialization, and Azadeh Moghtaderi, vice president of data science and analytics at Ancestry.

THE AI MARKETING CANVAS: Ancestry				
	AI ACQUISITION	**AI RETENTION**	**AI GROWTH**	**AI ADVOCACY**
STAGE 4: TRANSFORMATION Uses AI to automate across complete set of marketing activities across one Customer Relationship Moment or deeply in one or two moments. Most capabilities in-house or with partner whose advanced development product is under marketing's control.	ML-driven search advertising	Uses in-house data scientists to develop churn propensity models that use all aspects of customer behavior to make predictions	Use customer information and web signals to present the right information at the right time in the right order to the right customers	Connects customers; promotes WOM
Key Questions				
Should I build in-house or buy a company with the capabilities?	The level of customization of algorithms would require development of in-house AI/ML capabilities executed by in-house data scientists			
Where will I find the talent required?	Expand centralized data science team with expertise that could solve problems of interest			
What AI practices set our marketing practices apart?	Find similarities in customer behaviors to identify customer segments, and identify the unique needs and preferences of the segments	Personalize website based on the unique customer segment needs	Our ability to effectively predict interests and best product offers	Relationships with consumers lead to them to advocate on our behalf

Figure 28. AI marketing canvas: Ancestry.

Todd and Azadeh indicated that the company has invested time and effort into three main areas:

1. acquiring deep knowledge about what AI and machine learning are and can do,
2. establishing trust between the marketing and data science teams, and
3. formulating a strategic vision for the use of AI in marketing.

To the third point, Azedeh added, "People tend to think more tactically than strategically. AI is a strategic function; you have to think one year ahead. I don't think it's possible now to do great marketing without AI."

Let's look at what Ancestry has done vis-à-vis the AI Marketing Canvas and the various Customer Relationship Moments. The first place where

Todd and Azadeh collaborated was in using machine learning for search advertising. Like most companies, Ancestry first relied on a partner's machine-learning capabilities to supercharge an aspect of marketing—in this case, Stage 2, Acquisition—and since it works, the company continues to do that. At this juncture, however, Ancestry is applying AI and machine learning across the Customer Relationship Moments with much of the programming and algorithms generated in-house—a good example of Stage 4. For example, the website content served to Ancestry subscribers is personalized on the basis of their needs and preferences, which are predicted from their search keywords (Acquisition).

Ancestry also is continuously improving the customer experience. For example, image recognition is used to crop images from old high school and college yearbooks, and match them to user profiles by simple name-to-image linking. Ancestry also uses image recognition to extract familial relationships from obituaries and wedding announcements from Newspapers.com, which it owns. AI and machine learning is then used to help users find relationships between relatives, extract unique and interesting facts (the color of flowers at your great-aunt's wedding), and increase the accuracy of user trees, thus improving the overall quality of the big tree, which has network effects. (New users benefit when the relationships in the big tree are more accurate.) Also, this content is more recent what is found in old high school and college yearbooks, increasing the likelihood that younger users will make discoveries when using the service because more recent historical documentation benefits newer generations (Advocacy).

Ancestry's AI and machine-learning technology also predicts a customer's interest. For example, are they looking to go as far back as possible in their family tree, or do they want to go deep into the stories of a few people in the family tree? The system provides the user with personalized hints on the website, and prompts them to check in by sending personalized emails (Retention). Finally, Ancestry uses different aspects of customer behavior as input data to predict the lifetime value of revenue (Growth).[16] In this way, it has built on its strong foundation of data and data analytics and its in-sourced AI and machine-learning capabilities to provide personalized customer experience at all moments of the customer relationship.

In the next chapter we'll show you how some brands have monetized the AI models they've created to create a brand new source of revenue—and how you can do the same.

CHECKLIST

- Gather learning and wins you can share in a business case for the need to customize algorithms beyond what existing models can provide.
- Determine what models you want to create that will lead to personalization consumers will find valuable, and which your current vendors do not currently offer.
- Conduct research to see whether there is a company you can buy to fill that gap, or whether building the models in-house makes more sense.

SUMMARY

- Stage 4: Transformation—With at least one Customer Relationship Moment fully automated, or one initiative automated across adjacent moments, you're getting a feel for how to progress up and across the AI Marketing Canvas.
- You're now consistently deploying AI and machine learning, but focus is now on increasing the returns curve to compete, because in the end, winner takes all.
- Look for proprietary AI capabilities that, if developed, will set your marketing practice and business apart, or eventually become a new source of revenue.
- Create a plan to either bring capabilities in-house, partner with a vendor whose advanced development product is under marketing's control, or buy a company (maybe even the vendor, as Ulta did).
- The strategy is to create a "center of excellence" whose objective is competitive advantage.
- Determining whether to buy a company or build in-house is a matter of examining combinations of cost, timing, and degree of difficulty, as well as company culture.

12 Stage 5: Monetization

*Focus on the customer value imperative—creating new products
or business models that deliver value for the market before your
current or potential competitors do.*

—David Rogers, Columbia Business School faculty
and author, *The Digital Transformation Playbook*[1]

WITH MOST OF THE CUSTOMER RELATIONSHIP now automated, you're
ready to maximize the ways the firm can use the AI models you've created to
drive profitable growth and generate new revenue streams—the core of Stage
5 (figure 29). Strategically, in the words of former P&G chief A. G. Lafley and
professor Roger L .Martin, you need to know *where to play* and *how to win*.

Remember networks and nodes? Stage 5 is the land of networks—
Amazon, Google, Netflix, Airbnb, etc.—companies whose entire businesses
were driven by data from day one. And they continue to level up all the time.
Think of Airbnb Experiences, Google Maps, Gmail, YouTube, and Netflix
original content—and of Amazon, laddering back to grab even more market
share from retail nodeland, with its own clothing labels. If you're a node,
can you compete? And if so, how?

Consider Marriott, which has its own trove of customer data gleaned
from its customer loyalty program, Bonvoy. The hotel chain has recently
entered the home sharing space with its Homes & Villas platform, thereby
competing with Airbnb and others. It's taking a different approach than

Airbnb and other hotels chains, however. Instead of making equity investments into home-sharing platforms, Marriott's model is to create a marketplace for consumers to find homes by partnering with property-management
companies.[2] Bonvoy members who stay at a Homes & Villas property earn
and redeem loyalty points, as they do with other brands Marriott owns,
including Sheraton, W Hotels, and Ritz-Carlton.

Said Michael Bellisario, VP and equity research senior analyst at Baird,
in a 2019 interview with *Hotel News Now*, ". . . [The] scale component [is] vital
for the future of Marriott's platform. . . . Marriott has been building this
loyal base for decades. This is what they're trying to leverage. Airbnb, do
they have that? Maybe for certain guests, but it's not the same deep-rooted
loyalty, with the credit card and loyalty program like Marriott has, and that's
the differentiator."[3]

Stage 5 is about looking at your platform, data, and potentials, and finding ways to create additional value for your firm—and possibly others like

STAGE 5
STAGE 4
STAGE 3
STAGE 2
STAGE 1

THE AI MARKETING CANVAS				
	AI ACQUISITION	AI RETENTION	AI GROWTH	AI ADVOCACY
STAGE 5: MONETIZATION Uses AI to drive significant new revenue streams and/or new business models. Serve external customers as a platform.				
Key Questions: • What is the business model? • How could AI generate a new revenue stream?				

Figure 29. AI Marketing Canvas, Stage 5

it—with what you've created in Stages 2 through 4. Beware; it is not easy to become a network. Nowhere is this more apparent than in the struggles that even mighty GE has faced with its software arm GE Digital, which in 2015 aimed to become one of the top ten software platforms in the world by 2020. That did not happen, as the division was hampered by (among other things) old-guard thinking that prevented it from following the Agile processes its competitors were busily embracing.

The following are a few examples of firms that have used AI and machine learning to create new business models and sources of revenue either in their core business or by extending the model or capabilities to other businesses—a source of revenue that can fuel additional development.

STAGE 5 EXAMPLES: ALIBABA AND COCA-COLA

Alibaba, which started life in 1999 as an e-commerce site connecting buyers and sellers of goods, is now a data-driven network of sellers, marketers, service providers, logistics companies, manufacturers, and financial services. It engages in a "smart business" model in which all entities driving toward a common business goal are connected through an online network where machine-learning technology allows them to leverage data in real time to make strategic business decisions at every level.[4]

In addition to using AI in its core business, Alibaba engages in many AI-driven initiatives. One is the City Brain Project, which is helping cities run their operations by artificial intelligence. Every vehicle in the Chinese city of Hangzhou, for example, is monitored by AI, giving Alibaba control of more than 104 traffic light junctions. This has helped the city reduce traffic jams by 15 percent in the project's first year of operation. Alibaba Cloud provides the software, but the city owns the data. Alibaba also has introduced a state-of-the-art digital store option to one million small shops and one hundred superstores across China, where retailers get all of their goods through Alibaba's platform and use its Alipay app.[5]

Coca-Cola has leveraged the learning and capabilities of its Freestyle soft drink dispenser, discussed in chapter 10 as an example of Stage 3, to create the *Powerade Command Center*, which coaches and athletic trainers can use to design highly personalized drinks for individual athletes. Currently, the station is in permanent place at Louisiana State University (LSU) only, but it has previously appeared at the 2018 World Cup in Russia, among other venues, according to Thomas Stubbs, vice president of engineering at Coca-Cola Freestyle. The machine creates singular custom cups of Powerade, with settings that can be adjusted on a digital touchscreen. It is a countertop unit which connects to athlete management systems. It is portable, so that when not in the locker room it can reside on a cart on the sidelines, powered by a battery. Drinks such as LSU's custom mix "Tiger Juice" are prescribed for consumption before, during, and after workout and competition, personalized to the performance and needs of each individual athlete. The athlete can then adjust the level of sweetness and flavor profile of the drink. LSU is leveraging this personalized capability to care for its athletes in its recruiting efforts, and it's easy to imagine its massive potential for a new revenue stream for Coke from professional sports and beyond.[6]

Let us be clear. Stage 5 is not for everyone. If you are a node focused on mastering Stage 4, tirelessly asking how AI can further personalize the customer experience and supercharge every Customer Relationship Moment, that may be challenging and profitable enough! That said, let's look at the *Washington Post* one more time, because it is a prime example of a firm using the AI and machine learning it initially developed for its own use and now offers as a service to others.

STAGE 5 IN PRACTICE: *THE WASHINGTON POST*

At the *Post*, AI and machine learning powers everything from personalized recommendations and comment moderation to story-writing and more. All are housed under Arc Publishing, a flexible publishing platform the *Post* built for its own newsroom, which is now licensed to and generating revenue from top publishers, broadcasters, and brands.[7] To gain more insight into the firm's ascension to Stage 5, we spoke with Patrick Cullen, director of data science and artificial intelligence for the *Washington Post*. Spoiler: The *Post* followed a progression that in many ways parallels the AI Marketing Canvas (figure 30).

THE AI MARKETING CANVAS: The Washington Post

	AI ACQUISITION	AI RETENTION	AI GROWTH	AI ADVOCACY
STAGE 5: MONETIZATION Uses AI to drive significant new revenue streams and/or new business models. Serve external customers as a platform.	Zeus Insights (ad delivery)	Heliograf (robot writing assistance)	Zeus Insights (article and topic recommendation engine)	Comment Moderation System
Key Questions				
What is the business model? Generally: Provide value-added services to other publishers with a subscription plan. Allows customer (i.e., publication that uses The Post's technology) to provide more value to reader/subscribers.	Increase publishers' ability to connect with prospective readers and draw them into the fold.	Free up reporters to work on higher value and more unique projects to increase the value of the publication to the reader.	Get consumers to the content they are most interested in, quickly so readers will feel compelled to subscribe.	Allow consumers to become part of the editorial process by providing expert moderation.
How could AI generate a new revenue stream?	The AI/ML technologies developed in-house can help other publishers. An API to access the algorithms can provide a subscription-based model which enables a new revenue stream beyond customer newspaper subscriptions and advertisers. The business model includes other publishers as a new group of customers.			

Figure 30. AI Marketing Canvas, *The Washington Post*

Patrick says the story starts small:

A few years ago, like other companies, we were using off-the-shelf software to deliver value to subscribers and advertisers, but we quickly realized its limitations, particularly when it came to recommendations. Recommendations are key, because they lead the reader to purchase subscriptions and consume more pages. The more pages readers consume, the more advertising they see and respond to, which leads advertisers to buy more media on the site.

Rather than switching software or trying to customize what was in place, we decided to see what we could accomplish if we brought the development of the models in-house. We chose to focus on the recommendation system first, because it was the answer to the questions "What could we do now to provide best value to readers and the business?" and "What could we develop where we could have a success we could talk about?" We also had a lot of trust that we could build the technical teams internally and, over time, improve and even exceed the capabilities of third parties, because we understand our systems, our data, and our users better than a third party does.

We started small: one or two people. At first our algorithms did not perform well, but we kept iterating and combining different algorithms, and we got better as we began to better understand our readers. Page views increased. We kept experimenting, and stayed focused on improving the reader experience. Not everything worked. Some of the things we looked at doing ended up being too difficult from a technical point of view, or we didn't have the data to power the algorithms. We try not to put too many eggs in one basket until we actually know how the system could benefit the business.

Another interesting technology we built was a topic classification system called Zeus Insights. It's a model that uses machine learning to assign topics names from a taxonomy—politics or weather, for example—to create metadata around an article. We actually built it first and then started looking around to see where we could use that algorithm in other areas. We ended up using it in our recommendation system, because it allows us to automatically surface content related to a topic similar to what a reader is already consuming, making readers more likely to stay on the site longer, consume more content, and potentially become paying subscribers. In addition, advertisers get a better return [Growth].

"Another way that algorithm got pressed into service was the *Post*'s new ad delivery platform called Zeus Insights," Patrick added. According to a July 2019 press release, Zeus Insights is part of a platform that creates a focused ad experience centered on user consumption patterns, allowing advertisers to tailor their message for specific segments of the *Post*'s audience or align with specific types of content (Acquisition). It is also designed to reduce the industry's reliance on cookies, using machine learning to move to a cookieless targeting system in future iterations. It will eventually be available to the *Post*'s publishing clients through the Zeus Technology Suite platform.[8]

Patrick continued: "Naturally, advertisers want to have some control over the context where their ads show up—or where they don't show up—for brand safety purposes. An added bonus is, since the recommendations are context-oriented, it really helps to make advertising more relevant for users who don't want to be tracked or opt out of tracking while continuing to respect their privacy settings."

A dozen or so engineers and data scientists on the *Post*'s team are now working on Zeus, notes Patrick, as well as on its automated publishing system Heliograf and its comment moderation system. Patrick says the goal with AI is not to replace people, but to enhance their capabilities and free them to work on more interesting and in-depth assignments. "When we talked to people in the newsroom, they mentioned that for reporting on elections and sporting events there's a very short time window to cover it so they have to write and publish the content very quickly," he says. "It's very stressful, and there's no time for creativity. Readers expect us to report the results quickly and accurately.

"The Heliograf system takes in data from the sources and then converts it into sentences that flow into a template that sits on a web page. Heliograf continuously updates the template, meaning the sentences actually change as the data changes. We've also built a similar system that allows us to live-stream the news, which we did for the last presidential election, which updated automatically in real time as the results came in." Patrick adds that the *Post*'s comment moderation system was also conceived from the desire to help journalists. "The *Post* has over two million comments on our site every month," he says, "and it's just not possible for the staff to review and approve them all. This ensures the user generated content that shows up on our site is of the highest value."

The *Post* also has a section where the best reader comments are rolled up and sent out to subscribers, enabling them to participate in the process (Advocacy). Says Patrick:

> Our comment moderation system is a tool that assigns a probability to whether the comment is one that should be filtered, or not shown on the site. The people in charge of moderating comments can control the filter and the probability that they trust. For example, staff can create parameters such as, if the probability the comment is a bad one is 0.8, then automatically block the comment. But if the probability is only 0.1, automatically approve

it. Anything in between those two numbers is sent to a human to review. If something does get through that shouldn't have, they can adjust the thresholds, and those adjustments help to improve the algorithm over time.

The most important thing about both Heliograf and the comment moderation system is that they free up the staff to do more interesting work. That's really where we see AI fitting in into the newsroom. It takes away a lot of the undifferentiated grunt work and gives it to computers, which are very good at it.

In terms of what we focus on and why, our first priority is always our readers. How can we build technology that improves their reading experience? Then we think about our journalists. What do they need to enhance or expand news coverage? And can we deliver the news faster to readers? Lastly, these technologies are part of our SaaS business. If we're developing technology and we're sharing it across multiple publishers, we can actually build a better system than if we just built it for the *Washington Post*. The algorithms that are working on behalf of each publisher are only using that publisher's data.

As you can imagine, it's expensive to build these custom systems. Not just the cost of building them, but also the cost of continuing to evolve and improve them. Adding additional publishers creates a flywheel effect, because we are helping to offset that cost and build a better system for everyone. And we all benefit.[9]

By this point, you have a solid understanding of what artificial intelligence and machine learning are all about, and why these technologies will be increasingly important for you as a marketer. You also know how your marketing organization can build AI and machine learning into its marketing tool kit by energizing the five stages of AI and machine learning, using the AI Marketing Canvas as your road map. In the next chapter we'll take a close look at a brand that has "ground" through all five stages and is using AI and machine learning to win customer's hearts and minds with personalization: Starbucks.

CHECKLIST

- Examine your current AI platform and data stores, and figure out what it would take to extend them to create additional value for consumers and also demonstrate a positive impact on the business.

SUMMARY

- Stage 5, Monetization, uses AI to drive significant new revenue streams and/or new business models, and serves external customers as a platform.
- Stage 5 is not for everyone. If you are a node focused on mastering Stage 4, that may be challenging—and profitable—enough!
- At this level, AI and machine learning are used to create new business models and sources of revenue, either in the core business or by extending the model or capabilities to other businesses, thereby creating a source of revenue that can fuel additional development (the flywheel effect).
- Likely most development at this point will be in-house, because the models you are creating now represent a strategic and competitive advantage.
- The advantage of developing in-house is that you have the freedom to experiment—to combine and repurpose models to achieve different outcomes.
- Keep experimenting while staying focused on activities that will improve the Customer Relationship Moments and consumer experience, and create value you can talk about.

13 Putting It All Together

STARBUCKS

WHEN WE ARE ASKED by marketing leaders for an example of a great brand example to emulate, one that successfully combines AI and machine learning, big data, and personalized marketing to drive business results, and that does it in a way which tracks with our AI Marketing Canvas, the brand we point to is Starbucks—the place to get a great cup of coffee, meet a friend to catch up, or write your latest screenplay. In fact, some of this book was written in a Starbucks cafe. Starbucks has been connecting people over coffee for nearly fifty years, and serves more than a hundred million customers every week.

Invariably, some of those customers are our caffeine-fueled graduate students. When asked in class, "Who has been to a Starbucks in the last week?" nearly all hands go up. And when asked, "How many of you have the Starbucks app?" most of those hands remain raised. Students say they use the app because it makes it more convenient for them to order and pay. They can earn rewards, and they receive personalized offers. Indeed, the customer service section of the Starbucks website states: "We want to provide you with promotions and offers that are personalized for your Starbucks Experience. So the specifics of our offers, promotions and coupons vary by customer. While you may not receive a particular offer or promotion, there may be another offer that is personalized for you to take advantage of."[1]

It's not just our venti latte–driven graduate students who are using the Starbucks app to receive personalized offers, however. As of November 2019, Starbucks announced it had 17.6 million active rewards members, up 15 percent year-over-year. Rewards members now account for roughly a fifth of all customers, who are responsible for an astonishing 40 percent of total sales. Says Kevin Johnson, COO of Starbucks, "We are not alone among global retailers turning to AI, nor are we the first to incorporate this kind of technology. But at Starbucks, we are on a quest to leverage world-class technology in support of our mission: to inspire and nurture the human spirit—one person, one cup, and one neighborhood at a time."[2]

To get a feel for how you might approach implementation of the five stages, let's take a closer look at Starbucks's progression. Keep in mind that, though we've represented the five stages as discrete and sequential, the way you actually work through them will likely involve working within some stages concurrently. Starbucks is no different. The Starbucks Rewards program, however, fits neatly into Stage 1: Foundation.

STARBUCKS REWARDS

In 2019, Starbucks Rewards was the most popular loyalty app among quick-service restaurants, according to a study from technology survey data company The Manifest.[3] Every aspect of the Starbucks Rewards program is available through a smartphone app, eliminating the need to carry a physical rewards card or anything else in your wallet to pay or earn stars. Today, in addition to the ability to earn stars for purchasing products, rewards membership offers a birthday reward, early access to certain promotions and offers, personalized offers and coupons, and a "double star" day.[4]

Matthew Ryan, Starbucks chief marketing officer said, "Since introducing Starbucks Rewards ten years ago, we've experienced tremendous growth and continued to evolve the program to meet the changing needs and purchase patterns of our customers. These new updates put choice in the hands of our customers and a personal touch they can only get from Starbucks."[5] Because of its rewards program, Starbucks now has a huge customer database that includes not only contact information but also a record of customer behaviors such as how often they purchase, what they purchase and repurchase, where they purchase, what days and times they purchase, what offers they redeem, and how long they've been members, as well as their locatione, obtained from mobile device ID.

In other words, check Starbucks off as having successfully fulfilled all the criteria in Stage 1 of the AI Marketing Canvas, which is to have accumulated an "adequate amount of quality data to begin training machine-learning models and supercharge Customer Relationship Moments." Starbucks didn't get there overnight, however. In fact, the app and its data-collection abilities—and the ability to make predictions and offer personalized suggestions, for that matter—are the results of more than a *decade* of trial and error.

STARBUCKS AI MARKETING CANVAS TIMELINE

See if you can identify activities consistent with Stages 1 through 5 in this timeline.

- **2007:** Starbucks begins experimentation with mobile applications.[6]

- **2008:** Launches the My Starbucks Idea website to gather product suggestions submitted by consumers. (Note: Idea #202 was the ability to make mobile payments at drive-throughs.)[7]

- **2009:** Launches My Starbucks Rewards loyalty program and Starbucks Card mobile payment.[8]

- **2010:** Rolls out a stand-alone payments app using QR code, which only works on the iPhone, and only at sixteen stores.
- Adapts its stand-alone app to work with bar code scanners at Target, which at the time houses about one thousand Starbucks stores.
- Links mobile payments to a loyalty app.[9]

- Adds Blackberry as a secondary platform; sends cease-and-desist letter to a creative Starbucks shift supervisor who develops an unauthorized mobile app for the Android.
- Consolidates the two Starbucks cards into one Starbucks Rewards program.[10]

- **2011:** Rolls out Starbucks for Android app, a Starbucks Card eGift feature. Develops the Starbucks Cup Magic app to share augmented reality experiences in its stores and beyond.

- **2012:** Combines loyalty program and payments app, and takes development in-house.[11]

- **2013:** Invests $25 million in Square and begins using it to process its payments, but never uses its interface.

- **2014:** Confronts password security issues on its app.
- Launches Starbucks Mobile Order and Pay.[12]
- Cuts ties with Square, and moves processing to JPMorgan Chase.
- Retires My Starbucks Idea platform, and invites consumers to pitch ideas via Twitter and on its website.[13]

- **2015:** Hires CTO Gerri Martin-Flickinger.
- Takes strategic decision to move away from building its own technical infrastructure, in favor of using the "cloud."

- **2016:** Changes its rewards from a visit-based structure to a purchase-based structure so that it can use spending patterns "to have people try things they wouldn't try otherwise, or to put something quietly on sale to create incentives to desired behaviors."[14]
- Begins offering personalized serving suggestions of foods that customers they might like with their drink, automatically generated by artificial intelligence on the basis of weather, buying history, and choices that others with similar preferences have made.[15]

- Designs its new line of products to complement the habits it has gleaned from its own stores, and using data from traditional consumer research.[16]
- Reworks its email program using a real-time, artificial intelligence–based personalization engine, which is tied to reward cards' spending data, allowing the automatic creation of 400,000 personalized variants per week.[17]

- **2017:** Offers shoppers the ability to earn rewards from Starbucks products purchased in grocery stores, by going to www.Starbucks.com/Rewards and entering its "star code." This action also adds them to the Starbucks Rewards program.[18]
- Partners with Microsoft to develop Deep Brew, its next-generation personalization engine.

- **2018:** Launches its first credit card, which allows customers to earn stars with every use.[19]

- **2019:** Consolidates Rewards into a single-level program. "With these updates we wanted to provide an assortment of options for members to choose from, giving them choice and the ability to make their Rewards meaningful to them and to meet their needs," Kyndra Russell, vice president, global marketing says.[20]
- Apple Pay overtakes Starbucks mobile app to become the top mobile payment app in the United States, marking the *first time* a generic mobile payment app has led Starbucks in the domestic market.[21]
- Recognizes strong correlation between Starbucks partner (barista) engagement and customer connection, which leads to higher customer frequency. Allocates additional store labor, increases store-level training, and simplifies in-store tasks with technology.[22]
- Partners with Brightloom to make its personalization technology available to other retailers.

You get the idea. The point is that Starbucks committed early to a mobile-first strategy that would allow it to collect data (Stage 1) that would eventually allow it to hyper-personalize the consumer experience using AI and machine-learning capabilities (Stages 2 through 4) and ultimately resell its personalization technology (Stage 5).

EXPERIMENTATION AND EXPANSION

As you can see from the timeline, Starbucks is constantly experimenting with different ways to use its data (Stage 2), and it constantly applies AI across a broader set of marketing abilities. It also has worked to develop in-house capabilities (Stage 3). Stages 2 and 3 in this example are commingled. As outsiders, we offer here our best inference from the aforementioned timeline.

At the beginning of 2016, Starbucks was sending thirty handcrafted emails per week. The process was spreadsheet-driven, and there was a two-week lag. By mid-2016 Starbucks had reworked the system to apply AI to rewards spending data, which allowed marketers to send four hundred thousand hyper-personalized email variants in real time. This shift addresses the Retention and Growth relationship moments, and could be an example of Stage 2.[23]

Starbucks was among the first to offer customers the ability to order and pay in advance from a mobile device. Starbucks Mobile Order and Pay launched in 2015, extending the capabilities of its app, which was already on customers' phones (Stage 3). Starbucks also uses data to help align its menu and product lines with consumer preferences. For example, when building out its grocery lines of K-Cups and bottled beverages, Starbucks both data from its stores as well as customer market research to decide which products to create, personalizing the Growth relationship moments. One finding was that many tea drinkers don't put sugar in their tea, so Starbucks created two unsweetened tea K-Cups (Stage 3).[24]

The Starbucks "Deep Brew" personalization engine also has one foot in Stage 3, in regard to developing in-house capabilities. However, its impact extends far beyond that to Stage 4 and even Stage 5.

DEEP BREW

As you'll remember from the timeline, in 2017, Starbucks partnered with Microsoft to build Deep Brew, the company's in-house "personalization engine," which we can attribute to Stage 4. The Deep Brew platform allows the Starbucks Rewards app to provide customers with hyper-relevant product recommendations across a variety of channels, including in-app ordering. The system can adapt to customer preferences and context over time through factors such as ingredients, price sensitivity, time of day, weather, location, and type of product, resulting in beverage and food recommendations for each user. It can provide customized discounts and emails based on the user's behavior. The app can also track the customer's location, to provide directions to the closest Starbucks store and order from the store specifically. In addition, Starbucks has given users the opportunity to engage with a "virtual barista" on the app by ordering online ahead of time through voice command, or by clicking through the menu.

The platform is backed by Microsoft's Azure infrastructure. In addition to personalization for consumers, the company is looking to Deep Brew to "optimize store labor allocations, and drive inventory management" in stores. Starbucks wants to use artificial intelligence—and other advanced technologies related to the "Internet of Things"—to remove friction, streamline production of food and drinks, decrease equipment downtime, and handle other repetitive tasks so that its "partners" (i.e., employees) have more time to connect with customers—thus amplifying its technological personalization with human-to-human connection.

Starbucks CTO Gerri Martin-Flickinger said, "When you walk around the store, you see a lot of people talking to people, a lot of engagement between the baristas and the customers, . . . and for tech to be done well at Starbucks means tech needs to enhance that experience, not get in the way of that experience."[25]

MONETIZING DEEP BREW

Starbucks is also in the process of monetizing its technology by investing in a company called Brightloom—helmed by the former chief digital officer at Starbucks, Adam Brotman.[26] Brotman called the agreement historic because it will give the industry an all-in-one digital solution that includes Starbucks's industry-leading customer engagement software. It plans to sell the combined system at an affordable price to brands of all sizes, including competitors—a clear execution of Stage 5, which is using AI to drive significant new revenue streams and/or new business models, and serve external customers as a platform.[27]

We hope that seeing what Starbucks has done with AI and machine learning through the lens of the five stages of the AI Marketing Canvas has made it clearer how AI and machine learning can be used to successfully supercharge Customer Relationship Moments, and business results along with it.

BUSINESS IMPACT

This deep level of personalization continues to benefit the company, which it applies to the growing number of active members in the Starbucks Rewards loyalty program, some 17.6 million at Q4 2019 (up 15 percent year-over-year). As a marketer, you may find it interesting to note that Starbucks is achieving revenue growth despite a marked *decrease* in US advertising spending over the past two years (figures 31 and 32). Its strategy of using technology in as many ways as possible to supercharge its Customer Relationship Moments is delivering business results, and as such it is a great model to study for any brand looking to use technology to bring consumers closer and make relationships stronger. So, the next time your team or your CFO asks you

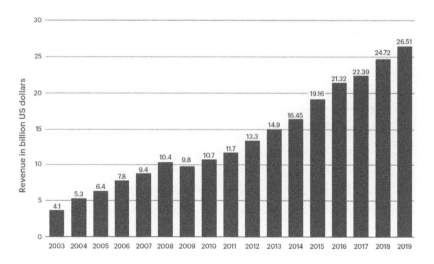

Net revenue of Starbucks worldwide from 2003 to 2019 (in billion US dollars)

Figure 31. Starbucks net revenue. Source: Starbucks 10-K, September 2019.

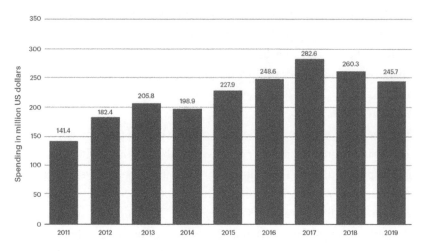

Starbucks Corporation's advertising spending worldwide in the fiscal years 2011 to 2019 (in million US dollars)

Figure 32. Starbucks ad spending. Source: Starbucks 10-K, September 2019.

who is doing this successfully, you can tell them about Starbucks—and the *Washington Post*, Ancestry, Coca-Cola, JPMorgan Chase, and Unilever, along with all the other examples we've provided throughout this book. And say we can do this too!

You may be thinking, "Well of course, big global premium brands such as Starbucks can do this; they have momentum. It's not so easy, or maybe not even possible, for my brand." Based on our knowledge of where many brands big and small are on this continuum, we remain confident that you can achieve what the other brands described in this book have achieved, which is the ability to personalize all your Customer Relationship Moments with AI and machine learning, in the service of long-term profitable growth. You won't do it the same way they did, because your brand and your business are different from theirs. Be inspired and informed by how other brands have done this, but don't obsess over following in their footsteps. Rather, double down on your commitment to do what your brand and business can do to take steps forward using the canvas—starting now.

Again, applying AI and machine learning to marketing can be considered a competitive advantage today, but very soon it will be table stakes and something that all successful brands are doing. This means that engaging with AI and machine learning is not just about the return on investment; it's also about the "risk of ignoring"—meaning the consequences you'll face if you choose not to act while all your competitors do. The exponential returns from using AI and machine learning in marketing implies that the "risk of ignoring" is very high.

Another reason to invest is that you can bet consumers will increasingly be benchmarking your ability to anticipate and fulfill their needs on the basis of their experiences with such front-runners as Starbucks, the *Post*, Ancestry, Coca-Cola, JPMorgan Chase, Unilever, and others—including the FANGs.[28]

Finally, take note of Starbucks' new focus on using AI to reduce repetitive tasks so that its baristas can spend more time with customers, making one-to-one *human* connections. They are using AI not only to achieve one-to-one personalization online, but to increase the volume of the ultimate in personalized experiences—those experiences that only another unique human being who knows you can create. It's a tall (maybe we should say grande?) order that Starbucks has been working on for more than a decade, with more than one misstep. So you won't be able to get to that point overnight, particularly if you are still pulling together your digital foundation. That's OK. You don't have to do it all this month, but you do have to *start*. The risk of being left behind is real.

By now you have a firm grasp on the "why" and the "what" with respect to AI in marketing—especially the "why *now!*" Other things we hope you've gotten down:

- the difference between a network and a node, and which one you are;
- the three forces—technology, customer connectivity, and information abundance—and how they're impacting your business today;
- context for how this evolved, based on a historical progression of the three waves composed of four eras of mass marketing, to segmented marketing, digital marketing and where we are today, which is to one-to-one fully personalized marketing;
- the basic computer science underpinning AI and ML (which we hope wasn't too painful);

- a basic understanding of how to use the AI Marketing Canvas framework to create a strategic road map for incorporating AI and machine learning into your marketing tool kit;
- inspiration and clarity, based on examples of what dozens of brands are doing at each of the five stages in the AI Marketing Canvas.

Next, in part 4, we will turn our attention to "How?" Chapter 14, "Managing Change," is devoted to addressing the key change management issues you will face not just in work flow and processes and in people required, but also in the cultural changes that will be required to effectively implement the AI Marketing Canvas and make the shift to AI-powered marketing.

PART 4

Implementation

14 Managing Change

AI and machine learning is shuffling the deck on every level and in every category, just like digital and big data did a few decades back. This seismic shift will require new thinking, skill sets, strategies, systems and will require the organizational culture to evolve as well.

— Nicolas Darveau-Garneau, chief evangelist, Google[1]

BECOMING AN AI- AND MACHINE learning–driven organization is a tough pivot for any organization—even Google. Yes, even Google had to make the shift to being an AI- and machine-learning-first organization. Let's take a look at how they made the shift, so that you can get a sense of the changes your organization will also need to go through.

GOOGLE'S TECHNICAL SHIFT TO AI

Google is the largest subsidiary of Alphabet, Inc., a holding company based in Mountain View, California. Recently Alphabet's market cap surpassed $1 trillion, making it just the fourth US company to achieve that milestone (along with Apple, Amazon, and Microsoft).[2]

Google's main source of revenue is search and ads. When it was founded in 1998 by Larry Page and Sergey Brin, Google's original innovation was an algorithm called PageRank, which better identified the most relevant websites to return as search results by examining relationships among websites. PageRank was a rules-based algorithm that looked at the number of pages in a given site, and the importance of the pages that linked to them. When you entered a search, Google's machines would crunch millions of "if-then" statements in milliseconds, and return you the best search results.

In Google's earliest days, there was no machine learning involved in this process; it was all about computations on a massive scale. At the time, this was a huge step forward from other early search engines which either used human editors who hand-determined which search results to show, or used simple rules like how many times your search term appeared on a page to determine the search results you would see. At least since 2006, however, Google search has been undergoing a substantial change in the way it works. Increasingly, machine learning and neural networks now determine the search results you see. This focus on machine learning intensified with the advent of the ImageNet project in 2012 (discussed in chapter 6) and Google's 2014 acquisition of a company called DeepMind.[3]

The search results you see today are the result of what Google calls RankBrain. The experts at Moz.com describe RankBrain as "a component of Google's core algorithm which uses machine learning (the ability of machines to teach themselves from data inputs) to determine the most relevant results to search engine queries."[4] So the search results you see today when you search for "best hotel in Paris" (Hotel George V, of course!) or "What 1940s Hollywood actress was also an inventor?" (Hedy Lamarr, featured in a Google homepage Doodle in 2015) appear because of machine learning. That's how Google search results continue to get better and better.

GOOGLE'S CULTURAL SHIFT TO AI

While Google's engineers were able to make large advances with machine learning, that's just half of the story. Making technical progress with machine learning is one thing, but managing the organizational change to bet your company's future on machine learning, as Google is doing, is another challenge altogether. That takes leadership, and a new way of thinking about your people, your processes, your culture, and your potential sources of profit.

Recognizing the need to drive this change across Google, Eric Schmidt, then executive chairman of Alphabet (Google's parent company) and Google CEO Sundar Pichai began making the external and internal case several years ago. At Google's Cloud Next conference in 2017, Schmidt very directly declared, "I'll bet the rest of my professional career that the future of your business is big data and machine learning applied to the business opportunities and customer challenges . . . before you. You're going to use machine learning to take that data and do something that's better than what the humans are doing." He predicted that it would "create huge new platforms, companies, IPOs, wealth, and enormous things going on in the future."[5]

While the staff at Google were generally aware of machine learning before 2017, most saw it merely as something interesting or evolving or worth keeping an eye on, but did not yet see it as the main focus of the company—or their own personal future. So that statement by Schmidt *rocketed* through Google. It was a clarion call to employees, motivating them to start focusing on machine learning. It's when everyone at Google recognized, "This is our future as a company, and it's critical to my future career as a working professional."

Echoing and amplifying Schmidt's statement, Sundar Pichai, then Google's CEO (now Alphabet's CEO) declared during a 2017 analyst call, "I do think in the long run we will evolve in computing from a mobile-first to an AI-first world." And then, at a town hall in January 2018: "AI is one of the most important things humanity is working on. It is more profound than, I dunno, electricity or fire." These statements really got the attention of Google's staff, and change began to happen rapidly. Sundar pushed teams to revamp all of Google's products and services to be AI-powered, and pushed for every Google employee to personally become versed in the fundamentals of machine learning. Google launched the website https:// ai.google/ for its employees and the world to start to learn more about this advanced approach to computing and problem solving. Perhaps most important was that Sundar put machine-learning expert John Giannandrea in charge of Google search, firmly establishing machine learning as its core product to power both search results and ads, thus further shifting the collective mindset.[6] The point is that, even Google has had to change the way it thinks and shift its corporate mindset to ensure that it can continue to deliver the machine learning–powered personalization required to succeed now and in the future.[7]

Now, we know that every company is not a trillion-dollar global company like Google. You may be working at a midsized company or a start-up, or you may be the sole proprietor of a one-person consulting firm. Regardless of your size, the kind of transformation to AI and machine learning that happened internally at Google will also need to happen in your organization, within your team. From the story of Google's transformation to an AI platform we can see that Schmidt and Pichai followed the eight-step change model John Kotter laid out in his 1996 book *Leading Change* (figure 33).[8] The first three steps—increasing urgency, determining management, and establishing vision—are about creating the climate for change. The next three steps—communicating buy-in, enabling authorization, and creating short-term wins—are about engaging and enabling the organization. The seventh step is not easing up, and the eighth is finally reinforcing the course once it is set. Google's leaders created the climate for change, then engaged and enabled the organization, created short-term wins, and didn't ease up. They kept reinforcing the new direction!

Similarly, we argue that you as a marketing leader, and as a leader within your organization, will need to make the case for a shift to AI- and machine learning–powered marketing, and then create the climate for change, engage

Figure 33. Kotter's eight-step change model

PEOPLE, PROCESS, CULTURE, PROFIT		
	Before	**After**
People	Brand Marketers and Digital Marketers	Data Scientists, Brand Managers, Digital Marketers, Technology
Process	Single campaign; long term annual planning; the "big idea"	Agile projects; many "little ideas"; focus on metrics; long-term strategic outcomes and let the machines run and test the campaigns
Culture	Decisions are intuition and experience-driven; deliberate, highly considered debate; Friday meetings with spreadsheets; being right the first time	Test and learn; speed is important; generating reasonable hypotheses and testing them fast; data-driven decisions; continuous improvement; "data beats opinion"
Profit	Bigger margins, lower volume	Smaller margins, bigger volume

Figure 34. People, process, culture, profit

and enable your organization, create some short-term wins (Stages 1 and 2 on the Marketing Canvas), and then refuse to ease up, reinforcing the new direction, pushing the team up to Stages 3, 4, and, if appropriate, 5!

Specifically, this will require you facilitating very specific changes across multiple dimensions. Let's have a look.

PEOPLE, PROCESS, CULTURE, PROFIT

It's not enough for you, as a leader, to make general statements like "Our organization needs to change," or "We need to make AI more of a priority in marketing." You will need to lead the shift from hand-curated marketing to machine-led marketing across four specific dimensions: people, process, culture, and profit (figure 34). Here's an overview of the shift you will need to make on each of those dimensions.

People

Energizing the AI Marketing Canvas will require a different kind of marketing team with new skill sets and philosophy, different from that of traditional marketing teams.

The first big "people" step in this process is to appoint the AI Marketing Champion you learned about in chapter 2. The Champion's job is to oversee all of your AI and machine-learning marketing initiatives, and function as a translator between marketing and data science. (Note: A complete list of things this role should be responsible for is located in chapter 10.) The best time to appoint this person typically is when you are moving from Stage 2, working with external partners and vendors, to Stage 3, where you are beginning to in-source more and more of the capabilities needed to perform AI-powered marketing in-house.

The qualities you are looking for in an AI Marketing Champion are as follows.

- **Project management expertise** and relevant prior experience. Although you may want to seek someone who is well credentialed, don't get hung up on requiring certifications such as project management professional (PMP). Some of the best and most effective project managers we know do not have this designation.
- **Comfort on both sides of the fence.** You want someone who is well-versed in data and technology, but also in marketing and creative skills—and who speaks both "languages" fluently.
- **Excellent communication skills.** They should be proactive about communicating not only to the team, but also to you.
- **Proven ability to be a self-starter.** The whole purpose of putting someone in this role is so you don't have to micromanage them. Look for a *proven* self-starter who will embrace this assignment with enthusiasm.
- **Natural collaborative skills**. This person likely will be the one you'll work with to hash out first-draft plans; and good collaboration fosters synergy and creativity.
- **Relationship-building skills.** The Champion will be the one tasked with getting people across functions to *do* the things on the plan, so they need to be someone who knows how to nurture those relationships and can charm people to do things that may not appear to be directly in their best interests.
- **Agile friendliness.** You want someone who has a sense of urgency and has a reputation for delivering fast, because the success of these

initiatives hinges on the need for speed. This person needs to think in terms of driving progress weekly, or even daily—not monthly or, heaven forbid, yearly.

- **Persistence.** You need someone who can forge ahead in the face of challenges and obstacles without getting discouraged or giving up, because change of this magnitude will be *hard*.

In this "marketing technologist" role, the Champion will act as an advocate for all of your AI and machine-learning marketing efforts, and will work with internal staff to reinforce how important these initiatives are to you and the firm. That means you must always have the Champion's back; you must consistently and publicly support this person in everything they do. If there are missteps or doubts, you resolve them privately. The organization must accept this person as your proxy. If you cast doubt or aspersions on their abilities, two things may happen. In the best-case scenario, people will disengage and the Champion won't be able to get anything done without involving you in every request (exactly what you don't want); and in the worst case, they will infer that the AI and marketing transition is just not that important to you.

So give your Champion airtime in your weekly team meetings, and showcase them in your all-hands-on-deck meetings, in company newsletters, and at company offsites. Do everything you can to signal to the organization that this person is leading your number-one most mission-critical priority for the future! As important as the Champion is—and we cannot emphasize that enough—you and the Champion alone cannot accomplish this shift. Your whole team will need to be "in the boat" together with you.

As Google's Schmidt and Pichai did, you will need to broadly communicate the new focus on AI and get everybody on board rowing in the same direction. Dedicating an "all-hands" meeting is a good moment to do this. You can also announce your Champion at that time too! Next, carve out some budget to send people to as much training as they can absorb; it's an investment that will pay big dividends in the future as you work your way up and across the stages of the AI Marketing Canvas. Consider bringing in an expert to talk to your team about AI at an upcoming offsite, and/or having the entire team read a book or watch a YouTube video each month about AI in marketing. Also consider including an aspect of AI in your employee evaluations. Most quarterly or annual evaluations already have a dimension around "learning and development" that measures how much an employee is growing their skill set. Tell your team that you'll be evaluating their Growth in AI as part of this dimension. We even know of a marketing leader who has established an "AI Star of the Quarter" award for her team, honoring the staffer each quarter who has made the greatest strides in AI.

In short, you must signal in all your communications that making progress on the AI Marketing Canvas is a priority for you!

Beyond your current staff, you will also need to begin screening prospective new team members for their knowledge and capabilities in data, computer science and AI and machine learning. In fact, it's our position that from here on out, every new person you hire needs to come in with some existing machine-learning competence. We know that sounds extreme. But if you really believe this is the future—and by this point, we hope we've convinced you that it is—then the sooner your entire team is fluent in AI and machine learning, the better and faster you will get to that future state.

By the way, most MBA students in our classes now are learning what AI is and how it can be applied to marketing. You'd be surprised how many newly minted MBA's can work in Python and R to build machine learning models!

Internal transfers are another opportunity to quickly add expertise in AI and machine learning to your marketing team. For example, is there someone on your firm's data science team who might be interested in a marketing role? In the past, you may have given them a "hard pass" for lack of marketing experience. Now, if there is someone on the data science side who wants to jump, and if they have strong data and computer science skills (with good communication skills a plus), giving them a chance to join your team could be a good move for both of you.

Now that you've communicated that the shift to AI/ML marketing is your priority, named a Champion, started to train your marketing team, and started selecting new hires and transfers based on their skills in machine learning, the next step is to get your team to start working in a different way with new processes.

Process

Marketing with AI requires a process more like software development than like traditional of long-term campaign planning. Traditional marketing, at least before the advent of digital marketing, was about conducting extensive primary research and planning every detail before launching a campaign. If a marketing campaign involved buying TV ads during the Super Bowl, the stress levels were even higher. The long-term planning was also reflected in new product innovation and product pricing. Until recently, it was not uncommon for marketing teams to spend up to a year planning before executing major initiatives.

Digital marketing introduced the idea of rapid experimentation. The medium was conducive, because it was both cheap and fast to conduct experiments online. You could now for the first time change your creative, your offer, your targeting, and your media placement during the course of a single day—or even a single hour—to optimize your results. Accordingly, marketing began to shift from a researching, planning, and debating discipline to a test-and-learn discipline. With digital marketing, instead of having to debate the right answer, your job becomes to generate reasonable hypotheses and quickly test them, expand on the approaches that work better, and pull back on the approaches that work less well. In our experience, most marketing teams now are increasingly fluent and comfortable with this approach, though most often it involves a single marketing moment such as "acquisition" or "conversion," in which the team rapidly iterates to find the most new customers at the lowest possible cost per acquisition. This is known as lower-funnel marketing. In other areas, such as "brand marketing," many marketing teams continue to use the traditional quarterly/annual approach with some pre-testing and conference room debate and decision making. This is known as upper-funnel marketing.

So what is the best *process* for AI-powered marketing? AI has taken the experimentation mindset that began with digital marketing even further. For example, instead of meeting every morning to review the responses to your campaign and decide on how to revise and update your campaigns, with AI in place, the machine just runs in the background and updates itself constantly, making continuous optimizations instead of episodic decisions. This process, of course, has the potential to further improve your marketing results, because we are more frequently running the optimal right message to the right person at the right time, in the right place.

This sentiment is also reflected in the quote below from Katherine Johnson, director of emerging technologies at IT solutions provider Trace3, reacting to a question about companies understanding the process necessary to bring AI into the enterprise: "They don't. They don't! I think [companies] form a lot of committees on how is the best way to bring [AI] in, and then it is indecision by committee, as opposed to looking for those quick wins. . . . Companies tend to look for areas of pain instead of areas of gain. And [areas of gain are] key to [AI] success. Don't try to fix something that is a huge area of pain; start with the areas of gain."[9]

The AI Marketing Canvas suggests a lot of rapid experiments to learn quickly about customers. To achieve this, you'll want to focus on two main things:

- developing an Agile marketing process similar to software development, and
- cultivating a multidisciplinary team of marketers, vendors, data scientists, and IT professionals.

Step one is to replace quarterly initiatives with Agile sprints. For example, a company we have worked with runs two Agile sprints at the same time every two weeks. One sprint designs a new marketing initiative, and another tests the marketing initiative designed in the previous sprint. The members of each sprint team present the results from their work every second Monday at a company-wide town hall. The company also has a review committee that ensures that the machine learning and AI follow proper and consistent principles. Any employee can propose a marketing sprint. The review committee evaluates the priority of the suggestion for the firm, and then, if it approves, puts the suggestion for design and testing in the Agile-sprint pipeline. This process of rapid and constant experimentation allows firms to quickly obtain feedback from customers and build on quick wins. As these sprints and quick wins culminate, the firm changes its marketing process to be more data- and customer insight–driven.

Again, your Champion will be immensely helpful to you and your team here. A skilled and carefully selected Champion will already be familiar with this evolved approach to process, and will help you implement it in a standardized and scalable way across the team as you implement more and more AI-powered marketing.

Culture

Becoming a world-class AI marketing organization requires more than just evolving the people on your marketing team and the processes by which they work. To be successful in the long term, you'll also need to transform the team's mindset and attitude—a shift that will require cultural change. Yet according to a recent study by Accenture, 55 percent of CMOs say they don't have a culture that inspires innovation or experimentation.[10]

The new culture must be one that embraces data, experimentation, probabilities and speed—just like the companies we've featured in this book. But where do you start? Answer: Start with what you and your team *values*.

Naturally, you value results and ROI. The difference is that in an AI marketing organization you also especially need to value how you *get* to those results. You might also value intuition and experience; and though those things still matter, with AI in place you now also need to value data, data models, and the scientific method. Optimally, your culture will become one that uses its intuition and experience to generate a continuous stream of hypotheses, where all reasonable ones get tested and the data ultimately determines the outcome of the experiment—win, lose, or draw.

Data beats opinion. Encourage your team to experiment, to view every marketing problem as a prediction problem in which machine learning can provide a better answer than a human-driven answer. A question such as "Who should we target?" becomes "What is the highest-probability target for us to engage?" This way of thinking is the hallmark of a culture that sees the world in terms of data and probabilities. One way to help your marketing team start to understand this cultural mindshift toward thinking in probabilities is to have them all read Annie Duke's excellent book *Thinking in Bets* (Portfolio, 2018).[11] Annie is a world champion poker player (poker players see the game in terms of probabilities), and her book does an excellent job of laying out how most of us are used to thinking in terms of "success or failure," "yes or no," and "right or wrong." Think about how many marketing meetings you've been in recently where those words were used!

In reality, the world around us is actually all about gauging probabilities—just like machine learning!

As a leader you need to continuously challenge and reinforce a culture of data, experimentation, probabilities, and speed by asking questions such as:

- Is this opinion, or is there a machine model that suggests this?
- Are we experimenting enough? Should we run more experiments?
- What is the probability of that outcome?
- How can we move faster, reduce cycle times, and try more things?

Marketing organizations that ask these questions will create a culture that can support the shift to a successful AI and machine-learning future.

One cultural watchout that often stymies the shift from hand-curated to machine-powered marketing is the feeling across the team that everything revolves around data and computer science, and that creativity, intuition, and experience no longer matter. This can alienate team members and give them a feeling of whiplash: "Wait—now only data matters? I thought marketing was about big ideas and creativity." To address this, get in the habit of responding with, "Yes, and. . . ." In this case the response would be, "Yes, big ideas and creativity still matter; *and* now data, AI, and machine learning matter, too."

Profit

The final dimension you'll need to address—often the one management cares about most—is profit. Traditionally, firms operating in the human-driven model have relied on fewer higher-margin sales to make their revenue goals. A marketer's main goal has been to create a brand that is so strong and has such emotional resonance that consumers are willing to pay a price premium for it, well above and beyond the cost of goods.

While that continues to be important, we foresee the possibility that firms in this new AI-driven marketing world may realize smaller unit margins and returns from their campaigns because the personalization is serving up a unique campaign for each individual. If you focus on margin impact only, this seems negative—until you consider that marketing with AI will allow you to launch multiple campaigns at the same time to a lot of customers with minimal cost outlay.

The profit model then switches from large ROIs from a few segment-driven campaigns to smaller ROIs from many campaigns, which optimally are personalized to each individual customer through the power of AI and machine learning—thereby shifting the focus from profit *margin* to *total profit*. This will require marketing and finance leaders alike to shift their mindsets. The ROIs or unit margins from traditional campaigns cannot be easily compared with those from AI campaigns. Further, AI campaigns require time to learn, so their initial ROI might be *negative*. The firm will need to have patience while marketing and data science fine-tunes the AI machine, allowing time for it to learn and for you to guide the organization through the various stages of the AI Marketing Canvas.

We predict that most firms can create this total profit scenario by mastering Stages 1 through 4. However, if your firm commits to the AI Marketing Canvas and builds the right tools, you may be able to open a new profit stream by selling your AI marketing tools to other firms (Stage 5) just as Starbucks and the *Washington Post* have done. It may or may not be right for your firm, but it is something to aspire to. Thus, the concept of "profit" in a world of strong AI-powered marketing is not just about selling more products and services more quickly. It's ultimately about expanding the pie *beyond* products or services to monetizing your AI and machine learning platforms so you can sell them to others too.

As we've mentioned previously, this journey is not an easy one. In the next chapter, we've provided a guide to an assessment meeting as well as a diagnostic you can do to get things in motion. We also discuss four gaps you'll likely have to bridge, which will require shifts in the internal culture and mindset.

15 Getting Started

The danger is to cling to comfort and custom at a time when events demand breaking away from both.
—Geoffrey Moore, professor and author of
Crossing the Chasm: Marketing and Selling High-Tech Products to Mainstream Customers[1]

NOW, WITH A SENSE OF THE TRANSITION you will have to make when it comes to people, processes, culture, and your approach to profit, it's time to get your team in a room and really get started. Enough researching, thinking, and reading (the rest of this book excepted). It's time to take action.

THE AI IN MARKETING ASSESSMENT MEETING
Start by scheduling a ninety-minute AI-in-marketing "assessment meeting" with your immediate marketing team. Roles you should include are

- your immediate marketing core team leaders,
- your marketing operations leaders,
- your data analysis leaders,
- your representative from the CIO team,
- your representative from the CFO team (i.e., your finance partner), and
- your representative from the project management office, or project manager

The purpose of this meeting is to agree on exactly which stage you are at on the AI Marketing Canvas, what you need to do to move to the next stage, who will own that effort, and on what time horizon. To help guide your discussion in this assessment meeting, we've developed a quiz to use as a diagnostic tool. You also can use it to guide the discussion in cross-functional team meetings about "Where are we at?" and "What do we need to do here?"

One method we like is for the team leader to distribute the quiz to each team member in advance. Collect the results and compute the average score and range for each item. Then create some slides you can project onscreen, and refer to them as you talk through each diagnostic item together. Having hung in there with us this far, you will find that much of this looks familiar. That's OK. It'll likely be your team's first exposure to these concepts.

This set of diagnostic quiz items need not be reviewed at *every* meeting. They are discussion starters meant to help you start to explore, and begin to plan your journey toward AI. The key items are 6 and 7, where we ask whether the data covers sufficient customers over enough time to reliably develop algorithms and test their efficacy. If your organization is not currently focused on customers—"customer-centric," as Wharton's Peter Fader calls it— then personalizing customer experiences with AI probably isn't right for you at this time.

THE AI AND MACHINE-LEARNING DIAGNOSTIC TOOL

Based on your understanding of your organization's strategy, select your level of agreement with the following statements using a five-point scale in which 1 means you strongly agree and 5 means you strongly disagree.

1. Long-term customer relationships are a strategic priority for our firm.
2. Developing data-driven customer insights is a priority for our firm.
3. Our customers prefer that we provide products that are personalized to their preferences.
4. Our customers only prefer low prices.
5. Our firm faces competition from technology platforms (e.g., Google, Amazon, Facebook, Apple, Microsoft).

Stage 1: Foundation

6. Please indicate on a scale of 0 to 100 percent the level of first-party data you collect for prospects (i.e., data you directly collect about individuals' actions that can be attributed to them).

7. Please indicate on a scale of 0 to 100 percent the level of first-party data (i.e., data you directly collect about individuals' actions that can be attributed to them) you collect for customers about
   - their transactions with you
   - their communications with other customers (i.e., reviews, social media posts, etc).

Please state your level of agreement with the following statements, based on your understanding of your organization's data structures, using a five-point scale in which 1 means you strongly agree and 5 means you strongly disagree.

8. Our database can identify each customer's transactions with the firm.

9. Our database can identify each of the firm's actions directed to a customer.

10. Our database can identify each prospect's transactions with the firm.

11. Our database can identify each of the firm's actions directed to a prospect.

12. Our database can easily access information about customers.

13. Our database can easily access information about prospects.

14. Our firm tracks customer actions over time.

15. Our firm tracks prospects' interactions with the firm over time.

Stage 2: Experimentation

Please respond yes or no to the following statement.

16. We expect to conduct experiments with AI solutions from third-party vendors that personalize our interactions with at least one Customer Relationship Moment (i.e., Acquisition, Retention, Growth, Advocacy).

If the response to item 16 is yes, please state your level of agreement with the following statements in reference to the experiments identified in item 16, using a five-point scale in which 1 means you strongly agree and 5 means you strongly disagree.

17. We have identified a vendor to develop AI systems that can be tested in the experiments.
18. We have allocated a budget to conduct the experiments.
19. We have identified metrics to evaluate the performance of the experiments.
20. We have approval for running more than one cycle of the experiments.

Stage 3: Expansion
Please respond yes or no to the following three statements.

21. We have conducted experiments with AI solutions from third-party vendors that personalize our interactions with at least one Customer Relationship Moment (i.e., Acquisition, Retention, Growth, Advocacy).
22. We anticipate developing AI-based systems that personalize more aspects of the Customer Relationship Moment that was tested in item 21.
23. We anticipate developing AI-based systems that personalize the Customer Relationship Moment other than the one was tested in item 21.

If you responded yes to item 21 and to either item 22 or item 23, please select your level of agreement with the following statements, using a five-point scale where 1 means you strongly agree and 5 means you strongly disagree.

24. We have identified an AI Marketing Champion: an individual responsible for leading the AI marketing initiatives in the firm.
25. We are investing in talent to develop AI marketing capabilities in-house.
26. We have compiled a summary of the results from AI experiments to present to top management.

27. We are developing a budget for building AI marketing capabilities across all Customer Relationship Moments.
28. We are refining the AI models based on feedback from the experiments.
29. We have a cross-functional team of C-level executives collaborating to develop AI marketing capabilities.
30. We are developing an Agile methodology to conduct multiple AI marketing experiments
31. We are developing an Agile methodology to track the performance of AI marketing experiments.
32. We are developing an Agile methodology for conducting marketing experiments quickly, with no experiment lasting longer than one month.

Stage 4: Transformation

Please respond yes or no to the following statements.

33. We have developed AI-based systems that personalize one or more Customer Relationship Moments.
34. We anticipate using AI to personalize all moments of the customer relationship (Acquisition, Retention, Growth, and Advocacy).

If you answered yes to items 33 and 34, please indicate your level of agreement with the following statements, using a five-point scale where 1 means you strongly agree and 5 means you strongly disagree.

35. We are tracking outcomes from our AI and machine-learning experiments so that we can prepare a solid business case for top management to fund additional AI and machine learning for marketing initiatives.
36. Our business case will recommend building an AI marketing group in-house.
37. Our business case will recommend buying an AI marketing firm.
38. We have identified areas where external vendor solutions are not sufficient to personalize Customer Relationship Moments.

Stage 5: Monetization

Please indicate your level of agreement with the following statements, using a five-point scale where 1 means you strongly agree and 5 means you strongly disagree.

39. We are actively engaged in discussions to develop a new revenue stream that leverages our capabilities in AI marketing from existing customers.
40. We are actively engaged in discussions to develop a new revenue stream that leverages our capabilities in AI marketing from new customers.
41. We are actively engaged in discussions to level our AI marketing capabilities to develop a network-based business model that connects our different stakeholders.

This set of statements should provide the basis of robust discussion for your team. It's OK if you don't march through every single item in order. But during the course of the discussion it should become clear at what point your scores start to decline from all 4's and 5's to 1's and 2's. For instance, if you answer an average of 4.8 for the Stage 1 items, and 4.2 for the Stage 2 items, but only 2.6 for the Stage 3 items, that point of drop-off means you are currently in Stage 2 and need to plan to move into Stage 3. Then you can refer back to chapter 10 of this book, where we discuss all things Stage 3 to build your to-do list.

Some teams we know measure a diagnostic like this twice a year, to track their overall progress toward becoming AI-powered marketing organizations. Knowing this, you can tell your CEO or your board of directors about your strategic plan for AI in marketing and your progress against it. "We began the year at Stage 2, and our goal is to be solidly Stage 3 by the end of this year." In this way, "becoming better at AI in marketing" no longer is something fuzzy and abstract; it's a goal that can be measured using the AI Marketing Canvas and this diagnostic.

THE FOUR GAPS

As you think about this diagnostic quiz and move up the AI Marketing Canvas, we want to alert you to four gaps you'll likely have to bridge, which will require shifts in the internal culture and mindset (figure 35). In deference to Geoffrey Moore, we don't want to exactly call them "chasms." But in a loose sense of the term, you can think of them in that way. Imagine that between each stage there's a gap, a chasm, a barrier you will need to overcome to move to the next stage. These natural separations are in fact what create and define the five discrete stages, rather than all the stages oozing or blending from one into the next. The gaps are hard lines between the stages. So once you've identified which stage you are in at your assessment meeting, we'd like you to think about the gap you must overcome to get to the next stage.

Let's dive a little deeper into each of these gaps. The first gap, between Stages 1 and 2, is between human-driven and data-driven marketing. To close this gap, your firm must invest resources in shoring up its digital foundation. If your firm is still in the midst of this, use what you learn from

THE FOUR GAPS		
STAGE	GAP TYPE	KEY QUESTIONS
STAGE 5		MONETIZATION
GAP 4	Business model	Monetize offerings or not? This is a CEO/Board level discussion.
STAGE 4		TRANSFORMATION
GAP 3	World-class talent, capabilities	Build models in-house or buy a company? This is a CFO + CIO level discussion.
STAGE 3		EXPANSION
GAP 2	Process/culture	Changes needed with people, processes, and culture change managed? CMO + Data team.
STAGE 2		EXPERIMENTATION
GAP 1	Mindset, priorities	Prerequisite. How will we move from human-driven to data-driven marketing? CMO.
STAGE 1		FOUNDATION

Figure 35. The four gaps

your vendor-driven AI marketing efforts to make a case for what is possible now, what is coming, and why management should make it a priority to complete this process.

The second gap occurs between Stages 2 and 3, and largely has to do with anticipating culture changes and finding the right talent to move forward.

In between Stages 3 and 4 there's a gap where you are grappling with the decision of whether to begin building models in-house or buy and integrate another company into your firm. This is a strategic decision, the implications of which call for a thorough study by the strategy committee and the board of directors. (As a starting point, the decision matrix in chapter 11 [figure 25] could prove useful!)

Finally, a fourth gap occurs between Stages 4 and 5, where you decide whether it makes sense to monetize the systems you've created to create additional revenue for the firm. This one is tough, and could legitimately be considered a chasm rather than a gap; not every firm can or should aspire to Stage 5, because it will very likely involve changing the company (as in the cases of Google, the *Washington Post*, and Starbucks).

All firms who want to win in this new AI arena have faced or will face these challenges. The key is to look for the challenges and anticipate them, and to craft a plan for overcoming them. In all cases, these are strategic discussions you will need to have, which go beyond tactical, operational, or executional questions—so it's critically important to involve the right stakeholders. Especially as you deliberate about the gaps between Stages 4 and 5, C-suite involvement becomes increasingly important.

Now that you've had your assessment meeting and are aware of the four gaps, it's time to fill out the canvas. To keep it simple, let's look at how you might work through completing the canvas for a mythical local small business called Raj's Bakery (figure 36), which is currently focused on Stage 3.

SAMPLE OF COMPLETED AI MARKETING CANVAS: RAJ'S BAKERY

The canvas provides the road map, but that's just the first part of the process. Here are seven key questions you also need to consider as you begin to *operationalize* the canvas.

THE AI MARKETING CANVAS: Raj's Bakery				
	AI ACQUISITION	**AI RETENTION**	**AI GROWTH**	**AI ADVOCACY**
STAGE 3: EXPANSION Uses AI across a broader set of marketing activities; beginning to in-source development and capabilities.	FB targeting prospects	Rewards for loyalty points on the app	Targeted recommendations on the app (additional cookies)	
Key Questions				
Do I go deeper into the Customer Relationship Moment or branch over to the next one?	Focus on building look-alike audiences (Dig deeper)	Develop a set of rewards that recognizes repeat customers (Branch over)	Develop predictive models of next products customers would buy based on their transactions (Branch over)	
Who is my internal core competency team across functions?	Social marketing	IT, sales and marketing	App development, IT	

Figure 36. Raj's Bakery at Stage 3

1. What is the expected outcome?
2. Who is in charge?
3. Who is the vendor?
4. What are the experiments, and do they have pilot dates?
5. What is the scope of the data? Does it have enough numbers of customers, and a long enough period of coverage?
6. What is the expected completion time for each experiment?
7. What are the metrics by which we'll evaluate success, failure, and learning?

The good news is that you no longer need to start from scratch. You are now privy to the patterns, paths, and methods that both networks and nodes have used to supercharge their Customer Relationship Moments with AI and machine learning. More importantly, you now have the AI Marketing Canvas, a tool you can use to guide strategic choices as your firm embraces new ways to optimize people, processes, and culture in service of creating more powerful, enduring, and profitable one-to-one customer relationships. In the next and final chapter you will learn what you need to do *personally* as a marketing *professional* to ensure that you not only survive but thrive in this new world of modern marketing.

16 A Call to Action

The best investment you can make is an investment in yourself.
—Jim Lecinski's frequent advice to his team at Google

THE PRIMARY PURPOSE OF THIS BOOK is to assist you in your role as a marketing leader by providing you with a solid *strategic* framework you can use to supercharge each moment in your customer's decision journey, and succeed in this new world of AI and machine learning in marketing—no matter where you're starting from. We also hope our plain-language approach to explaining the key computer science and data concepts of AI and machine learning will allow you to better understand what you're reading in the trades, and will lead to more informed conversations with vendors, staff, and management alike.

Before we go, we want to acknowledge how much is at stake personally for you and your career in this new world—not just as a marketer, but as an individual who aims to build a successful career in this industry, and in the new machine-assisted, data-first world of marketing. Here are what a few industry leaders whose thinking we respect have told us during interviews:

It is imperative marketers become more comfortable, knowledgeable, and well-versed in the area of technology. Achieving credibility with internal IT leads and important technology partners—not to mention advancing in their careers—depends on it. Young marketers should enroll in continuing education classes that help build their competencies in this important area, and seek exposure to technology-related projects within their organizations. As they progress in their careers, more tenured marketers should nurture important IT relationships internally, and pursue informal mentorships from outside the organization (from subject matter experts, technology thought leaders, and strategic vendor relationships, etc.).

—Mitch Duckler, author of *The Indispensable Brand* and managing partner at brand strategy consultancy Full Surge[1]

To prepare for the future, the best thing that marketing leaders can do today is find data scientists and ask them questions. If you have these people in your organization, then consider yourself lucky. Make them your best friends. See if you can recruit one onto your team. I've done this at 4C and it's made all the difference. I now have a go-to person to explore all the "what if" questions that come up on a daily basis.

If you don't have data scientists in your organization, go out and meet some. Attend a local meetup. Hang around the engineering department of your local university. Offer someone an internship. Join some webinars. But make it a priority. Then, once you've established relationships, ask those questions. They don't have to be specific to your company or your marketing plans. See what trends these people are paying attention to and throw out some hypotheticals. The answers will be illuminating and help get you comfortable with the language of artificial intelligence and machine learning.

—Aaron Goldman, CMO at data science and marketing technology company 4C Insights, and author of *Everything I Know about Marketing I Learned from Google*[2]

With machines that can experiment with tactical marketing execution far more speedily, systematically, and consistently than any human, the marketers that want to make best use of these machines will require frameworks (and mindsets) that support and encourage iterative learning and experimentation. The leverage here is huge; if machines can execute tactical marketing experimentation, us humans get to focus on strategic marketing experimentation, made possible by the enormous reduction in operational costs associated with the tactical piece.

When it comes to data assimilation, mathematics, and repetition the machines are already superior, but in areas requiring disparate skills—handling ambiguity, empathy, creativity, and strategy—humans will have the edge for some time. The great gains will be in how these two complementary processing approaches are combined.

—Konrad Feldman, founder and CEO of Quantcast[3]

Get laser-focused on your consumer. Know what makes them tick and what experiences matter to them. Learn how to connect with them in new and meaningful ways. We're going back to the future a bit now. Thanks to AI, we can focus more on smart strategies and breakthrough creative.

—Kristen D'Arcy, chief marketing officer at Pac-Sun[4]

Here's our take: To be a successful marketer in the coming years, you must decide now whether you will engage and become an expert AI marketer, or sit on the sidelines and watch the "AI bus" pass you by—or worse, run you over.

You've likely seen this movie before. Remember, you had to decide whether to become a digital marketer or just stay in the realm of traditional marketing, and then decide again whether to become a data marketer or just stay in the realm of intuition. Most marketing job descriptions now list digital and data as a requirement, and you've also probably noticed that those who jumped in and embraced those things early now have a leg up. The difference is that this time, the changes are happening at ten-plus times the velocity of those that came earlier.

As Jenifer Berman, CMO of Insider Inc. (parent of Business Insider) recently told an audience at the Consumer Electronics Show in Las Vegas, "Whether we're talking about 5G or AI, or privacy issues, it is about helping the navigating change piece of it. And being an organization that needs to be at the front of that, you have to be able to walk the walk yourself, right? You have to be an organization that can iterate really quickly and move quickly."[5]

That's why we believe that fluency and experience with AI in marketing (i.e., leading, developing, and implementing AI Marketing Canvas–based programs like the ones we've described in this book) will become part of your job sooner than later. What you decide to do about your knowledge of AI and machine learning for marketing today will impact what you're able to achieve in the years to come, along with your ability to weather crises and respond to the changes in customer behavior that occur during those times.

This is your personal AI Moment of truth. A moment that is happening *right now*. There are any number of things you could do to address your AI Moment of truth, but the most important and powerful thing you can do right now is look for ways to experience how AI and machine learning works, beyond just reading about it—this book included! In fact, if you take nothing else away from this chapter (so far) let it be impetus to engage and take a first step by familiarizing yourself with these tools.

You can't learn to drive a car by just reading the manual. At some point you have to actually put your hands on the wheel. It's the same for us as marketers; we know it's critical to *experience* the tools in our marketing tool kits. Because the application of AI and machine learning in marketing is still so nascent, the time invested now to really understand how it works will pay you *big* dividends later.

The good news is that there's an easy way to get your hands in the dirt right now in the form of Google's Teachable Machine tool. Teachable Machine (teachablemachine.withgoogle.com) is a "web-based tool that makes creating machine learning models fast, easy, and accessible to everyone."[6] The tool allows you to actually train a computer to recognize your own images, sounds, and poses, resulting in a functional machine learning model; and no special expertise or coding is required. One exercise you can do—the one we use in our executive education classes—is to build a simple visual-recognition machine-learning model that can distinguish between a car or a truck. The best part is that this tool is free and Web-based, and requires no software or installation.

You can experience machine learning firsthand by playing the kid's game "rock, paper, scissors." Let that sink in. There's a *children's game* that involves building a machine-learning model to recognize pictures of hand shapes.

You've heard of "digital natives." Enter "machine learning natives" who will grow up to become the next wave of marketers. The rock, paper, scissors and other exercises were developed by Dale Lane, using APIs from IBM Watson. It's an awesome Web-based experience designed for use in the classroom by schools and volunteer-run coding groups for children, but it's a great way to introduce machine learning to anyone.

Navigate to machinelearningforkids.co.uk and select the "rock paper scissors" exercise. Download the step-by-step "how to play" guide and begin! The exercise takes just a few hours, and by the end you will have trained your very own model. More importantly, not only will you have gained valuable first-hand experience about how machine learning works, but you'll have moved from just *reading* about AI and machine learning to actually having *done* it. That's a huge step toward preparing yourself for the future of marketing.

USING AI TO NURTURE AND ENHANCE HUMANITY

There's one more aspect of AI we want to touch on before we wrap things up. That is the huge potential for you to use AI and machine learning to allow your brand to participate in a way that nurtures people and enhances your brand's overall *humanity*.

JPMorgan Chase is already using AI to do this. At the 2019 Websummit in Lisbon, JPMorgan Chase's then-CMO Kristen Lemkau said, "I believe deeply to my bones that the most important development in the history of marketing is machine learning." Under her guidance, Chase is using AI to discover ways to serve customers with ads that "feel like a choice not an ad," and she expects those more human-sounding ads to continue to differentiate Chase and drive business growth.[7]

Consider Starbucks's mission statement: "To inspire and nurture the human spirit—one person, one cup and one neighborhood at a time." Perhaps more telling, however, are its stated values, particularly this one: "We are performance driven, through the lens of humanity."[8] That's why there is so much focus on using AI to free up its baristas to spend more time making connections with customers.

It doesn't stop there. Starbucks CEO Kevin Johnson was introduced by a friend to renowned neuroscientist Richard Davidson, a professor of psychology and psychiatry at the University of Wisconsin–Madison and founder and director of the Center for Healthy Minds. Among their many conversations about helping Starbucks partners find ways to more deeply connect with customers, Johnson and Davidson have been dreaming about another idea: What if customers also were able to change how they interact with each other in the stores?[9] It's a big idea that starts with using AI to help facilitate deeper, more authentic, and ultimately more rewarding connections with the human beings who are experiencing your products and services—and a refusal to capitulate to the fearmongers who insist that the future of AI in marketing can only result in a cold, quasi-personal, robot-driven "Matrix" future. Marketing technology veteran (Google, Instagram, YouTube) and consultant Dr. Eric Solomon put it this way in his January 16, 2020, article for Entrepreneur.com:[10]

> The reality is that marketers have long understood the need to build and foster meaningful emotional connections between businesses and customers. The quality of these connections helps to define the world's most iconic brands. But as technology, data, and metrics have moved to the forefront of corporate discourse, the context in which to establish these emotional relationships has changed. The net result of the connected world is that people are producing more signals about who they are, what they talk about, and the things they like.
>
> So the temptation—one I understand all too well—is to move away from individuals and to look for human patterns in the tangled web of data. There is value in doing that, of course. I'm not saying that advertising is pointless, or that targeted marketing doesn't work. But I am saying that you can't confuse those tools for what it means to build relationships with humans.
>
> So how do businesses do the more important work? First, they need to acknowledge that there are living, feeling human beings at the beginning and end of every transaction—and that a shift in thinking must be employed to really build emotional connections with their customers.

We urge you to become that marketing leader whose obsession is to find ways to use AI and machine learning not only to personalize the customer journey at every juncture, but also to add humanity back into your brands wherever possible.

One more thing: Center for Health Minds director Richard Davidson said, "I really believe it's possible to cultivate and scale well-being. [Starbucks CEO] Kevin totally gets this. It's one of the things I love about him."[11]

Can one company doubling down on human connection make a difference?

"It can change the world," Davidson said. "It can totally change the world."[12]

A CLOSING THOUGHT

We hope this book has inspired you to move quickly and strategically into this world of AI and machine learning for marketing, and to get down to business using AI to supercharge all your Customer Relationship Moments. We wish you luck on this mission, which has the potential to deliver value and positive change to your organization in ways you can't imagine. To that end, we look forward to hearing your great success stories and including them in our future writings, talks, and classes about the AI Marketing Canvas.

Please connect with us on LinkedIn, and comment on our posts using the hashtag #AIMarketingCanvas—or send us a message. We promise to respond.

RAJ VENKATESAN: www.linkedin.com/in/education-marketing-consultant/
JIM LECINSKI: www.linkedin.com/in/jimlecinski
HASHTAG: #AIMarketingCanvas

We've shown you a way forward that is grounded in sound marketing principles and strategy, supported by dozens of real examples. Now it's up to you to take it from here—to use the AI Marketing Canvas to win your AI Customer Relationship Moments, and ultimately win it all.

Acknowledgments

We owe a heartfelt "thank you" to a long list of people who have collaborated with us to make this book possible. In a new, complex and fast-moving area like AI in Marketing, no one person, nor even any duo of coauthors, yet has a complete view of what's happening and where things are heading in the future. We can only provide such a view here thanks to the many contributors who have helped us along the way. We'd like to say a few special thank-yous:

to Helena Bouchez, our cowriter and project manager, who kept us on track and helped bring our vision to paper;

to Ping (Lisa) Li, Sarah Han, and Hong Jik Lee, our research assistants who unearthed the details, backstories, and facts behind this book's content;

to Alex Modie, graphic designer extraordinaire, who brought our sketches to life with her wonderfully clear charts and exhibits, which you see throughout the book;

and to Steve Catalano, our editor, and all the great folks at Stanford University Press. Steve's strong and steady belief in us and this project, along with his editorial direction, made this book possible.

Thanks also to Peter ter Kulve and Jim Jansen, Todd Pollak and Azadeh Moghtaderi, Prama Bhatt, Dave Edington, Patrick Cullen, Kent Landers and Thomas Stubbs, and Van Diamandakis—the business leaders we interviewed in depth for their brand stories, featured in each of the five stages of the AI Marketing Canvas. We are forever grateful for the extended time they spent with us, sharing their personal and brand journey in implementing AI in their marketing.

Thanks to Paul Roetzer, Konrad Feldman, Aaron Goldman, and Chris Penn, industry experts on AI in marketing, who patiently talked with us about their thinking and gave us helpful critical feedback.

Thanks to our university colleagues and faculty, especially Vijay Viswanathan and Florian Zettlelmeyer at Northwestern University who encouraged Jim to pursue this project. Florian and IBM generously sponsored an AI in Marketing conference at Kellogg in 2019, where many of these initial ideas first surfaced. Thanks also to the 3M Corporation for funding Raj Venkatesan's research at the University of Virginia's Darden School of Business; to the brave students in Raj Venkatesan's course in marketing technology products, where many of the ideas for this book surfaced; to Sean Carr, Robyn Swift, and MJ Toms at the University of Virginia's Batten Institute, for not only providing funding for the course in marketing technology products, but also for connecting Raj with leaders in the technology industry. Thanks to Robert Bruner, Scott Beardsley, Yiorgos Allayanis and Jim Detert at the Darden School of Business, for encouraging Raj to pursue the path of technology/AI and offer technology related courses at Darden. Thanks to Paul Farris, who read an early version of our book proposal and manuscript, and offered us his sage thoughts and advice. Thanks to Steve Momper at Darden Business Publishing for advising us about the book publishing process. And thanks also to David Rogers at Columbia University, whose *Digital Transformation Playbook* was an inspiration and model to us for this book.

Thanks to Jim's former colleagues at Google, especially Eric Schmidt and Nicolas Darveau-Garneau, whose early recognition and evangelism for AI and ML applied to marketing were highly instructional and inspirational.

Thanks to our students, past, present and future. Our interactions with you inspire us every day to continue our own learning journeys, to continue to dig deeper, and to ask how and how—and why not. Your energy, interest, and interaction with us is why we do what we do.

Thanks to our families, especially Raj's wife Disha and Jim's wife Annette, for their unconditional love and support in this project and all of our professional endeavors over the years. Thanks also to Raj's sons, Neel and Rohan, for reinforcing the critical role of technology among digital natives.

And thanks finally to you, our readers. We know your time is precious; you have many pressing priorities and demands on you. And the books you chose to read are the ones you deem special and interesting. We hope we have lived up to that expectation.

Warmest personal thanks to each and all of you.

—RAJ and JIM

Notes

CHAPTER 1

1. Jeff Bezos, "Jeff Bezos on Post Purchase," *Washington Post*, August 5, 2013, accessed June 15, 2020, https://www.washingtonpost.com/national/jeff-bezos-on-post-purchase/2013/08/05/e5b293de-fe0d-11e2-9711-3708310f6f4d_story.html.

2. Claire Atkinson, "The Washington Post Still Plays Catch-Up, but Is Gaining on The Times," NBC News, December 28, 2017, accessed November 1, 2019, https://www.nbcnews.com/news/us-news/washington-post-still-plays-catch-gaining-times-n833236.

3. "Arc Publishing Unveils State-of-the-Art Commerce Platform Arc Subscriptions," *Washington Post*, May 16, 2019, accessed November 4, 2019, https://www.washingtonpost.com/pr/2019/05/16/arc-publishing-unveils-state-of-the-art-commerce-platform-arc-subscriptions/.

4. "Arc Publishing Licenses Technology to Global Brand BP," *Washington Post*, September 25, 2019, accessed May 22, 2020, https://www.washingtonpost.com/pr/2019/09/25/arc-publishing-licenses-technology-global-brand-bp/.

5. "NPR: At 'Washington Post,' Tech Is Increasingly Boosting Financial Performance," *Washington Post*, June 14, 2017, accessed November 1, 2019, https://www.washingtonpost.com/pr/wp/2017/06/14/npr-at-washington-post-tech-is-increasingly-boosting-financial-performance/.

6. Sara Fischer, "Scoop: WaPo Hits 2nd Year of Profitability, Plans Expansion," Axios, January 9, 2018, accessed November 1, 2019, https://www.axios.com/washington-post-1515418495-9c9dc541-165f-4e99-b002-ad41416737ef.html.

7. Barry Schwartz, *The Paradox of Choice: Why More Is Less* (New York: Ecco, 2004), 2.

8. Rick Press, "Wonder Why You Dread Car Buying? A Famous Psychologist Explains," Capital One, March 28, 2018, accessed January 23, 2020, https://www.capitalone.com/cars/learn/getting-a-good-deal/wonder-why-you-dread-car-buying-a-famous-psychologist-explains/1030.

9. Lee Breslouer, "Starbucks Baristas Name Their Favorite Drinks," Thrillist, November 10, 2016, accessed January 23, 2020, https://www.thrillist.com/drink/nation /best-starbucks-drinks-according-to-baristas-who-serve-them.

10. Jim Lyski, "Don't Settle for the Best Customer Experience in Your Industry, Deliver the Best One—Period," Think with Google, October 2017, accessed November 4, 2019, https://www.thinkwithgoogle.com/marketing-resources/experience-design/carmax -industry-consumer-experience/.

11. Lauren Hirsch, "After Brutal Year, Kraft Heinz Taps AB InBev's Miguel Patricio to replace CEO Bernardo Hees," CNBC, April 22, 2019, accessed January 23, 2020, https://www.cnbc.com/2019/04/22/kraft-heinz-taps-new-ceo-ab-inbevs -miguel-patricio.html.

12. Martin Giles, "Kraft Heinz Appoints New CIO to Deliver an AI Growth Recipe," *Forbes*, November 14, 2019, accessed May 22, 2020, https://www.forbes.com/ sites/martingiles/2019/11/14/kraft-heinz-cio-uses-ai-machine-learning/#148c96f c28f6.

13. "Contrary to Hype, Advertisers Divided on AI," *Advertiser Perceptions*, March 3, 2020, accessed March 4, 2020, https://www.advertiserperceptions.com/advertisers -divided-on-ai/.

14. Lynne Galia and Lainie McKeague, "Kraft Heinz Rebrands Kraft Recipes Website as 'My Food and Family,' Adds New Features," Kraft Heinz, March 21, 2019, accessed October 31, 2019, http://ir.kraftheinzcompany.com/news-releases/ news-release-details/kraft-heinz-rebrands-kraft-recipes-website-my-food-and-fami- lytm; Peter Eavis, "Kraft Tests How Much Costs Can Be Cut as Tastes Change," *New York Times*, February 22, 2019, accessed October 31, 2019, https://www.nytimes .com/2019/02/22/business/dealbook/3g-capital-buffett-kraft-heinz.html; Martin Giles, "Kraft Heinz Appoints New CIO to Deliver an AI Growth Recipe," *Forbes*, November 14, 2019, accessed January 23, 2020, https://www.forbes.com/sites/ martingiles/2019/11/14/kraft-heinz-cio-uses-ai-machine-learning/#4d4f0e9e28f6.

15. Sunil Gupta, *Driving Digital Strategy: A Guide to Reimagining Your Business* (Boston: Harvard Business Review Press, 2018), 192–94.

16. Ben Unglesbee, Cara Salpini, and Kaarin Vembar, "The Running List of 2018 Retail Bankruptcies," *Retail Dive*, November 21, 2018, accessed Octo- ber 31, 2019, https://www.retaildive.com/news/the-running-list-of-2018-retail -bankruptcies/516864/;. Daphne Howland, Ben Unglesbee, Cara Salpini, Kaarin Vembar, and Caroline Jansen, "The Running List of 2019 Bankruptcy Victims," *Retail Dive*, October 23, 2019, accessed October 31, 2019, https://www.retaildive. com/news/the-running-list-of-2019-bankruptcy-victims/545774/; Ben Ungles- bee, "One Year Later: Toys R Us' Fatal Journey through Chapter 11," *Retail Dive*, September 18, 2018, accessed October 31, 2019, https://www.retaildive.com/news/ one-year-later-toys-r-us-fatal-journey-through-chapter-11/532079/.

17. Ben Unglesbee, "Sears Filed for Chapter 11 with Plans to Close 142 Stores—Now What?" *Retail Dive*, October 15, 2018, accessed October 31, 2019, https://www.retaildive.com/news/sears-filed-for-chapter-11-with-plans-to-close -142-stores-now-what/539654/.

18. Emily Price, "Teen Discount Jewelry Favorite Claire's Emerges from Chapter 11 Bankruptcy," *Fortune*, October 15, 2018, accessed January 23, 2020, https://fortune. com/2018/10/15/claires-emerges-from-chapter-11-bankruptcy/.

19. Matthew Townsend and Joe Deaux, "Toys 'R' Us, Back from the Dead, Will Open U.S. Stores in 2019," *Bloomberg*, June 21, 2019, accessed January 23, 2020, https://www. bloomberg.com/news/articles/2019-06-21/toys-r-us-back-from-the-dead-will-open -u-s-stores-in-2019.

20. "Tru Kids Teams with Candytopia for Toys R Us Adventure," PYMNTS, September 19, 2019, accessed January 23, 2020, https://www.pymnts.com/news/retail/2019/tru -kids-teams-with-candytopia-for-toys-r-us-adventure/.

21. Lauren Hirsch and Lauren Thomas, "Life after Liquidation: Toys R Us Stores Will Be Back This Holiday Season, This Time with a Tech Partner," CNBC, July 18, 2019, accessed January 23, 2020, https://www.cnbc.com/2019/07/18/toys-r-us-plots-comeback -with-smaller-stores-in-partnership-with-b8ta.html.

CHAPTER 2

1. Paul Roetzer, The Future Is Marketer + Machine," Marketing Artificial Intelligence Institute, July 17, 2019, accessed November 4, 2019, https://www.marketin-gaiinstitute.com/blog/the-future-is-marketer-machine-maicon-2019-video.

2. "AI Adoption Advances, but Foundational Barriers Remain," McKinsey & Company, November 13 2018, October 31, 2019, https://www.mckinsey.com/featured-insights /artificial-intelligence/ai-adoption-advances-but-foundational-barriers-remain.

3. Laurence Goasduff, "3 Barriers to AI Adoption," Smarter with Gartner, September 18, 2019, accessed May 20, 2020, https://www.gartner.com/smarterwithgartner /3-barriers-to-ai-adoption/.

4. V. Kumar, Bharath Rajan, Rajkumar Venkatesan, and Jim Lecinski, "Understanding the Role of Artificial Intelligence in Personalized Engagement Marketing," *California Management Review* 61, no. 4 (July 4, 2019): 7, https://doi.org/10.1177 /0008125619859317.

5. Philip Kotler, Hermawan Kartajaya, and Iwan Setiawan, *Marketing 4.0: Moving from Traditional to Digital* (Hoboken, NJ: Wiley, 2016), xvi, 23.

6. Jacques Bughin, Jeongmin Seong, James Manyika, Michael Chui, and Raoul Joshi, "Notes from the AI Frontier: Modeling the Impact of AI on the World Economy," McKinsey & Company, September 4 2018, accessed October 31, 2019, https://www.mckinsey.com/featured-insights/artificial-intelligence/notes-from -the-ai-frontier-modeling-the-impact-of-ai-on-the-world-economy.

7. Jack Kornfield, *Buddha's Little Instruction Book* (New York: Bantam, 1994), 9.

CHAPTER 4

1. Peter Fisk, "Network Effects Drive Over 70% of the Value of Technology-Based Companies . . . Time to make Metcalfe's Law Work for You!" accessed July 10, 2020, https://www.thegeniusworks.com/2018/06/network-effects-drive-over-70-of-the-value -of-technology-based-companies-time-to-make-metcalfes-law-work-for-you/.

2. Geoffrey G. Parker, Marshall W. Van Alstyne, and Sangeet Paul Choudary, *Platform Revolution: How Networked Markets Are Transforming the Economy and How to Make Them Work for You* (New York: W. W. Norton, 2016), 3.

3. "Uber of X," PYMNTS, accessed January 23, 2020, https://www.pymnts.com/ category/uber-of-x/.

4. "YouTube for Press," YouTube, accessed December 17, 2019, https://www. youtube.com/about/press/.

5. Nathan Lasche, "YouTube Music Makes Discovery More Personal with Playlists Mixed for You," YouTube Official Blog, December 17, 2019, accessed January 23, 2020, https://youtube.googleblog.com/2019/12/youtube-music-makes-discovery -more.html.

6. "YouTube Originals," YouTube, accessed January 23, 2020, https://www.youtube .com/originals.

7. Michael Schneider, "'Ryan Hansen,' 'Champaign ILL' Canceled as YouTube Prepares for New Originals Strategy," *Variety*, April 10, 2019, accessed January 23, 2020, https://variety.com/2019/tv/news/ryan-hansen-solves-crimes-on-television-champaign-ill-canceled-youtube-1203185818/.

8. Rajkumar Venkatesan, Paul Farris, and Ronald T. Wilcox, *Cutting-Edge Marketing Analytics: Real World Cases and Data Sets for Hands On Learning* (New York: FT Press, 2014), 149.

9. "Number of Netflix Paying Streaming Subscribers Worldwide from 3rd Quarter 2011 to 2nd Quarter 2020," Statista, accessed July 21, 2020, https://www.statista .com/statistics/250934/quarterly-number-of-netflix-streaming-subscribers -worldwide/.

10. Peter Kafka and Rani Molla, "Netflix Shows Off the Numbers behind Its Global Growth Story for the First Time," Vox, December 17, 2019, accessed January 23, 2020, https://www.vox.com/2019/12/17/21025154/netflix-global-growth -numbers-sec-streaming-investors.

11. Julia Alexander, "Netflix Is Removing Subscribers' Ability to Leave Movie Reviews," *Polygon*, July 6, 2018, accessed January 30, 2020, https://www.polygon.com /2018/7/6/17539918/netflix-movie-reviews-feature-rating.

12. Twitch, accessed January 23, 2020, https://www.twitch.tv/p/en/about/.

13. "25 Useful Twitch Stats for Influencer Marketing Managers," *Influencer*

Marketing Hub, January 3, 2020, accessed January 23, 2020, https://influencermarket inghub.com/twitch-stats/.

14. "Twitch 101," Twitch, accessed January 23, 2020, https://www.twitch.tv/ creatorcamp/en/learn-the-basics/twitch-101/.

15. Jeremy Chow, "Building a Growth-Focused Game Recommender for Twitch Streamers," Medium, October 25, 2019, accessed January 23, 2020, https://towardsdatascience.com/building-a-growth-focused-game-recommender -for-twitch-streamers-7389e3868f2e.

16. AJ Willingham, "What Is eSports? A Look at an Explosive Billion-Dollar Industry," CNN, August 27, 2018, accessed January 23, 2020, https://www.cnn. com/2018/08/27/us/esports-what-is-video-game-professional-league-madden-trnd/ index.html.

17. Lucas Fortney, "How Amazon's Twitch Platform Makes Money," *Investopedia*, October 20, 2019, accessed January 23, 2020, https://www.investopedia.com/investing/ how-does-twitch-amazons-video-game-streaming-platform-make-money/.

18. Tiffany Hsu, "Twitch Users Watch Billions of Hours of Video, but the Site Wants to Go beyond Fortnite," *New York Times*, September 26, 2019, accessed January 23, 2020, https://www.nytimes.com/2019/09/26/business/media/twitch-twitchcon- ads-redesign.html.

19. Andrew Webster, "Ninja Announces He Is Leaving Twitch to Stream Exclu- sively on Mixer," The Verge, August 1, 2019, accessed January 23, 2020, https://www. theverge.com/2019/8/1/20750393/ninja-mixer-exclusive-twitch-fortnite-streaming -gaming-announcement; Sarah Perez, "Twitch's Loss of Top Streamers Impacts Hours Watched and Streamed in Q4 2019, Report Says," TechCrunch, January 16, 2020, accessed January 23, 2020, https://techcrunch.com/2020/01/16/twitchs-loss -of-top-streamers-impacts-hours-watched-and-streamed-in-q4-2019-report-says/.

20. Torque Esports Corp., "NFL Football on Twitch Gaining Yards According to Torque Esports Data Experts," Cision, December 20, 2019, accessed January 23, 2020, https://www.prnewswire.com/news-releases/nfl-football-on-twitch-gaining -yards-according-to-torque-esports-data-experts-300978223.html.

21. Robert Williams, "NFL's Audience on Twitch Livestream Rises 45% from Last Year," *Mobile Marketer*, December 23, 2019, accessed January 23, 2020, https://www. mobilemarketer.com/news/nfls-audience-on-twitch-livestream-rises-45-from-last -year/569579/.

22. Gennaro Cuofano, "TikTok Business Model: The Rise of Creative Social Media Powered by AI," FourWeekMBA, accessed January 23, 2020, https://fourweekmba .com/tiktok-business-model/.

23. Manish Singh, "TikTok Tops 2 Billion Downloads," *TechCrunch*, April 29, 2020, accessed May 13, 2020, https://techcrunch.com/2020/04/29/tiktok -tops-2-billion-downloads/.

24. Deanna Ting, "Ad Buyers to TikTok: Make It Easier to Buy Ads," Digiday, November 18, 2019, accessed January 23, 2020, https://digiday.com/marketing/ad-buyers-tiktok-make-easier-to-buy-ads/; Traci Ruether, "How Artificial Intelligence Is Transforming Live Streaming," Wowza Media Systems, July 8, 2019, accessed January 23, 2020, https://www.wowza.com/blog/artificial-intelligence-transforming-live-streaming.

25. "Our Businesses," Alibaba Group, accessed January 23, 2020, https://www.alibabagroup.com/en/about/businesses.

26. J. Clement, "Number of Available Apps in the Apple App Store from 2008 to 2019," Statista, September 2019, accessed January 23, 2020, https://www.statista.com/statistics/268251/number-of-apps-in-the-itunes-app-store-since-2008/.

27. "About Poshmark," Poshmark, accessed January 23, 2020, https://poshmark.com/about.

28. "About: Keep Commerce Human," Etsy, accessed January 23, 2020, https://www.etsy.com/about?ref=ftr.

29. Sarah Perez, "Walmart to Expand In-Store Tech, including Pickup Towers for Online Orders and Robots," TechCrunch, April 9, 2019, accessed January 23, 2020, https://techcrunch.com/2019/04/09/walmart-to-expand-in-store-tech-including-pickup-towers-for-online-orders-and-robots/.

30. Véronique Hyland, "Walmart Officially Bought ModCloth, and Some Customers Are Freaking Out," *The Cut*, March 17, 2017, accessed October 31, 2019, https://www.thecut.com/2017/03/wal-mart-buys-modcloth.html.

31. Melissa Repko, "Walmart Winds down Jet.com Four Years after $3.3 Billion Acquisition of E-Commerce Company," CNBC, May 19, 2020, accessed May 28, 2020, https://www.cnbc.com/2020/05/19/walmart-winds-down-jetcom-four-years-after-3point3-billion-acquisition.html.

32. Kristina Monllos, "'Brands Start DTC': Inside Procter & Gamble's Startup Brand Studio P&G Ventures," Digiday, September 30, 2019, accessed January 23, 2020, https://digiday.com/marketing/brands-start-dtc-insid-procter-gambles-start-brand-studio-pg-ventures/; Kristina Monllos, "Procter & Gamble Is Looking to Add More Direct-to-Consumer Brands to Its Roster," Digiday, May 1, 2019, accessed January 23, 2020, https://digiday.com/marketing/procter-gamble-looking-add-direct-consumer-brands-roster/.

33. Lauren Hirsch, "Edgewell's Acquisition of Harry's 'Not a Good Comparison' to Unilever's Dollar Shave Club Deal," CNBC, May 9, 2019, accessed January 23, 2020, https://www.cnbc.com/2019/05/09/dont-compare-harrys-to-unilevers-dollar-shave-club-deal-edgewell-ceo.html.

34. Nicole Lee, "Netflix User Reviews Weren't Useful Anyway," Engadget, July 6, 2018, accessed July 10, 2020, https://www.engadget.com/2018-07-06-netflix-user-reviews-weren-t-useful-anyway.html.

35. Rajkumar Venkatesan, Paul Farris, and Ronald T. Wilcox, *Cutting-Edge*

Marketing Analytics: Real World Cases and Data Sets for Hands On Learning (New York: FT Press, 2014).

36. David B. Yoffie, Annabelle Gawer, and Michael A. Cusumano, "A Study of More Than 250 Platforms Reveals Why Most Fail," *Harvard Business Review*, May 29, 2019, accessed January 23, 2020, https://hbr.org/2019/05/a-study-of-more -than-250-platforms-reveals-why-most-fail.

37. Paul Ausick, "Who Loses as Nike Parts Ways with Amazon?" 24/7 Wall St., November 13, 2019, accessed January 23, 2020, https://247wallst.com/retail/2019/11/13/who-loses -as-nike-parts-ways-with-amazon/.

38. Khristopher J. Brooks, "Nike Will No Longer Sell Its Shoes and Swag on Amazon," CBS News, November 14, 2019, accessed January 23, 2020, https://www.cbsnews.com /news/nike-shoes-no-longer-on-amazon/.

39. Anita Elberse and Monica Cody, "The Video Streaming Wars in 2019: Can Disney Catch Netflix?" HBS no. 519–094 (Boston: Harvard Business School Publishing, 2019), 7.

40. "How Disney Plus Personalizes Your Viewing Experience," *Forbes Insights*, April 21, 2020, accessed May 13, 2020, https://www.forbes.com/sites/insights-teradata/2020 /04/21/how-disney-plus-personalizes-your-viewing-experience/#13f9ff5d3b6e.

41. Véronique Hyland, "Walmart Officially Bought ModCloth, and Some Customers Are Freaking Out," The Cut, March 17, 2017, accessed October 31, 2019, https://www.thecut.com/2017/03/wal-mart-buys-modcloth.html.

42. Sarah Perez, "Walmart Partners with Shopify to Expand Its Online Marketplace," TechCrunch, June 15, 2020, accessed June 20, 2020, https://techcrunch.com /2020/06/15/walmart-partners-with-shopify-to-expand-its-online-marketplace/.

43. "About," Verizon Media, January 23, 2020, https://www.verizonmedia.com/.

44. "Using Alexa with Your Whirlpool Appliances," Whirlpool, accessed October 31, 2019, https://producthelp.whirlpool.com/Connected_Appliances/Product_Info /Connected_Support/Using_Alexa_with_Your_Appliances.

45. Richard Best, "Harry's Shave Club Review: Is It Worth It?" Investopedia, August 11, 2019, accessed January 23, 2020, https://www.investopedia.com/articles /personal-finance/012516/harrys-review-it-worth-it.asp.

46. Rachel King, "Exclusive: The Makers of BarkBox Are Moving into an Often Overlooked Space in Pet Wellness," *Fortune*, October 30, 2019, accessed January 23, 2020, https://fortune.com/2019/10/30/barkbox-bark-bright-dogs-dental-care/.

47. "How to Boost Your Brand Equity through Brand Partnerships," Pica9, August 27, 2019, accessed October 31, 2019, https://www.pica9.com/blog/boost-brand-equity-brand -partnerships.

48. Sophia Bernazzani, "18 Examples of Successful Co-Branding Partnerships (and Why They're So Great)," HubSpot, June 28, 2019, accessed October 31, 2019, https://blog.hubspot.com/marketing/best-cobranding-partnerships.

49. Bernazzani, "18 Examples."

50. Hilary Milnes, "How Target Is Getting More DTC Brands to Sell in Its Stores," Digiday, March 14, 2019, accessed October 31, 2019, https://digiday.com/retail/target-getting-dtc-brands-sell-stores/; Marty Swant, "As Digital Payments Grow in the U.S., Banks and Tech Companies Are Forging Partnerships," *Adweek*, October 8, 2018, accessed October 31, 2019, https://www.adweek.com/digital/as-digital-payments-grow-in-the-u-s-banks-and-tech-companies-are-forging-partnerships/.

51. Swant, "As Digital Payments Grow."

52. "Case Studies," Numerator, accessed January 23, 2020, https://www.numerator.com/resources/success-story.

53. Brooks Barnes, "How Disney Wants to Take on Netflix with Its Own Streaming Service," *New York Times*, August 8, 2017, accessed November 5, 2019, https://www.nytimes.com/2017/08/08/business/media/disney-streaming-service.html.

54. Thomas Franck, "Disney's Streaming Service Will Rival Netflix with 160 Million Subscribers, JP Morgan Says," CNBC, March 6, 2019, accessed November 5, 2019, https://www.cnbc.com/2019/03/06/disneys-streaming-service-will-rival-netflix-says-jp-morgan.html.

55. Julia Alexander, "AT&T Will Pull Popular Shows Like Friends from Streaming Competitors, Says CEO," The Verge, May 14, 2019, accessed November 5, 2019, https://www.theverge.com/2019/5/14/18623082/att-streaming-warnermedia-netflix-hulu-friends-er-disney-comcast-nbc-universal.

56. Todd Haselton, "Verizon Will Offer Customers a Year of Disney+ for Free," CNBC, October 22, 2019, accessed November 5, 2019, https://www.cnbc.com/2019/10/22/verizon-will-offer-customers-a-year-of-disney-for-free.html.

57. *Bird Box*, Netflix, accessed January 31, 2020, https://www.netflix.com/title/80196789.

58. Aja Hoggatt, "*Bird Box* Is a Triumph of Netflix's Data-Driven Content Machine," Slate, December 28, 2018, accessed October 31, 2019, https://slate.com/culture/2018/12/bird-box-netflix-diversity-audience.html.

CHAPTER 5

1. Nick Edouard, "How to Know if AI Will Work for You," Marketing Artificial Intelligence Institute, October 29, 2019, accessed October 31, 2019, https://www.marketingaiinstitute.com/blog/how-to-know-if-ai-will-work-for-you.

2. Rajkumar Venkatesan, "Executing on a Customer Engagement Strategy," *Journal of the Academy of Marketing Science* 45 (January 2017): 289–93, https://doi.org/10.1007/s11747-016-0513-6.

3. Salman Aslam, "Facebook by the Numbers: Stats, Demographics & Fun Facts," Omnicore, January 13, 2020, accessed January 28, 2020, https://www.omnicoreagency.com/facebook-statistics/.

4. "1969 Sears Craftsman Drill Ad 'Look again,'" Vintage Adventures, accessed January 18, 2020, https://www.vintage-adventures.com/vintage-tool-hardware-ads/5267-1969-sears-craftsman-drill-ad-look-again.html; or https://www.pinterest.com/pin/262827328240057850/

5. "1952 Lustre Creme Shampoo: Bette Davis Vintage Print Ad," eBay, accessed January 28, 2020. https://www.pinterest.com/pin/22588435606948467/.

6. Ronald D. Michman and Edward M. Mazze, *Specialty Retailers: Marketing Triumphs and Blunders* (Westport, CT: Quorum Books, 2001), 67.

7. Beth Berselli, "Retooling at Black & Decker," *Washington Post*, February 9, 1998, accessed January 28, 2020, https://www.washingtonpost.com/archive/business/1998/02/09/retooling-at-black-decker/ecbccdb3-09d9-4fb3-b65f-e7dcf4f33fbe/.

8. Karl Wirth, "What McDonald's Latest Acquisition Means for Marketers," *Entrepreneur*, June 26, 2019, accessed January 28, 2020, https://www.entrepreneur.com/article/332239.

9. "Peloton Changes Entire Marketing Strategy," Lightning AI, accessed January 28, 2020, https://lightningai.com/case-studies/peloton/; Adam Coombs, "Big Data and the Smart Gym: Leveraging Your Customer Data [webinar]," IHRSA, accessed January 28, 2020, https://www.ihrsa.org/publications/big-data-and-the-smart-gym-leveraging-your-customer-data/.

10. Courtney Carlisle, "Super Hi-Fi Signs Peloton to Deliver Next Generation Audio Experiences for Its Live and On-Demand Fitness Classes," *Business Wire*, March 13, 2019, accessed January 28, 2020, https://www.businesswire.com/news/home/20190313005270/en; Anthony Vennare, "The Peloton of 'X,'" *Fitt Insider*, accessed January 28, 2020, https://insider.fitt.co/peloton-home-workout-equipment/.

CHAPTER 6

1. Cade Metz, "DeepMind Can Now Beat Us at Multiplayer Games, Too," *New York Times*, May 30, 2019, accessed November 4, 2019, https://www.nytimes.com/2019/05/30/science/deep-mind-artificial-intelligence.html.

2. Rajkumar Venkatesan, Jenny Craddock, and Noreen Nagji, *Automation of Marketing Models* (Charlottesville, VA: Darden Business Publishing, 2018).

3. Martin Childs, "John McCarthy: Computer Scientist Known as the Father of AI," *Independent*, November 1, 2011, accessed November 4, 2019, https://www.independent.co.uk/news/obituaries/john-mccarthy-computer-scientist-known-as-the-father-of-ai-6255307.html.

4. John McDermott, "R1: An Expert in the Computer Systems Domain," *Proceedings of the First Annual National Conference on Artificial Intelligence* (Menlo Park, CA: AAAI Press, 1980), 269–71, https://web.archive.org/web/20171116060857/http:/aaai.org/Papers/AAAI/1980/AAAI80-076.pdf.

5. McDermott, "R1: An Expert in the Computer Systems Domain."

6. "AI: 15 Key Moments in the Story of Artificial Intelligence," BBC, accessed November 4, 2019, https://www.bbc.co.uk/teach/ai-15-key-moments-in-the-story -of-artificial-intelligence/zh77cqt#zcpkj6f.

7. Joe Osborne, "Google's Tensor Processing Unit Explained: This Is What the Future of Computing Looks Like," TechRadar, August 22, 2016, accessed November 4, 2019, https://www.techradar.com/news/computing-components/processors /google-s-tensor-processing-unit-explained-this-is-what-the-future-of-computing -looks-like-1326915.

8. John Markoff, "Seeking a Better Way to Find Web Images," *New York Times*, November 19, 2012, accessed November 4, 2019, https://www.nytimes.com/2012/11/20/ science/for-web-images-creating-new-technology-to-seek-and-find.html; Dave Gershgorn, "The Data That Transformed AI Research—and Possibly the World," *Quartz*, July 26, 2017, accessed November 4, 2019, https://qz.com/1034972/the-data -that-changed-the-direction-of-ai-research-and-possibly-the-world/.

9. Muneeb ul Hassan, "AlexNet: ImageNet Classification with Deep Convolutional Neural Networks," *Neurohive*, October 29, 2018, accessed November 4, 2019, https://neurohive.io/en/popular-networks/alexnet-imagenet -classification-with-deep-convolutional-neural-networks/.

10. Rajkumar Venkatesan, Jenny Craddock, and Noreen Nagji, *Automation of Marketing Models* (Charlottesville, VA: Darden Business Publishing, 2018).

11. "What Is a Computer Algorithm? Design, Examples & Optimization," Study. com, January 14, 2014, accessed November 4, 2019, https://study.com/academy/lesson/ what-is-a-computer-algorithm-design-examples-optimization.html.

12. Jason Brownlee, "A Tour of Machine Learning Algorithms," Machine Learning Mastery, August 12, 2019, accessed November 4, 2019, https://machinelearningmastery .com/a-tour-of-machine-learning-algorithms/.

13. Cassie Kozyrkov, "9 Things You Should Know about TensorFlow," Hackernoon, August 3, 2018, accessed November 4, 2019, https://hackernoon.com /9-things-you-should-know-about-tensorflow-9cf0a05e4995.

14. Master Blaster, "Japanese Bakeries Can Now Use a Robocop-Style Bread Recognition Checkout System," SoraNews24, April 12, 2017, accessed November 4, 2019, https://soranews24.com/2017/04/12/japanese-bakeries-can-now-use-a-robocop-style -bread-recognition-checkout-system/.

15. Xulei Yang, Zeng Zeng, Sin G. Teo, Li Wang, Vijay Chandrasekhar, and Steven Hoi, "Deep Learning for Practical Image Recognition: Case Study on Kaggle Competitions," *KDD '18: The 24th ACM SIGKDD International Conference on Knowledge Discovery & Data Mining* (New York: ACM, 2018), 923–31, https://doi. org/10.1145/3219819.3219907.

16. Ralitsa Golemanova, "The Top 5 Uses of Image Recognition," Imagga Blog, June 6, 2019, accessed November 4, 2019, https://imagga.com/blog/ the-top-5-uses-of-image-recognition/.

17. Shea Gibbs and Rajkumar Venkatesan, *Have Text, Will Travel: Can Airbnb Use Review Text Data to Optimize Profits?* (Charlottesville, VA: Darden Business Publishing, 2015).

18. George Seif, "The 5 Clustering Algorithms Data Scientists Need to Know," Medium, February 5, 2018, accessed November 4, 2019, https://towardsdatascience.com/the-5-clustering-algorithms-data-scientists-need-to-know-a36d136ef68.

19. Chris Nicholson, "A Beginner's Guide to Neural Networks and Deep Learning," Pathmind, accessed November 4, 2019, https://pathmind.com/wiki/neural-network.

20. Simon Löfwander, "About Artificial Intelligence, Neural Networks & Deep Learning," Ayima, January 24, 2017, accessed November 4, 2019, https://www.ayima.com/uk/insights/artificial-intelligence-neural-networks-deep-learning.html.

21. Shijing Yao, Dapeng Li, and Shawn Chen, "Amenity Detection and Beyond: New Frontiers of Computer Vision at Airbnb," Medium, July 16, 2019, accessed November 5, 2019, https://medium.com/airbnb-engineering/amenity-detection-and-beyond-new-frontiers-of-computer-vision-at-airbnb-144a4441b72e.

22. Shijing Yao, Qiang Zhu, and Phillippe Siclait, "Categorizing Listing Photos at Airbnb," Medium, May 2, 2018, accessed November 4, 2019, https://medium.com/airbnb-engineering/categorizing-listing-photos-at-airbnb-f9483f3ab7e3.

23. Dave Gershgorn, "The Data That Transformed AI Research—and Possibly the World," *Quartz*, July 26, 2017, accessed November 4, 2019, https://qz.com/1034972/the-data-that-changed-the-direction-of-ai-research-and-possibly-the-world/.

24. Jo Best, "IBM Watson: The Inside Story of How the Jeopardy-Winning Supercomputer Was Born, and What It Wants to Do Next," TechRepublic, September 9, 2013, accessed November 4, 2019, https://www.techrepublic.com/article/ibm-watson-the-inside-story-of-how-the-jeopardy-winning-supercomputer-was-born-and-what-it-wants-to-do-next/.

25. Sean Silverthorne, "Deep Blue Put Out to Digital Stud," ZDNet, September 24, 1997, accessed November 1, 2019, https://www.zdnet.com/article/deep-blue-put-out-to-digital-stud/.

26. Stephen Shankland, "IBM Details Blue Gene Supercomputer," ZDNet, May 9, 2003, accessed November 1, 2019, https://www.zdnet.com/article/ibm-details-blue-gene-supercomputer/.

27. Maris van Sprang, "Watson and Other Impossible Grand Challenges," IBM, October 20, 2014, accessed November 4, 2019, https://www.ibm.com/blogs/think/nl-en/2014/10/20/watson-and-other-impossible-grand-challenges/.

28. Best, "IBM Watson."

29. Aatash Shah, "Machine Learning vs. Statistics," KDNuggets, August 1, 2016, accessed November 4, 2019, https://www.kdnuggets.com/2016/11/machine-learning-vs-statistics.html.

30. Larry Wasserman, "Statistics versus Machine Learning," Normal Deviate, June

12, 2012, accessed November 4, 2019, https://normaldeviate.wordpress.com/2012/06/12/statistics-versus-machine-learning-5-2/.

31. George Seif, "The 5 Clustering Algorithms Data Scientists Need to Know," Medium, February 5, 2018, accessed November 4, 2019, https://towardsdatascience.com/the-5-clustering-algorithms-data-scientists-need-to-know-a36d136ef68.

32. Manish Kumar, "Understanding Genetic Algorithms in the Artificial Intelligence Spectrum," Medium, September 5, 2018, accessed November 4, 2019, https://medium.com/analytics-vidhya/understanding-genetic-algorithms-in-the-artificial-intelligence-spectrum-7021b7cc25e7.

33. "Vitamix," Optimizely, accessed November 4, 2019, https://www.optimizely.com/customers/vitamix/.

CHAPTER 7

1. Author interview with Konrad Feldman via email, October 2019.

2. Paul Sawers, "YouTube Taps Machine Learning to Serve the Best Contextual Ads for Each User," *Venture Beat*, September 23, 2019, accessed January 28, 2020, https://venturebeat.com/2019/09/23/youtube-taps-machine-learning-to-serve-the-best-contextual-ads-for-each-user/.

3. A. G. Lafley and Roger L. Martin, *Playing to Win: How Strategy Really Works* (Boston: Harvard Business School Publishing, 2013), 3.

4. Alexander Osterwalder, "The Business Model Ontology: A Proposition in a Design Science Approach," *Research Gate*, January 2004, accessed November 4, 2019, https://www.researchgate.net/publication/33681401_The_Business_Model_Ontology_-_A_Proposition_in_a_Design_Science_Approach.

5. A. Osterwalder and Y. Pigneur, "Business Model Canvas," via DIY Toolkit, accessed January 28, 2020, https://diytoolkit.org/tools/business-model-canvas/; Used by permission with credit: strategyzer.com.

CHAPTER 8

1. Sunder Madakshira, head of marketing, Adobe India, direct quote to authors via email July 23, 2020.

2. Saleh Alitr, "Starbucks: Analyze-a-Coffee," Medium, July 18, 2019, accessed January 28, 2020, https://towardsdatascience.com/starbucks-analyze-a-coffee-b4eef811aa4a.

3. "Starbucks Reports Q4 and Full Year Fiscal 2019 Results," Starbucks Stories and News, October 30, 2019, accessed November 4, 2019, https://stories.starbucks.com/press/2019/starbucks-reports-q4-and-full-year-fiscal-2019-results/.

4. David L. Rogers, *The Digital Transformation Playbook* (New York: Columbia Business School Publishing, 2016).

5. José Antonio Martínez Aguilar, *The Data Advantage* (Seattle: Amazon Digital Services, 2018), 38 (Kindle edition).

6. "The Difference between First, Second, and Third Party Data and How to Use Them," ReTargeter, accessed November 1, 2019, https://retargeter.com/blog/difference-first-second-third-party-data-use/.

7. Crissi Cupak, "Why Retail Marketers Can't Dismiss Third-Party Data," Digital Commerce 360, March 19, 2019, accessed January 28, 2020, https://www.digitalcommerce360.com/2019/03/19/why-retail-marketers-cant-dismiss-thirdparty-data/.

8. Nicki Franz, "Moving from Analyzing Datasets to Decisions in DPL," Syncopation Software, July 18, 2017, accessed November 1, 2019, https://www.syncopation.com/blog/moving-analyzing-datasets-decisions-dpl.

9. Steven Chabinsky and F. Paul Pittman, "USA: Data Protection 2019," *ICLG*, March 7, 2019, accessed November 1, 2019, https://iclg.com/practice-areas/data-protection-laws-and-regulations/usa.

10. Neil Irwin, "Why Surge Prices Make Us So Mad: What Springsteen, Home Depot and a Nobel Winner Knew," *New York Times*, October 14, 2017, accessed October 7, 2019, https://www.nytimes.com/2017/10/14/upshot/why-surge-prices-make-us-so-mad-what-springsteen-home-depot-and-a-nobel-winner-know.html.

11. Robert W. Palmatier and Kelly D. Martin, *The Intelligent Marketer's Guide to Data Privacy: The Impact of Big Data on Customer Trust* (London: Palgrave Macmillan, 2019), 170–78.

12. Deborah O'Neill and Nick Harrison, "If Your Company Isn't Good at Analytics, It's Not Ready for AI," *Harvard Business Review*, June 7, 2017, accessed October 7, 2019, https://hbsp.harvard.edu/product/H03PKC-PDF-ENG.

13. Derek du Preez, "Unilever Teams Up with Microsoft to Deliver AI-Assisted Decision Making to Users," Diginomica, May 24, 2018, accessed January 28, 2020, https://diginomica.com/unilever-teams-microsoft-deliver-ai-assisted-decision-making-users.

14. Unilever, "Peter ter Kulve: Advantage at Scale in the AI & Handheld Economy," YouTube, December 5, 2018, accessed November 4, 2019, https://www.youtube.com/watch?v=VRSfXwiDIJw; Seb Joseph, "How Artificial Intelligence Is Influencing Unilever's Marketing," Digiday, April 8, 2019, accessed September 9, 2019, https://digiday.com/marketing/artificial-intelligence-influencing-unilevers-marketing/.

15. Jennifer Smith, "Unilever Uses Virtual Factories to Tune Up Its Supply Chain," *Wall Street Journal*, July 15, 2019, accessed January 28, 2020, https://www.wsj.com/articles/unilever-uses-virtual-factories-to-tune-up-its-supply-chain-11563206402.

16. Jennifer Sokolowsky, "Now It's Personal: Unilever's Digital Journey Leads to Real Results for Consumers and Employees," Microsoft, July 15, 2019, accessed January 28, 2020, https://news.microsoft.com/transform/now-its-personal-unilevers-digital-journey-leads-to-real-results-for-consumers-and-employees/.

17. Gautam Naik, "New CEO Alan Jope Puts Digital Transformation at Heart of Unilever's Strategy," S&P Global Market Intelligence, January 22, 2019, accessed January 28, 2020, https://www.spglobal.com/marketintelligence/en/news-insights/latest-news-headlines/49355732; Unilever, "Making Sustainable Living Commonplace: Unilever Annual Report and Accounts 2018," accessed January 28, 2020, https://www.unilever.com/Images/unilever-annual-report-and-accounts-2018_tcm244-534881_en.pdf.

18. Rebecca Stewart, "Unilever Ups Ad Spend by €300M in 2 Years Thanks to Agency Cutbacks," The Drum, April 19, 2019, accessed January 28, 2020, https://www.thedrum.com/news/2019/04/19/unilever-ups-ad-spend-300m-2-years-thanks-agency-cutbacks.

19. Karlene Lukovitz, "The Tao of Unilever, Part 2: Amazing AI Applications," MediaPost, May 7, 2019, accessed January 28, 2020, https://www.mediapost.com/publications/article/335552/the-tao-of-unilever-part-2-amazing-ai-applicatio.html.

20. "Dove Line Sticker," Spikes Asia, accessed January 28, 2020, https://www2.spikes.asia/winners/2016/promo/entry.cfm?entryid=898&award=101&order=6&direction=1.

21. Gautam Naik, "New CEO Alan Jope Puts Digital Transformation at Heart of Unilever's Strategy," S&P Global Market Intelligence, January 22, 2019, accessed January 28, 2020, https://www.spglobal.com/marketintelligence/en/news-insights/latest-news-headlines/49355732; "Dove Line Sticker," Spikes Asia, accessed January 28, 2020, https://www2.spikes.asia/winners/2016/promo/entry.cfm?entryid=898&award=101&order=6&direction=1.

CHAPTER 9

1. Peter ter Kulve, president of home care at Unilever, via email to Jim Lecinski, July 2019.

2. Jane Ho, "Introducing MiniBot: Chatbots in Mini Program," Medium, May 14, 2018, accessed January 28, 2020, https://medium.com/rikai-labs/introducing-minibot-chatbots-in-mini-program-3022b41083bf; "Analytics for WeChat Mini-Programs: Where Do We Stand for Performance Tracking?" Solutions Benchmark, December 2018, accessed January 28, 2020, http://313ct818yszd3xd6xa2z47nm-wpengine.netdna-ssl.com/wp-content/uploads/2018/12/31Ten-WeChat-Mini-Program-Analytics-v1.pdf.pdf.

3. Team Linchpin, "A Beginner's Guide to the Agile Method & Scrums," pin SEO, accessed August 13, 2019 (updated June 5, 2020), https://linchpinseo.com/the-agile-method/.

4. Monica Georgieff, "Book Roundup: 8 Must-Reads for Agile Marketers," AgileSherpas, accessed January 28, 2020, https://www.agilesherpas.com/8-books-for-agile-marketers/.

5. Jamie Tero, "JPMorgan Chase Announces Five-Year Deal with Persado for AI-Powered Marketing Capabilities," Persado, July 30, 2019, accessed November 1,

2019, https://www.persado.com/press-releases/jpmorgan-chase-announces-five-year -deal-with-persado-for-ai-powered-marketing-capabilities/.

6. AdLingo, "AdLingo: Join the Conversation," YouTube video, October 16, 2018, accessed November 4, 2019, https://www.youtube.com/watch?v=z3Zj1NgA4_c&feature =youtu.be.

7. Brock Ferguson, "Introducing Optimail: Email Marketing Powered by Artificial Intelligence," Strong, September 28, 2016, accessed November 1, 2019, https:// www.strong.io/blog/optimail-email-marketing-artificial-intelligence.

8. "Alaska Improves Its Mileage Plan Offering with Optimizely," Optimizely, accessed November 4, 2019, https://www.optimizely.com/customers/alaska-airlines/.

9. "AI-Powered Search for Digital Commerce," Lucidworks, accessed November 4, 2019, https://lucidworks.com/digital-commerce/; Ingrid Lunden, "Lucidworks Raises $100M to Expand in AI-Powered Search-as-a-Service for Organizations," TechCrunch, August 12, 2019, accessed November 1, 2019, https://techcrunch .com/2019/08/12/lucidworks-raises-100m-to-expand-in-ai-powered-search-as-a -service-for-organizations/.

10. "Quantcast Drives New Customers for Bonobos," Quantcast, accessed November 1, 2019, https://www.quantcast.com/case-studies/quantcast-drives-new-customers -bonobos/.

11. Shareen Pathak, "'Home Run for Us': Inside Chase's In-House Agency," Digiday, May 30, 2018, accessed November 1, 2019, https://digiday.com/marketing/home-run -us-inside-chases-house-agency/.

12. Adrianne Pasquarelli, "Chase Commits to AI after Machines Outperform Humans in Copywriting Trials," *AdAge*, July 30, 2019, accessed November 1, 2019, https://adage.com/article/cmo-strategy/chase-commits-ai-after-machines-outperform -humans-copywriting-trials/2187606.

13. Jaime Tero, "JPMorgan Chase Announces Five-Year Deal with Persado for AI-Powered Marketing Capabilities," Persado, July 30, 2019, accessed November 1, 2019, https://www.persado.com/press-releases/jpmorgan-chase-announces-five-year -deal-with-persado-for-ai-powered-marketing-capabilities/.

14. Tero, "JPMorgan Chase Announces Five-Year Deal."

15. Peter Adams, "JPMorgan Chase Inks 5-Year Deal to Generate Marketing Copy via AI," Marketing Dive, July 30, 2019, accessed November 1, 2019, https://www. marketingdive.com/news/jpmorgan-chase-inks-5-year-deal-to-generate-marketing -copy-via-ai/559836/.

16. Adams, "JPMorgan Chase Inks 5-Year Deal"; Pasquarelli, "Chase Commits to AI."

17. Tero, "JPMorgan Chase Announces Five-Year Deal."

18. Van Diamandakis, former Persado CMO-in-residence and CMO advisor for technology consultancy Firebrick, in email to author Jim Lecinski, October 19, 2019.

CHAPTER 10

1. "Ed Breault, CMO, Aprimo, direct quote to Jim Lecinski, July 14, 2020.

2. Anthony Ha, "Razor Startup Harry's Will Be Acquired by Edgewell Personal Care for $1.37B," TechCrunch, May 9, 2019, accessed August 13, 2019, https://techcrunch.com/2019/05/09/edgewell-acquires-harrys/.

3. Paul W. Farris, Dominique M. Hanssens, James D. Lenskold, and David J. Reibstein, "Marketing Return on Investment: Seeking Clarity for Concept and Measurement," *Applied Marketing Analytics* 1, no. 3 (April 2015): 270.

4. Paul Roetzer, "Machine Learning Made Easy for Marketers with Amazon Personalize," Marketing Artificial Intelligence Institute, June 13, 2019, accessed November 1, 2019, https://www.marketingaiinstitute.com/blog/machine-learning-made-easy-for-marketers-with-amazon-personalize. "AWS Announces General Availability of Amazon Personalize," *Business Wire*, June 10, 2019, accessed November 1, 2019, https://www.businesswire.com/news/home/20190610005788/en/AWS-Announces-General-Availability-Amazon-Personalize; "Amazon Personalize," Amazon, accessed November 1, 2019, https://aws.amazon.com/personalize/.

5. Bernard Marr, "The Fascinating Ways Warby Parker Uses Artificial Intelligence and AR to Change Retail," *Forbes*, April 18, 2019, accessed September 4, 2019, https://www.forbes.com/sites/bernardmarr/2019/04/18/the-fascinating-ways-warby-parker-uses-artificial-intelligence-and-ar-to-change-retail/#5070f07c4b2e. "Warby Parker: Customer Journey Breakdown and Marketing Review," *Retention Science*, accessed November 1, 2019, https://www.retentionscience.com/blog/warby-parker-marketing-review/."Data Science & Online Retail—At Warby Parker and Beyond: Carl Anderson Interview," *Data Science Weekly*, accessed November 1, 2019, https://www.datascienceweekly.org/data-scientist-interviews/data-science-transforming-online-retail-warby-parker-carl-anderson-interview.

6. Suman Bhattacharyya, "Warby Parker's David Gilboa: 'Every Retailer Is Facing Increasing Consumer Expectations,'" Digiday, December 27, 2018, accessed November 1, 2019, https://digiday.com/marketing/warby-parkers-david-gilboa-every-retailer-facing-increasing-consumer-expectations/.

7. "Sustainability Report 2018," Warby Parker, November 1, 2019, https://www.warbyparker.com/assets/img/sustainability/report-2018.pdf.

8. Ranjay Gulati, *Reorganize for Resilience: Putting Customers at the Center of Your Business* (Boston: Harvard Business School Publishing, 2010).

9. Rajkumar Venkatesan, Jenny Craddock, and Kyle Brodie, *Tackling Low Completion Rates—A Compare.com Conundrum*, case M-0947-1 (Charlottesville, VA: Darden Business Publishing, 2018).

10. Venkatesan, Craddock, and Brodie, *Tackling Low Completion Rates*.

11. Venkatesan, Craddock, and Brodie, *Tackling Low Completion Rates*.

12. Rajen Sheth, "How Unilever Uses Google Cloud to Optimize

Marketing Campaigns," *Google Cloud*, April 9, 2019, accessed November 1, 2019, https://cloud.google.com/blog/topics/customers/how-unilever-uses-google-cloud-to-optimize-marketing-campaigns.

13. Ellen Hammett, "How Retail Startup Thread is using AI to Solve the 'Choice Paradox,'" *Marketing Week*, February 6, 2019, accessed November 1, 2019, https://www.marketingweek.com/menswear-startup-thread-algorithm-fashion-tech/. Katie Strick and Samuel Fishwick, "Stitch Fix vs Thread: The AI Stylists to Help You Get Dressed in the Morning," *Evening Standard*, September 26, 2019, accessed November 1, 2019, https://www.standard.co.uk/tech/thread-vs-stitch-fix-reviews-2019-ai-fashion-stylists-a4247041.html.

14. Bernard Marr, "How Artificial Intelligence Is Used to Make Beer," *Forbes*, February 1, 2019, accessed November 1, 2019, https://www.forbes.com/sites/bernardmarr/2019/02/01/how-artificial-intelligence-is-used-to-make-beer/#77da858470cf.

15. IntelligentX, "IntelligentX promotional video," Facebook, accessed January 21, 2020, https://www.facebook.com/intelligentxai/.

16. Thomas Stubbs, vice president of engineering at Coca-Cola Freestyle, via direct interview with authors, November 3, 2019.

CHAPTER 11

1. Azadeh Moghtaderi, vice president for data science and analytics, Ancestry, from direct interview with authors.

2. Edgar Alan Rayo, "Artificial Intelligence at Disney, Viacom, and Other Entertainment Giants," Emerj, May 17, 2019, accessed November 1, 2019, https://emerj.com/ai-sector-overviews/ai-at-disney-viacom-and-other-entertainment-giants/.

3. Jane Doe, "Machine Learning at Disney: Solving Happiness," Digital Initiative, November 8, 2018, accessed November 1, 2019, https://digital.hbs.edu/platform-rctom/submission/machine-learning-at-disney-solving-happiness/.

4. "CarMax's New Omnichannel Shopping Experience," eTail, accessed November 4, 2019, https://etaileast.wbresearch.com/blog/carmax-omnichannel-strategy-used-car-shopping-online.

5. Jonathan Spiers, "CarMax Scouting Out Space Downtown," *Richmond BizSense*, December 14, 2015, accessed November 4, 2019, https://richmondbizsense.com/2015/12/14/carmax-scouting-out-space-downtown/.

6. David Muller, "Data Helps Solve Pre-Owned Sales Puzzle," *Automotive News*, November 12, 2018, accessed November 1, 2019, https://www.autonews.com/article/20181112/RETAIL04/181119976/data-helps-solve-pre-owned-sales-puzzle.

7. Dylan Haviland, "CarMax Innovates with Omnichannel Strategy," TTEC, accessed November 1, 2019, https://www.ttec.com/articles/carmax-innovates-omnichannel-strategy; Nicolas Wu, "Launching an Immersive Car Buying Experience

at CarMax," Adobe Blog, July 26, 2018, accessed November 1, 2019, https://theblog. adobe.com/launching-an-immersive-car-buying-experience-at-carmax/.

8. Databricks, "Creating an Omni-Channel Customer Experience with ML, Apache Spark, and Azure Databricks," SlideShare, May 6, 2019, Accessed November 4, 2019, https://www.slideshare.net/databricks/creating-an-omnichannel-customer -experience-with-ml-apache-spark-and-azure-databricks.

9. "McDonald's Corp. (MCD) Q2 2019 Earnings Call Transcript," The Motley Fool, August 15, 2019, accessed November 4, 2019, https://www.fool.com/earnings/call-transcripts/2019/08/15/mcdonalds-corp-mcd-q2-2019-earnings-conference-cal.aspx; Allison Schiff, "What's on Tap for Dynamic Yield after the McDonald's Acquisition," AdExchanger, June 24, 2019, accessed November 1, 2019, https://www.adexchanger. com/analytics/whats-on-tap-for-dynamic-yield-after-the-mcdonalds-acquisition/; Brian Barrett, "McDonald's Bites on Big Data with $300 Million Acquisition," *Wired*, March 25, 2019, accessed November 1, 2019, https://www.wired.com/story/mcdon-alds-big-data-dynamic-yield-acquisition/; Danny Klein, "How McDonald's Plans to Reinvent the Drive Thru," *QSR Magazine*, May 2019, accessed January 28, 2020, https://www.qsrmagazine.com/fast-food/how-mcdonalds-plans-reinvent-drive-thru.

10. David Yaffe-Bellany, "Would You Like Fries with That? McDonald's Already Knows the Answer," *New York Times*, October 22, 2019, accessed November 1, 2019, https://www.nytimes.com/2019/10/22/business/mcdonalds-tech-artificial-intelligence-machine-learning-fast-food.html.

11. Dan Berthiaume, "Ulta Beauty Shoppers Behold New AR, AI Features," *Chain Store Age*, June 4, 2019, accessed November 1, 2019, https://chainstoreage.com/ technology/ulta-beauty-shoppers-behold-new-ar-ai-features.

12. "Uruquay's GlamST Acquired by Ulta Beauty," *Endeavor*, November 20, 2018, accessed November 1, 2019, https://endeavor.org/blog/entrepreneurs/uruguays -glamst-acquired-ulta-beauty/.

13. Prama Bhatt, chief digital officer, Ulta Beauty, in interview with authors, October 17, 2019.

14. "Company Facts," Ancestry, accessed November 1, 2019, https://www.ancestry. com/corporate/about-ancestry/company-facts.

15. Gina Spatafore, "Ancestry Breaks November Sales Record," *Business Wire*, November 29, 2018, accessed November 4, 2019, https://www.businesswire.com /news/home/20181129005208/en/Ancestry-Breaks-November-Sales-Record.

16. Azadeh Moghtaderi, VP data science and analytics, Ancestry; and Todd Pollak, senior vice president for global customer success and product commercialization, interview with authors August 26, 2019.

CHAPTER 12

1. Direct quote from David Rogers, via email to Jim Lecinski, July 6, 2020.

2. Bryan Wroten, "How Marriott Will Differentiate Home-Sharing Platform," *Hotel News Now*, May 6, 2019, accessed January 28, 2020, https://www.hotelnewsnow .com/Articles/295132/How-Marriott-will-differentiate-home-sharing-platform.

3. Nadine El-Bawab, "Marriott Plans to Launch Home-Rental Market Platform That Would Compete with Airbnb, Report Says," CNBC, April 29, 2019, accessed November 1, 2019, https://www.cnbc.com/2019/04/29/marriott-to-launch-home-rental-platform -to-compete-with-airbnb-report.html.

4. Ming Zeng, "Alibaba and the Future of Business," *Harvard Business Review*, September-October 2018, 88–96, accessed November 1, 2019, https://hbr.org/2018/09/ alibaba-and-the-future-of-business.

5. Bernard Marr, "The Amazing Ways Alibaba Uses Artificial Intelligence and Machine Learning," LinkedIn, July 31, 2018, accessed November 1, 2019, https:// www.linkedin.com/pulse/amazing-ways-alibaba-uses-artificial-intelligence-ma- chine-marr/; Abigail Beall, "In China, Alibaba's Data-Hungry AI Is Controlling (and Watching) Cities," *Wired*, May 30, 2018, accessed November 1, 2019, https://www .wired.co.uk/article/alibaba-city-brain-artificial-intelligence-china-kuala-lumpur; Steve LeVine, "China's AI-Infused Corner Store of the Future," Axios, June 17, 2018, accessed November 1, 2019, https://www.axios.com/china-alibaba-tencent-jd-com -artificial-intelligence-corner-store-df90517e-befb-40ca-82d5-f37caa738d54.html.

6. Coca-Cola Freestyle team, interview by Raj Venkatesan and Jim Lecinski, October 18, 2019.

7. "The Washington Post Arc Publishing Case Study," Amazon Web Services, 2018, accessed November 1, 2019, https://aws.amazon.com/solutions/case-studies /washington-post-arc/.

8. "The Washington Post Introduces Next Generation Targeting for Marketers; Lay- ing Groundwork for Secure, Cookie-Free Ad Experiences," *Washington Post*, July 16, 2019, accessed November 1, 2019, https://www.washingtonpost.com/pr/2019/07/16/wash- ington-post-introduces-next-generation-targeting-marketers-laying-groundwork -secure-cookie-free-ad-experiences/.

9. Patrick Cullen, director of Data Science and Artificial Intelligence for the *Washington Post*, interview with authors, September 20, 2019.

CHAPTER 13

1. "Why Did I Not Get Certain Promotional Offers in My App?" Starbucks Cus- tomer Service Home, April 16, 2019, accessed January 29, 2020, https://customerservice .starbucks.com/app/answers/detail/a_id/5205/kw/promotions.

2. Kevin Johnson, "Can Artificial Intelligence Help Nurture Humanity?" Linke- dIn, October 23, 2019, accessed January 29, 2020, https://www.linkedin.com/pulse/can -artificial-intelligence-help-nurture-humanity-kevin-johnson/.

3. Riley Panko, "How Customers Use Food Delivery and Restaurant Loyalty

Apps," The Manifest, May 15, 2018, accessed January 29, 2020, https://themanifest.com/mobile-apps/how-customers-use-food-delivery-restaurant-loyalty-apps. Joanna Fantozzi, "The Evolution of the Starbucks Loyalty Program," *Nation's Restaurant News*, April 5, 2019, accessed January 29, 2020, https://www.nrn.com/quick-service/evolution-starbucks-loyalty-program.

4. "Starbucks Rewards Terms of Use," Starbucks, August 19, 2019, accessed January 29, 2020, https://www.starbucks.com/rewards/terms.

5. "Starbucks to Enhance Industry-Leading Starbucks Rewards Loyalty Program," Starbucks, March 19, 2019, accessed January 29, 2020, https://investor.starbucks.com/press-releases/financial-releases/press-release-details/2019/Starbucks-to-Enhance-Industry-Leading-Starbucks-Rewards-Loyalty-Program/default.aspx.

6. Stephanie Overby, "How Starbucks Brews Its Mobile Strategy," CIO, October 25, 2012, accessed January 29, 2020, https://www.cio.com/article/2390899/how-starbucks-brews-its-mobile-strategy.html.

7. Alexis Fournier, "My Starbucks Idea: An Open Innovation Case-Study," Braineet, March 20, 2019, accessed January 29, 2020, https://www.braineet.com/blog/my-starbucks-idea-case-study/.

8. "Starbucks Company Timeline," Starbucks, accessed January 29, 2020, https://www.starbucks.com/about-us/company-information/starbucks-company-timeline.

9. Daniel Wolfe, "Starbucks App Can Monitor Rewards," *American Banker*, May 13, 2010, accessed January 29, 2020, https://www.americanbanker.com/news/starbucks-app-can-monitor-rewards.

10. "Fact Sheet: My Starbucks Rewards Program," Starbucks Stories and News, July 25, 2013, accessed January 29, 2020, https://stories.starbucks.com/stories/2013/fact-sheet-my-starbucks-rewards-program/; Nitin, "The Science behind Starbucks' Massively Successful Customer Loyalty Program," Zeta Global, March 31, 2017, accessed January 29, 2020, https://zetaglobal.com/customer-retention/starbucks-reward-customer-loyalty-program-study/.

11. Daniel Wolfe, "Starbucks and Payments: Everything You Need to Know," PaymentsSource, accessed January 29, 2020, https://www.paymentssource.com/list/starbucks-and-payments-everything-you-need-to-know.

12. Paul Sawers, "Starbucks Launches Mobile Order & Pay for All U.S. Customers; U.K. and Canada coming in October," *Venture Beat*, September 22, 2015, accessed January 29, 2020, https://venturebeat.com/2015/09/22/starbucks-launches-mobile-order-pay-for-all-u-s-customers-u-k-and-canada-coming-in-october/.

13. "Ideas Page," Starbucks, accessed January 30, 2020, https://ideas.starbucks.com/.

14. Dan Richman, "How Starbucks Is Using Artificial Intelligence to Connect with Customers and Boost Sales," GeekWire, December 19, 2016, accessed January 29,

2020, https://www.geekwire.com/2016/starbucks-using-artificial-intelligence-connect -customers-boost-sales/.

15. Richman, "How Starbucks Is Using Artificial Intelligence."

16. Sarah Whitten, "Starbucks Knows How You Like Your Coffee," CNBC, April 6, 2016, accessed January 29, 2020, https://www.cnbc.com/2016/04/06/big-data-starbucks -knows-how-you-like-your-coffee.html.

17. Richman, "How Starbucks Is Using Artificial Intelligence."

18. Nitin, "The Science"; Megan Friedman, "It Just Got Way Easier to Rack Up Stars on the Starbucks App," *Seventeen*, May 5, 2017, accessed January 29, 2020, https://www. seventeen.com/life/food-recipes/news/a46962/starbucks-rewards-grocery-store/; Subrat Patnaik, "Starbucks Expands Rewards Program at Grocery Stores," Yahoo! Finance, May 4, 2017, accessed January 29, 2020, https://finance.yahoo.com/news/starbucks -expands-rewards-program-grocery-stores-151538534--sector.html.

19. Joanna Fantozzi, "The Evolution of the Starbucks Loyalty Program," *Nation's Restaurant News*, April 5, 2019, accessed January 29, 2020, https://www.nrn.com/quick -service/evolution-starbucks-loyalty-program.

20. Fantozzi, "The Evolution of the Starbucks Loyalty Program."

21. "Apple Pay Overtakes Starbucks as Top Mobile Payment App in the US," *Insider Intelligence,* October 23, 2019, accessed January 29, 2020, https://www.emarketer .com/newsroom/index.php/apple-pay-overtakes-starbucks-as-top-mobile -payment-app-in-the-us/.

22. "Starbucks US Rewards Membership Tops 17.6M," PYMNTS, October 31, 2019, accessed January 29, 2020, https://www.pymnts.com/earnings/2019/starbucks -us-rewards-membership-tops-17-6m/.

23. Richman, "How Starbucks Is Using Artificial Intelligence."

24. Rachel, "Starbucks' Secret Ingredient: Data Analytics," HBS Digital Initiative, April 9, 2018, accessed January 29, 2020, https://digital.hbs.edu/platform-digit/submission /starbucks-secret-ingredient-data-analytics/.

25. Harry McCracken, "Starbucks Brews a Tech-Infused Future, with Help from Microsoft," *Fast Company*, May 7, 2018, accessed January 29, 2020, https://www.fastcompany .com/40568165/starbucks-brews-a-tech-infused-future-with-help-from-microsoft.

26. Nancy Luna, "Starbucks Deal Expands Industry Access to Exclusive Tech," *Nation's Restaurant News*, July 22, 2019, accessed January 29, 2020, https://www.nrn .com/quick-service/starbucks-deal-expands-industry-access-exclusive-tech.

27. "Starbucks Backs Restaurant Tech Company in Creation of End-to-End Digital Platform," Starbucks Stories and News, July 22, 2019, accessed January 29, 2020, https://stories.starbucks.com/press/2019/starbucks-backs-restaurant-tech-company-in-creation -of-end-to-end-digital-platform-for-restaurant-industry/.

28. Nancy Koleva, "What Is Marketing AI and Why Does It Matter?" Dataiku, June 3,

2019, accessed January 30, 2020, https://blog.dataiku.com/what-is-marketing-ai-and-why
-does-it-matter.

CHAPTER 14

1. Nicolas Darveau-Garneau, chief evangelist, Google, directly to Jim Lecinski
via email, January 9, 2020.

2. Jennifer Elias, "Alphabet, Google's Parent Company, Hits Trillion-Dollar Market Cap for First Time," CNBC, January 16, 2020, accessed January 29, 2020, https://
www.cnbc.com/2020/01/16/alphabet-stock-hits-1-trillion-market-cap-for-first-time
.html.

3. Timothy B. Lee, "Why Google Believes Machine Learning Is Its Future," Ars
Technica, May 10, 2019, accessed November 1, 2019, https://arstechnica.com/gad-
gets/2019/05/googles-machine-learning-strategy-hardware-software-and-lots-of-
data/; Steven Levy, "How Google Is Remaking Itself as a 'Machine Learning First'
Company," *Wired*, June 22, 2016, accessed November 1, 2019, https://www.wired
.com/2016/06/how-google-is-remaking-itself-as-a-machine-learning-first-company/.

4. "Google RankBrain," Moz, accessed November 1, 2019, https://moz.com/learn/
seo/google-rankbrain.

5. Thomas Thoresen, "Eric Schmidt: Google Cloud Next 2017," YouTube, May 29,
2017, accessed November 4, 2019, https://www.youtube.com/watch?v=iIlkZoy6hiM.
Martyn Williams, "Eric Schmidt Sees a Huge Future for Machine Learning," *In-
foWorld*, March 23, 2016, accessed November 4, 2019, https://www.infoworld.com
/article/3047617/eric-schmidt-sees-a-huge-future-for-machine-learning.html.

6. Leena Rao, "Meet Google's Artificial Intelligence Chief," *Fortune*, October 27, 2015,
accessed November 1, 2019, https://fortune.com/2015/10/27/john-giannandrea-google
-artificial-intelligence/.

7. James Niccolai, "Google's CEO Sees A.I. as the Next Wave in Computing," *Com-
puterworld*, April 21, 2016, accessed November 1, 2019, https://www.computerworld.
com/article/3060285/googles-ceo-sees-ai-as-the-next-wave-in-computing.html; Cath-
erine Clifford, "Google CEO: A.I. Is More Important Than Fire or Electricity," CNBC,
February 1, 2018, accessed November 1, 2019, https://www.cnbc.com/2018/02/01/
google-ceo-sundar-pichai-ai-is-more-important-than-fire-electricity.html; Larry
Dignan, "Google Bets on AI-First as Computer Vision, Voice Recognition, Machine
Learning Improve," *ZDNet*, May 17, 2017, accessed November 1, 2019, https://www.
zdnet.com/article/google-bets-on-ai-first-as-computer-vision-voice-recognition
-machine-learning-improve/.

8. John P. Kotter, *Leading Change* (Boston: Harvard Business Review Press, 2012),
23; John P. Kotter, "Leading Change: Why Transformation Efforts Fail," *Harvard
Business Review*, January 2007, accessed January 29, 2020, https://hbr.org/2007/01/
leading-change-why-transformation-efforts-fail.

9. Linda Tucci, "Automation and AI Challenges: CIO Tips for Success," TechTarget, July 17, 2019, accessed November 1, 2019, https://searchcio.techtarget.com/video/Automation-and-AI-challenges-CIO-tips-for-success.

10. "Beyond the Brand: Marketing for Consumer Goods," *Accenture*, May 17, 2019, accessed November 1, 2019, https://www.accenture.com/us-en/insights/consumer-goods-services/beyond-brilliant-basics-consumer-goods-marketing.

11. Annie Duke, *Thinking in Bets: Making Smarter Decisions When You Don't Have All the Facts* (New York: Portfolio, 2018).

CHAPTER 15

1. Bob Morris, "Geoffrey Moore on Zone Management: An Interview by Bob Morris," Blogging on Business, November 29, 2015, accessed January 29, 2020, https://bobmorris.biz/geoffrey-moore-on-zone-management-an-interview-by-bob-morris.

CHAPTER 16

1. Via email to Jim Lecinski, used with permission from Mitch Duckler.

2. Via email to Jim Lecinski, used with permission from Aaron Goldman.

3. Via interview with Jim Lecinski, used with permission from Konrad Feldman.

4. Via email to Jim Lecinski, used with permission from Kristen D'Arcy.

5. MaryLee Sachs, "Putting the C in CMO," *Forbes*, January 20, 2020, accessed January 29, 2020, https://www.forbes.com/sites/maryleesachs/2020/01/20/putting-the-c-in-cmo/#1635b94d6b55.

6. "Teachable Machine," accessed January 29, 2020, https://teachablemachine.withgoogle.com/.

7. Kristin Lemkau, "Machine Learning Will Make Marketing More Human," Web Summit video, November 5, 2019, accessed January 29, 2020, https://www.sapo.pt/websummit/en/machine-learning-will-make-marketing-more-human_86714f34-c053-4ef6-bbb3-fa559a80d1ca.

8. "Our Mission," Starbucks, accessed January 29, 2020, https://www.starbucks.com/about-us/company-information/mission-statement.

9. Jennifer Warnick, "AI for Humanity: How Starbucks Plans to Use Technology to Nurture the Human Spirit," Starbucks Stories and News, January 10, 2020, accessed January 29, 2020, https://stories.starbucks.com/stories/2020/how-starbucks-plans-to-use-technology-to-nurture-the-human-spirit/.

10. Eric Solomon, "Your Data-Driven Marketing Is Harmful. I Should Know: I Ran Marketing at Google and Instagram," *Entrepreneur*, January 15, 2020, accessed January 29, 2020, https://www.entrepreneur.com/article/344399.

11. "AI for Humanity."

12. Jennifer Warnick, "AI for Humanity."

ABOUT THE AUTHORS

1. Stuart Elliott, "Google Offers Marketing Ideas, by the Book," *New York Times*, July 15, 2011, accessed January 28, 2020, https://mediadecoder.blogs.nytimes.com/2011/07/15/google-offers-marketing-ideas-by-the-book/.

Index

About the Authors

Rajkumar Venkatesan is the Ronald Trzcinski Professor of Business Administration at the Darden Business School at the University of Virginia. Raj has written about and taught quantitative marketing to MBA and executive education students worldwide. At Darden he has taught a course on marketing analytics for more than ten years, and a course on marketing technology products for five years. His experience in these courses translated into a book, *Cutting Edge Marketing Analytics,* published by Pearson Education in 2014. More than 235,000 individuals have participated in his Coursera course on marketing analytics. Please connect with Raj on LinkedIn: www .linkedin.com/in/education-marketing-consultant/.

Jim Lecinski is a clinical associate professor of marketing at the Kellogg School of Management at Northwestern University. Prior to this, he was vice president of customer solutions at Google, and also previously held leadership positions at the advertising agencies DDB, marchFirst, Young & Rubicam, and Euro RSCG (now Havas). Jim is a sought-after marketing advisor with thirty years of experience working with the world's top brands, and the author of *Winning the Zero Moment of Truth* (*ZMOT*) (Vook, 2011). Lauded by expert reviewers as "truly a paradigm shift in how marketers view buyer behavior," *ZMOT* has been read by more than three hundred thousand marketers worldwide, and has been featured in the *New York Times,*[1] *Advertising Age, Media Post,* and others. Please connect with Jim on LinkedIn: www .linkedin.com/in/jimlecinski.

Lightning Source UK Ltd.
Milton Keynes UK
UKHW011213050522
402497UK00004B/90/J